THE KICKS SERIES, VOLUME 3

Ground Kicks

Advanced Martial Arts Kicks for Groundfighting

Ne Geri Waza - The Art of Fighting from Down Under

With Hundreds of Applications
from Karate, Kung Fu, Krav Maga, Tae Kwon Do, MMA, Muay Thai, Capoeira and more

By

Marc De Bremaeker

Fons Sapientiae Publishing

Ground Kicks – Advanced Martial Arts Kicks for Groundfighting. 3rd Edition.
Published in 2017 by Fons Sapientiae Publishing, Cambridge, United Kingdom
The First Edition of this work was published in 2015.

Please note that the publisher and author of this instructional book are NOT RESPONSIBLE in any manner whatsoever for any injury that may result from practicing the techniques and/or following the instructions given within. Physical and Martial Arts Training can be dangerous, -both to you and others-, if not practiced safely. If you are in doubt as how to proceed or whether your practice is safe, consult with an accredited coach, physical trainer or a trained Martial Art teacher before beginning. Since the physical activities described maybe too strenuous in nature for some readers, it is essential that a physician be consulted prior to any type of training.

ISBN of the printed version: 978-0-9957952-2-8

__Recommended reading, by the same author:__
"Krav Maga Kicks -Tested in Battle: Kicking for No-nonsense Self-preservation (2017)
"Isoplex - Musculation Program for an Aesthetic and Truly Athletic Body" (2017)
"Sacrifice Kicks - Advanced Martial arts Kicks for Realistic Airborne Attacks" (2016)
"Stealth Kicks - The Forgotten Art of Ghost Kicking" (2015)
"Stop Kicks-Jamming, Obstructing, Stopping, Impaling, Cutting and Preemptive Kicks" (2014)
"Low kicks-Advanced Martial Arts Kicks for Attacking the Lower Gates" (2013)
"Plyo-Flex-Plyometrics and Flexibility Training for Explosive Martial Arts Kicks" (2013)
"The Essential Book of Martial Arts Kicks" (2010) by Tuttle Publishing
"Le Grand Livre des Coups de Pied" (2017) by Budo Edition (In French)
"Les Coups de Pied Bas" (2016 - in French)
"Les Coups de Pied d'Arrêt" (2017 - in French)
"i Calci nelle Arti Marziali" (2015) by Edizioni Mediterranee (in Italian)

DEDICATION

This book is dedicated to my Promising First Grandson
Oliver Maximillian Yiu Ting De Bremaeker

包耀庭

Family is not an important thing. It's everything.
~Michael J. Fox

Dear Reader,

In this day and age, the life of a serious author has become quite difficult. The proliferation of books and the explosion of internet content has made it nearly impossible to promote work based on extensive research and requiring complex lay-out.
Please enjoy this book. Once you are finished, I would ask kindly that you take a few short minutes to give your honest opinion. An unbiased Amazon review, of even a few words only, would be highly appreciated and encouraging.

Thank You,

Marc

Nothing is ever lost by courtesy. It is the cheapest of pleasures, costs nothing, and conveys much.
~Erastus Wiman

ACKNOWLEDGEMENTS

Without the active support of my wife and life companion, **Aviva Giveoni**, this book would not have come to life. Being an athlete in her own right, she understands the meaning of hard work and dedication.

Aviva

Sensei Shlomo Faige

Among many teachers and heads and shoulders above, my late Sensei, -**Sidney (Shlomo) Faige**-, should be mentioned with longing thankfulness. Sensei Faige founded the Shi-Heun style of Karate.

Special Thanks to my life-long friend and training partner, **Roy Faige,** for his help and support. Roy is now heading the Shi Heun school is also my co-author of *The Essential Book of Martial Arts Kicks*. His influence and advice is felt in nearly every page of this work and the previous books in the series.

Roy and Marc

Thank you to **Ziv Faige, Gil Faige, Shay Levy, Dotan De Bremaeker, Nimrod De Bremaeker and Itay Leibovitch** who helped by painstakingly posing for some of the photographs.

Most photographs have been taken by the author, by Roy Faige and by Aviva Giveoni. But special thanks have to be extended to talented **Grace Wong** for some long sessions. Thank you also to professional photographer **Guli Cohen**: some of the photographs in this book have been extracted from the photo sessions he gracefully did for previous volumes.

Grace Wong

The drawings in this book are mine. Everything that I have learned about line art, I have done so from professional Illustrator **Shahar Navot**, who illustrated *The Essential Book of Martial Arts Kicks.* Thanks Shahar!

Victorious warriors win first and then go to war, while defeated warriors go to war first and then seek to win.
~Sun Tzu

Contents

**The will to win is important, but the will to prepare is vital.
~Joe Paterno**

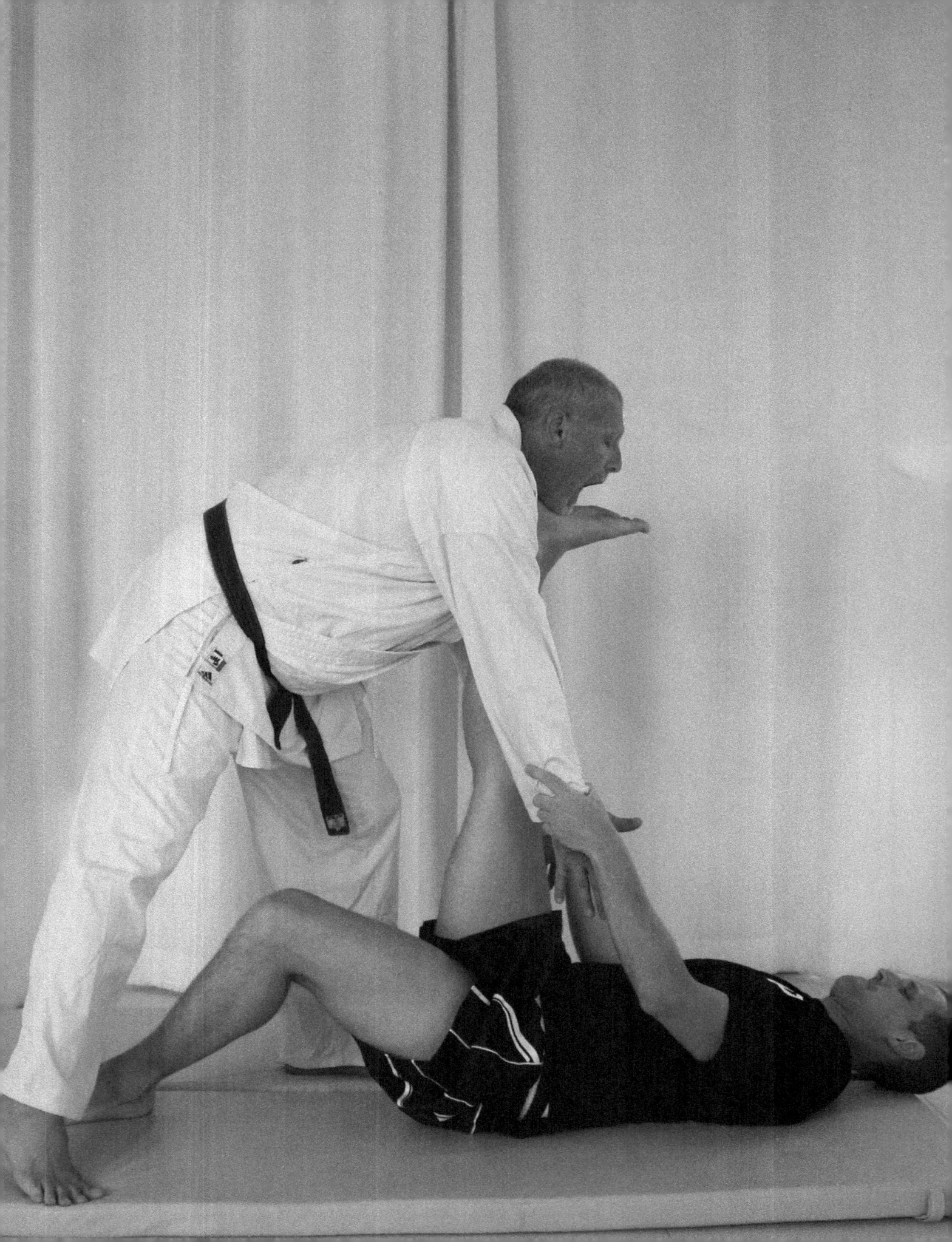

FOREWORD TO THE "KICKS" SERIES

A goal is not always meant to be reached, it often serves simply as something to aim at.
~Bruce Lee

The 'Foreword' and 'General Introduction' are very similar to those of the previous book in the 'Kicks' series. In order to spare a near re-read to our faithful readers of 'Low Kicks', 'Stop Kicks', 'Sacrifice Kicks' and 'Stealth Kicks', we invite you to go directly to the 'Introduction to Ground Kicks' on page xx.

My Martial Arts career started with Judo at age 6. Judo was pretty new Sixty years ago, and a bit mystical in the Western World. A mysterious Oriental Art teaching how to use one's opponent's strength against him was a pretty attractive proposition for a wimpy kid. And the decorum and costume trappings made it a unique selling proposition. That is, until the Kung Fu craze of the Seventies, starring Bruce Lee, and then others.

In my opinion, what fascinated the Western masses, and the teen-ager I was then, was mostly the fantastic kicking maneuvers in the spectacular fights of those Kung-Fu movies. The bulk of the fight scenes were based on spectacular exchanges, the likes of which we had never seen before. What was new and revolutionary back then, may seem banal and common to today's younger reader. But we had been raised in the era of boxing and we had been conditioned by the fair-play of *Queensburry's* rules: we had no idea one could fight *like that*!

It was also the first time that the general public in Europe and America had seen a well-rounded Martial Art in action: punching, but also striking, kicking, throwing down, grappling, locking... It comprised all fighting disciplines in seamless aggregation. Wow! Judo was great, but I now wanted to *kick* like Bruce Lee. I therefore took up *Shotokan Karate*. 'Shotokan-ryu' is not the most impressive kicking style, but it was then the most developed Kicking Art outside of Asia and the only one available to me. It is as well and I certainly do not regret it. Though it is not an art known for extravagant kicks, Shotokan is very well organized didactically. It also emphasizes tradition, hard training, focus (*Zanshin*) and mastery of basic work. In all athletic endeavors, the continuous drilling of basic work at all levels of proficiency is the only real secret to success.

...And traditional Shotokan Karate drills and low training stances definitely fit this bill. So, during the whole of my career, I kept practicing Shotokan Karate, or a Shotokan-derived style at all times. I also kept at Judo, my first love. But in parallel, I started to explore other Arts a few years at the time, as opportunities and geography allowed. During my long Martial Arts career, I also did practice assiduously Karatedo from the *Kyokushinkai, Shotokai, Wadoryu* and *Sankukai* schools. I also trained for long stints of *TaeKwonDo, Muay Thai (*in Thailand*), Krav Maga (*in Israel*), Capoeira, Savate-Boxe Française*, two styles of traditional *Ju-Jitsu* and some soft styles of *Kung Fu*. This search is where I developed my individual methods and my own understanding of the Art of Kicking and its place in complex fighting. It also provided the basis on which to build my own personal research. Of course, this is strongly accented towards the type of maneuvers and training that favor my personal physiology and personality, but I have tried very hard to keep an open mind, among others through coaching.

Sometimes during this maybe too eclectic career, my travels took me to the **Shi-Heun** School of the late *Sensei Sidney Faige*, mentioned in the Acknowledgements. The *Shi-Heun* style is *Shotokan*-derived and mixed with *Judo* practice. It emphasizes extreme conditioning, total fighting under several realistic rules sets and the personal quest for what works best for oneself. And its self-defense training is based on no-nonsense *Krav Maga*. As

Sensei Sidney Faige in action

this was only the early Eighties, this was definitely a prophetic ancestor of today's phenomena of Mixed Martial Arts of 'UFC' fame. The free-fighting rules in the *Dojo* were 'all-out' and 'to-the-ground', but this did not hinder the success of the School's students in more traditional tournaments under milder rules. The direct disciples of *Sensei Faige* did indeed roam the tournament scene undefeated for years.

In these days, points tournament fighting was mainly WUKO (World Union of Karate

Sensei Faige with the winning Israeli National Team; the author and Roy Faige are on the right

Organizations), with some notable exceptions like *Kyokushinkai* and *Semi-contact Karate* bouts. Unfortunately, WUKO generally (boringly) consisted in two competitors safely jumping up-and-down and waiting for the other to initiate a move, in order to stop-reverse-punch him to the body.

When my name was called up in these events, there was usually some spontaneous applause from the spectators; they knew they were going to see, finally, some kicking. I apologize if it sounds like boasting; the point I am trying to make is that Karate fans of these times came to see kicking and rich fighting moves, and not some unrealistic form of boxing. And this is not to denigrate *Karatedo*, but more to critisize the castrating effect of unintelligent rules sets.

Marc and Roy facing off at the finals of a 1987 Points Tournament

Marc, kicking in point tournament

...It is my strong belief that Kicking is what made the Oriental Martial arts so appealing. As I have already mentioned in articles and previous books, I do firmly argue that *kicking is more effective than punching.* This usually causes many to stand up, disagree and maybe want to *punch* me, pun intended. This is an old debate, still raging, and I respectfully ask to be allowed to complete the sentence. I strongly believe that kicking is more effective than punching, **but proficiency takes much more time and work**. When presented this way, I do hope that this opinion is more acceptable to most. Let me detail my position briefly.

Kicking is more efficient than punching:

1. Because of the longer range

2. Because the muscles of the leg are much bigger and powerful than those of the arms

3. Because kicking targets, unlike punching targets, go from head all the way down to toes

4. Because kicks are less expected and therefore more surprising than punches, especially at shorter ranges

One needs to drill kicks from very close ranges as well

I readily admit that the opponents of my position do have valid arguments. They will point out that kicks are inherently slower than punches and can be easily jammed because they start from longer ranges. They will also point out that kicking often opens the groin, while forgetting that so does punching usually as well. It is my experience that, - *after a lot of dedicated and intelligent work-,* many kicks can be as swift as punches and can be delivered at all ranges and from all positions.

...During all my training years, I invested a lot of time, personal drilling and original research into Kicking Arts from all over the world. I experimented with all training tips gathered and I endeavored to try all mastered new kick variations in actual free-fighting and competitive tournaments. Here is the place to note that this is *not* about a huge number of different techniques; it is about finding the best possible techniques suited to one's specific strength, physiology and affinities (Once you have found your **few** techniques and the best way to drill them, then you focus on a fast and perfect execution from all ranges and positions). During my quest in the realm of kicking, I slowly developed a personal kicking style based on my personal history and mindset. I researched most of the available literature, but very few treatises were actually *dedicated* to kicking. The few works I found about kicking were generally very good, but usually style-restricted and unorganized. I never found the kind of book that I would have liked to have at the start of my Martial arts career. And so I decided to write it myself and share my global view of the subject. To the best of my knowledge, there has never been an attempt to compile and organize all the different Kick types and variation in such a way that it could serve as a reference work and the basis for exploration for the kick-lover. I did try to start this potentially huge work, probably imperfectly, with a series of Books I chose to name the 'Kicks Series'. A global overview of Basic Kicks was presented in **'The Essential Book of Martial Arts Kicks'** (Tuttle), translated in several foreign languages. Its success lead me to follow with the important lower gates attacks in **'Low Kicks'**, and then **'Stop Kicks'** about preempting, jamming, impaling, obstructing and 'cutting' Kicks. This book about 'Ground Kicks' is in tune with our times of MMA fame . **'Stealth Kicks'** then endeavored to cover misdirection and dissimulation while kicking. Then came volume **'Sacrifice Kicks'** about Flying and Suicide Kicks. And we hope that all this work will be built upon by others in the future. As mentioned and underlined many times, kicking proficiency requires a lot of serious drilling. I have therefore also published a work about the basic general drills that will help you reach higher levels of proficiency. As in all athletic endeavors, it is the basic drills that will build the strong foundation needed; and it is to those basic drills that the truly good athlete will come back for further progress again and again. **'Plyo-Flex Training for Explosive Martial Arts Kicks and Other Performance Sports'** does present those general, basic but so-important exercises that one should regularly practice for continuous improvement of kicking proficiency.

And now last, but certainly not least: it is important to underline that my strong views do not try in any way or form to denigrate the Punching Arts. My personal philosophy is that Martial arts are a whole with a world of possible emphasis. A complete Martial artist should be proficient in punching, kicking, moving, throwing, grappling, evading and more. But every Artist will have his own preferences and particular skills in his own way to look at the Martial Arts as a whole.

➡

...And here must I add the obvious: *there is no kicking mastery* without punching proficiency! Even for a dedicated kicker, punching will be needed for closing the gap, feinting, setting up a kick, following it up and much more... This will be made abundantly clear from most of the applications presented in this volume, just as it is clear from all my previous work.

It must be said that Punching is sometimes the best or the only answer in some situations. I have known and met some extraordinary Punching Artists using kicks only as feints or set-ups. On the other hand, great kickers like legendary *Bill 'Superfoot' Wallace* were extremely skilled punchers and working hard at it, as I personally experienced in a few seminars. Kick and Punch, Punch and Kick: well-rounded is the secret.

And this leads me naturally to my last point. I would not want my books and my views to be misunderstood as an appeal to always kick when fighting, and especially not as an appeal to always high-kick. The best kicker in the world should not execute a high Kick, *just because he can*. A Kick should only be delivered *because and when it is suitable* to a specific situation! Obvious maybe, but certainly worth reminding. In someone else's words:

Take things as they are. Punch when you have to punch. Kick when you have to kick.
~Bruce Lee

GENERAL INTRODUCTION: THE 'KICKS' SERIES

This book is not a "How to" book for the beginner, but, hopefully, a reference work for the experienced Martial Artist. It presupposes the knowledge of stances, footwork, and concepts of centerline, guards, distance, evasions and more. It also expects from the reader a good technical level in his chosen Martial style, including kicking. As this work is building upon the *Essential* basic level towards more sophisticated kicking maneuvers, all *Essential Kicks* are considered mastered from the author's point of view. The reader is invited to consult previous work already mentioned above. This book is intended as a tool for self-exploration and research about kicking outside experienced Artists' specific style. Therefore, the description of the different kicks is very short and typical examples are only briefly explained. The author relies more on photos and illustrations to exemplify his point. Let the reader try it and adapt it to his liking and morphology. The author tends to prefer drawings over photographs to be able to underline salient points sometimes hidden in photos.

The experienced trainee will probably notice quickly that the basic background of the author is Japanese *Karate*. This cannot be avoided but was not deliberate. This book aspires to be as "style-less" as possible, as its purpose is to bridge across the different schools on the basis of common immutable principles. The author's philosophy is that Martial Arts are an interconnected whole, where styles are just interpretations of some principles and their adaptation to certain sets of strategies, rules, cultural constraints, or morphologies. It is one and same thing, although it may seem different from different angles. In the pictures and illustrations, the reader can see technical differences and adaptations from different styles. This is done on purpose to underscore the style-less philosophy of the treatise. Sometimes the foot of the standing leg is flat on the floor, as required in traditional Japanese styles, and sometimes the heel is up as in certain deliveries of Korean arts. It should be clear that the biomechanical principles are identical for trained artists and the small differences of emphasis are meaningless. It is more important for a trainee to adapt the technique to his morphology and preferences, once it is well mastered. This book definitely does not pretend to present an axiomatic way to kick! In the same vein, arms during kicking are sometimes close to the body in hermetic guard and sometimes loose and counterbalancing the kicking move. Hands can be open, or fists tight.

...Like in previous efforts, it has proved very difficult to name and organize the kicks into and within groups. The author has given the techniques descriptive names in English, whenever possible commonly used names. But the more complex, exotic and hybrid kicks have sometimes either several different appellations in use or none, while being difficult to describe. The names the author has chosen could certainly be disputed and improved upon by some. For the most basic kicks common to all styles, we have added the respective original foreign names. The author apologizes in advance to the purists of all styles: It is clear that the description of a technique cannot be in all details valid for all styles (For example, the basic Front Kick is taught differently in *Shotokan* karate than in *TaeKwonDo)*. The original foreign names in Japanese, Korean, Chinese or Portuguese are just there as an indication for further research by the reader. It should also be noted that some techniques have different names in different schools of the same Art! For the more complex or exotic kicks, we have purposely omitted original names. Only when a kick is especially typical of a certain style, did we mention it, as a tribute to the specific school. The author also apologizes for his arbitrary transcription of foreign names, as purists could dispute the way it was done.

The kicks presented in this volume are tagged "Advanced". This does not necessarily mean that they are more difficult to execute than the *Essential* basic kicks. On the contrary. Besides being a requisite of some form of classification, it mainly means that the principles behind the "basic" kicks should be first thoroughly mastered. A *Front Stop Kick* is relatively easy to perform and slightly different than a regular Front Kick. But for maximum power, it is important to follow the same principles of a basic Front Kick, with chambering, kicking through and chamber back. And the principles of the leg development stay the same for the Ground Front Kick. And even if a Low Front Kick seems easy to perform, it will be done so under the same principles already mastered for maximum speed and power. A typical Feint Kick, the Roundhouse-chambered Front Kick is slightly tricky to master, but it is more a question of hip flexibility and acquaintance drilling: the principles behind the power of what is ultimately a Front Kick stay the same. Once the principles behind the basic Front Kick are mastered, all other "Advanced" Kicks will be faster and more powerful. **This is all about mastering the basics and principles first,** and only later trying out variations in all kinds of situations, fancier or not. This is, by the way, true for any other physical activity. But because Advanced Kicks are more a variation on the theme of their underlying basic kicks, they will be presented in all their complexity by many variations in specific applications. *This* volume will not detail *Essential* basic kicks. If needed for the clarity of the narrative, some of them will be very briefly illustrated as a reminder...

➤

This volume deals with **Ground Kicks** only, as a variation of all six basic categories of Essential Kicks presented in previous work (Front, Side, Back, Roundhouse, Hook and Crescent Kicks). Further volumes are in preparation to present the complex Multiple kicks, the devastating Joint kicks and the no-nonsense Krav Maga Kicks.

Some Advanced Kicks have been omitted, as the author felt he had to draw the line somewhere. Again the decision was arbitrary, and could be considered as open for discussion. First have been omitted the whole range of nuances of a given kicks: As already mentioned, the same basic kicks are delivered in slightly different ways in all different styles and schools. The small differences come from the different emphasis of each style, and do not alter the basic principles. The author therefore described the kicks in the way his own experience dictates as best, and each reader can adapt it to his own personality. Many possible variations are presented for completeness in the applications though.

Secondly, hybrid kicks variations have been omitted, as the infinite number of intermediate possible deliveries in between two kicks would make this endeavor ridiculous. For example, many possible kicks as hybrids of Front and Roundhouse Kicks exist, each one with different levels of emphasis on the "front" side and the "roundhouse" side. In this specific book about Jumping Kicks of all types, it is even truer: there are a great number of deliveries possibilities to execute a Flying Front Kick, as the length and height of the jump is highly dependent on the circumstances and the reaction of the opponent.

Flying Knee Strike

Kicks combinations, and kick-punch combinations are infinite in numbers and will not be presented as such; *but hinted at in the Applications.* Knee strikes, although very effective and versatile, will not be presented; for the purpose of this work, they will not be considered as kicks.

The remaining **Ground Kicks** which will be presented in this work, will be so, generally, in a set descriptive way: After a brief **General** introduction and the **Description** of the kick (mainly by illustrations), the main **Key Points** to remember for a good execution will be noted. Please remember that the book is intended for conversant martial artists. The relevant **Targets** to be kicked in most applications will be mentioned, although only general targets will be mentioned: The specific and precise vulnerable points are out of the scope of this volume. Examples of **Typical Applications** will then be detailed and illustrated. The typical application will generally be, unless irrelevant, a detailed use or set up of the given kick in a tournament-type situation.

➤

This will generally be a movements combination based on alternating different attack angles or/and levels (For example: hi-lo-hi, or/and outside/inside/outside), or the Progressive Indirect Attack principle as it is called by *Jeet Kune Do* artists. The tactical principle involved will not be detailed or presented systematically though, as it is beyond the scope of this volume. Of course, those applications will also usually be relevant to real life situation, and training work.

Whenever possible, **Specific Training** tips to improve the given kick will be detailed. The specific training section will be brief and will only deal with the very specific characteristics of the kick and the ways to perfect them; general kick training guidelines are outside the scope of this book. The training of a *Ground Kick* is generally also the drilling of the corresponding Essential standing basic kick. Back to basics then! Last, and in order to widen the scope of applications, additional examples of the use of the kick will be presented, generally more suitable to a **Self-defense** or Mixed Martial Arts application.

And now the reader is asked to remember that the fact that this particular book (and the whole 'Kicks' Series) has cataloged a great number of kicks does not mean that he has to know and master them all. As already mentioned, a good Martial Artist must first master the basics of his chosen style by hard work on the *Essential* techniques. Only when he has done so, should he try advanced maneuvers and special techniques from other Arts. He should then drill new and unconventional techniques, and then try them in free fighting. A real Artist will then know how the choose only *a few* techniques that are suitable to his morphology, psychology and liking. These very few techniques will then have to be drilled for thousands and thousands of times until they become natural. During the fight, it the *body* that intuitively choses the best technique to be used. If you have to think about what to do, you have already lost! Practice makes perfect. Again, in other authors' words:

I fear not the man who has practiced 10,000 kicks once, but I fear the man who has practiced one kick 10,000 times.
~ Bruce Lee

Train hard, fight easy
~Alexander Suvorov

So drill the Kicks and Applications as presented. Then adapt them to your physiology and psychology. Keep drilling and try them in free fighting. The follow-up presented are indicative only and intended to make you think. Try them before replacing by your own. And now, let us go to GROUND KICKS...

INTRODUCTION TO GROUND KICKS

Foreword

Ground Kicks are an important skill to acquire for the well-rounded Martial Artist. These Kicks are usually not very prominent in most of the mainstream kickboxing arts, but it is mainly because of the strong competitive sport influence. This has changed recently, with the upcoming tsunami of MMA fighting and the ground submission craze: kicking from the ground has become more common. But, unfortunately, it is still mainly used to keep an opponent at bay, to create an opportunity to safely stand back up or to try to repel the 'advances' of a good grappler.

Some Traditional Arts do, on the contrary, emphasize ground fighting and ground kicking. One can think of some Chinese *Kung Fu* styles (Southern Shaolin Dog style, Drunken style, Monkey styles...) and some Indonesian *Pencak Silat* styles (*Tanjakan, Harimau,...*) for example. And usually, those are the styles basing their tactics on surprise and misdirection. *Capoeira* artists,-the foremost masters of deception-, never really lie or sit on the floor, but they hover very low, close to the ground, switching anchor points from hands, feet and head: their Art shows how effective it is to be able to move fast close to the floor and kick acrobatically from down under. Fighting systems like Russian *Systema* do encourage free-fighting with one protagonist on the floor and they teach many takedown techniques from the ground.

The complete Martial Artist should master ground-kicking, not only because some surprising and effective techniques can be used when going deliberately to the ground in certain situations (Stop-kicking comes to mind); but also because he could find himself down there unwillingly. One can slip, be thrown to the ground, be knocked down or even be attacked when just sitting around. One can also be fighting a better grappler than himself and would want to be able to keep his opponent away, especially when downed. One could be an excellent grappler and would prefer to be fighting from the floor, hoping to get his opponent to join him down. One could be a frequent user of Flying Kicks, at the end of which one often finds himself on the floor and in need of a follow-up. Going to the ground against a very skilled high-kicker will tend to neutralize his potential advantage; that is another good reason to drill Ground Kicks...

Going down against a skilled high kicker will neutralize his key advantage

... The reasons abound, and you could add, most importantly, that you should study and drill Ground Kicks **_because their practice also improves very much your general kicking skills_**. Because your position on the ground neutralizes some muscles groups, the Ground Kick from the floor will always be different from its standing counterpart. Compensation for the "un-usable" muscles will require more from other groups and a different delivery, although the underlying basic principles of effective kick delivery will stay the same. *This altogether makes the practice of Ground Kicks an excellent drill for general kicking proficiency*: just as bodybuilding exercises are based on focusing the effort on muscle groups, the Ground Kick will focus more power on less muscle groups and will complete general training. It will also teach the trainee multi-positional kicking, a basic tenet of kicking proficiency: being able to kick from any position, instinctively and at any angle necessary.

In our previous work about *Essential Kicks*, we have already described a few basic **Drop Kicks**. Those are basically the techniques in which you go down to the ground from a regular standing position, *while* delivering a "Ground Kick", usually to surprise the opponent by the change of plane, or to quickly remove your upper body from an area of danger. Please refer to those Kicks in previous work for a more complete picture. We shall mention the relevant individual Drop Kicks in this book at the corresponding sections, but succinctly and just for completeness. The practicing Martial Artist will understand easily that any Ground Kick can be delivered while dropping down and become a *Drop Kick*.

Side Drop Kick against high kicker

But in this book, we shall try to concentrate in describing the *pure* Ground Kicks as delivered from a set ground position.

The importance of ground-fighting skills is very clear in these days and age of *MMA*- and *Brazilian JuJitsu*-fame. In fact, kicking from the ground should be the prelude to ground submission fighting if possible. And a fighter who does not excel in ground grappling though, should better kick in order to allow for his going back to stand-up guard, as will be described later in this book.
I shall conclude this introduction, at the top of next page, with a personal anecdote illustrating, again, the importance of Ground Kicks.

➡

...Here it comes. In the 1980ies, already a skilled fighter, I had my first encounter with a *Capoeira* Artist. I was relatively adept at ground fighting, but of the then-common Judo-style type (*Ne Waza*); I had no idea people could kick from the ground with sophistication. *Karate* and *Kickboxing* were very set in their ways, and they were the fashionable items then. I agreed to some light free-fighting in the dojo with my new acquaintance to find myself at a loss of what to do from my standing position to a guy on the floor moving fast, crab walking-style, and kicking me in the knees. I became conscious of how close my groin was to his kicks while his vital targets were far from my natural weapons. I suddenly realized that being on the ground could be *far from a losing proposition* in the real world, something my tournament-winning Karate Sweeps had hidden from me. The importance of Ground Kicks and of Ground Submission Fighting are obvious today (like a TV remote or a cell phone); but it has not been eternally so... Learning and drilling Ground Kicking skills is definitely a requisite for the well-rounded modern Martial Artist.

The ground guard

Some styles do teach a *Ground Stance*. In my opinion, the term "Ground Stance", although not technically an oxymoron, should be considered one. The author strongly feels that there are two cardinal rules in ground fighting:

1.	**When in fighting range, always be on the move; preferably attacking.**
2.	**Never try to stand back up, unless you are totally out of range.**

Orthodox Ground Stances or Guards in Japanese Arts are codified, but the author does not feel it had a real martial meaning. Those were more meditation or intermediate dynamic stances: From *Seiza No Kamae* (Kneeling position, sitting on your heels) to *Hantachi* (kneeling on the balls of your feet, ready to stand up), and passing through *Suwari Gata No Kamae* (Crossed-leg sitting). Big names for trivial things...

Practically, the Ground Stances, described in the Figure at the top of next page, should be considered a reference point, or a starting position when hitting the floor: Your feet are close to the body, protecting it, chambered for kicking and away from possible stomps. One hand is in guard for blocks and stop-punches, and the other is on the floor for balance and ease of movement. You could be lying down fully, half-up on your elbow or fully up on your hand as illustrated. Just remember: *keep moving* and switch positions!

Should you be put on the defensive by being immediately hit and kicked, you should temporarily adopt the **"Shell" Stance** (at the bottom of the illustration), covering yourself with bent legs and arms; in this "Shell Position", you can roll away or move like "Humpty Dumpty". More on Ground Movement in a following section.

But in fact, as soon as your opponent gets into range, you should be kicking his ankles, knees and groin to keep him away and in front of you. Although it may not look so, you have the advantage: his vulnerable points are easy targets for you, while you are protected and are a difficult target. To get to you, he must bend forward and/or open himself. Just do not let him overtake you to your side and always keep on the move.

All this is true if you are a kicker and/or a poor grappler. Should you be an expert grappler, - a *Brazilian Ju-Jitsu* fighter or a *Ne-Waza Judo* specialist- , you then want to catch your opponent in between your legs and pull him to the floor.

Ground guard variations and the Shell Position

The "Ground Guard" for a grappler would then be controlling your opponent's limbs while having him between your legs, as commonly seen in *MMA* fights (See next Figure). This is, of course, outside the scope of this book, although a few examples will be given in context. There have been full books written about "The Guard", as keeping control and submitting an opponent from this position is a complex subject; this is what *BJJ* is all about, together with a lot of sweat and hard work.

The grappling Ground Guard

The secret of getting ahead is getting started.
~Mark Twain

Getting down to the ground

As mentioned, you should never be immobile on the floor, especially when in fighting range. There are many ways to move on the ground, and it is important to master them all: *you should be able to move quickly from any position you might find yourself in!* Moreover, the practice of this "Ground Footwork" is an extremely good exercise for warming-up, for muscle building and for general kicking proficiency. *Drilling ground-movement* is a highly recommended stamina and tactical training routine; the reader is encouraged to squeeze it in whenever he can. We will present here the most important ground-moving styles, as well as drills for *going down to the ground in a controlled way* if so you wish (Although it should be noted that, in the author's opinion, the best way to "go down to the ground" is with an *Offensive Drop Kick*!). Once you have mastered these moves, practice while capping 'going down' with an <u>immediate</u> follow-up Kick.

Here are presented the main "<u>To-the-ground-descents</u>" and then, further on, the main "<u>Ground-steps</u>". We present them in following sections because they are strongly related, as they are also related to the "Standing-back-up" moves presented later. It should be noted that the list is not exhaustive but only presents the most commonly occurring maneuvers.

a. Getting down to the ground:

- **The Front Roll** (*Mae Ukemi- Judo; Zen Po Kaiten – Nin Jitsu*). See Illustration. You roll forward on one shoulder and land on the ground in "guard". Of course, the *Full Front Roll* in which you finish back up on your feet as practiced in *Judo* sessions could be an evasive move and should be practiced as such as well. On the other hand, the Front Roll will be categorized as a <u>ground movement</u> if you start from a kneeling position and finish still on the ground. So you can basically start either standing up or kneeling down, and you can finish either back standing or lying on the ground; all four possibilities should be drilled for completeness and versatility. Finally, it should be noted that the Front Roll can easily be capped by an "*Axe Kick*" and we shall give such examples in the text's relevant kicking sections.

The stand-up to ground Front Roll

- **The Back Roll** (*Ushiro Ukemi- Judo; Tachi Nagare – Nin Jitsu*). See following Drawings. You bend your rear leg to land on the floor and roll rearwards on one shoulder. You can, again, stay on the ground or use the momentum to stand all the way back up (*Full Back Roll*). Just like the Front Roll, the Back Roll from the standing-up position can be an evasive maneuver like it is much-practiced in *Nin Jitsu*; it can also be simply a basic ground movement when starting from the ground. The Back Roll can be capped by a surprising kick, and a few examples will be provided in the text (Front Kick, Downward Roundhouse Kick and more).

The Full Back Roll, from standing to standing

- **The Side Breakfall** (*Yoko Ukemi - Judo*). You simply throw your straight rear-leg up while bending the standing knee to land on your side. From there on, you either can land while slapping the floor judo-style and stay down as illustrated by the first Figure; or you can roll your back and keep rolling 'Back Roll-style' (*Yoko Ushiro Ukemi*) as illustrated in the next set of Srawings. The Side Roll illustrated can lead you all the way back up (as illustrated), but can also let you settle on the ground after the roll.

Yoko Ukemi, the Side Breakfall

Yoko Ushiro Ukemi, the Side Roll all the way back up

- **The Bent-leg Back Descent**. The first Figure shows how you simply bend the rear leg to sit down on your rear foot, and then spread back. This is a very basic and natural sit-down. You can finish it with a *Back Roll* or even a *Full Back Roll* all the way back to standing. An intermediate step worth practicing is putting the rear knee on the floor before sitting back as illustrated by the second set of Drawings; in this case, you push back from the front leg while sitting down, which takes you a bit more rearwards.

Sit back down on your rear leg

Back knee to the floor, then push back to sit down

- **The Sit-down Descent**: See Illustration. You simply bend both legs and squat down, put your bottom down on the floor and either spread *or* roll back. If you roll back, of course you can then either spread after the roll or stand back all the way up. By working on both your flexibility and your stamina, you should become able to sit down on your bottom with no need for rolling back at all, as is routinely practiced in *Yoga* classes. It is recommended to practice the small up-and-down movement from squat-to-sit and back from sit-to-squat until it becomes easy (See next Figure).

Squat down and sit

The assiduous practice of P*lyometrics and Intense Stretching* will also help (refer to '*Plyo-Flex*' by the same author).

A great little drill: squat, sit, squat... with minimal movement

- **The Two-hand Descent**: See Illustrations. Pretty straightforward: you kneel and place both hands on the floor; you then use the hands as support to throw your legs to the front and roll on your back to guard position. Note that many *Drop Kicks* start from this Hands-on-floor position. Keep your eyes on your opponent and do not bend forward when squatting.

The simple Two-hand Descent

- **The Single-hand Descent**: See Figures. Just like the Two-hand Descent, but place only one hand on the ground. Keep the front hand *in guard* and throw the rear leg forward to roll back (which also allows you to keep one hand in guard).

The classic Single-hand Descent

- **The Crossed-leg Descent**. We have all done the drill (Illustrated by the Drawing) in Phys Ed at school when we were kids. Now, let us just practice it with *focus*, *explosiveness and without telegraph*: Cross legs and sit down into ("Indian") crossed-legs Sitting. From the sitting position, extend your legs into guard or start moving on the ground. This drill should be also done as a muscle-building exercise by going up and down with no pause until really exhausted.

- **Hand-on-floor Kicks**. As mentioned in the introduction, I think that the best and safest way to go down to the ground is *while being offensive*: Kick and go down while your opponent is hit and flustered. We are not talking here about the *Drop Kicks* already mentioned, where you drop first then kick; we are talking about *kicking first and then going down*!...

... Of course the distinction is often theoretical only as both actions take place more or less simultaneously, but the distinction is an important emphasis for practice and educational organization (As promised, examples of Drop Kicks will be presented for completeness at the end of the future sections about specific kicks). Going down to the ground will be best done after a kick executed with one or two hands already on the floor! You are kicking, but you are already half-way to the floor. Many examples of those "*Hand-on-floor-Kicks*" are presented in our previous book about Basic Kicks (*The Essential Book of Martial arts Kicks – Tuttle Publishing*); the reader is invited to refer to it for more information. The photographs below do illustrate only some of those important **Hand-on-floor Kicks**.

Hand-on-floor Kicks: Side Kick, Downward Back Kick, Overhead Back Kick, Drop Back Kick, close Hook Kick

-       **Face-down Descents**. In some cases, it is of interest to go to the ground fast and face-down; maybe the assailant is behind you, or you have tripped and have no choice. There are basically **2** basic ways: falling straight down as illustrated by the first Drawing (*top of next page*), or squatting before throwing the legs back as illustrated in the second Figure. *The first option* is the classic *Front Break-fal*l of older *Judo* and *Ju-Jitsu* (*Mae Ukemi*) which is important to practice as a break-fall, just in case: you fall straight down like a plank and brake the fall by bending your arms to dissipate the energy, as would your car's suspension. Start to practice from a high kneeling position and progress gradually to the throwing yourself up from stand-up position. *The second option* is the classic *Burpee* Callisthenic, presented here in its *Plyometric Drill* version where you jump up as high as possible from the kneeling position. For going to the ground, you will of course stop at the rearwards leg extension. Both options lead you to lying in prone position on the floor, <u>which is usually not an enviable position</u>: Get moving ASAP! The simplest follow-up would be to roll on your back and take the guard position (as illustrated in the next set of Drawings). An interesting alternative, especially if your assailant is on your head's side, would be a Yoga jump into sitting as illustrated by the following Figures. And, in any case, this *Yoga Jump* is a fantastic drill for flexibility, stamina and body awareness, especially if executed in proper classic form.

Ju-Jitsu's Mae Ukemi, a must-
practice

Classic Burpee drill

Do not stay face-down, simply roll onto your back

The classic Yoga 'Plank to Staff' transition

- **Submission pull-downs.** In this day and age of *MMA*, the reader will not be surprised that a Martial Artist can grab his opponent, throw himself down to the ground and pull the opponent with him while setting up a submission like an arm-lock, a leg-lock or a triangle choke. These take-downs are, of course, beyond the scope of this book but should be mentioned. The Figures below show an easy classic example from Ju-Jitsu; there are many more.

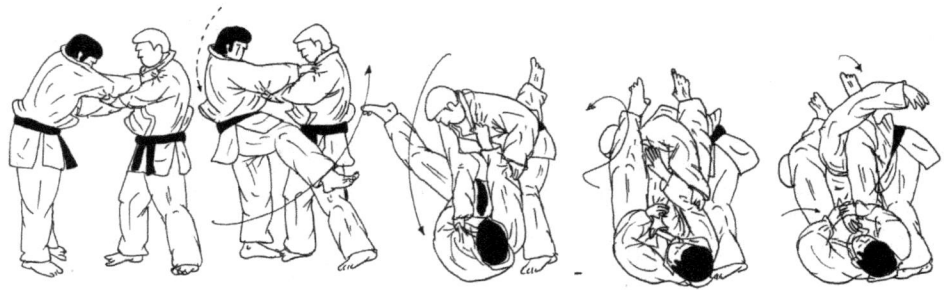

Juji-Gatame *arm-lock set up from standing*

- **Sacrifice throws.** These are the *Sutemi Waza* of *Judo* and *Ju-Jitsu* in which you "sacrifice" your standing position in order to take your opponent to the ground. We are presenting for illustration, in the coming Figures sets, two basic *Sutemi Nage* in their Judo form, starting from the Judo mutual hold in traditional *Judogi*. It is clear to the experienced Artist that many such Sacrifice Throws exist in

The Classic Tomoe Nage of Judo

many forms and without the necessity of traditional wear like the *Gi*. Enough to watch a recent *MMA* fight to realize that most throws are of the "Sacrifice" type and get both protagonists to the ground. It is also clear that you could kick your opponent from afar, then grab him and the take him down. For example, the first illustrated throw (*Tomoe Nage*) could come after bending the opponent over with a Front Kick to the solar plexus, then followed by a grab. These combinations are, though, far beyond the scope of this book and left to the own research or practice by the reader.

Tomoe Nage, the "Wheel" throw

The Classic **Yoko Otoshi** *of Judo*

- **Capoeira's Ginga**. As already mentioned in the Introduction, *Capoeira* is a fantastic Martial Art for lovers of ground- or quasi-ground-fighting. Needless to add that it is a great kicking art and an excellent physical condition training regimen. The *Capoeirista* hovers close to the ground and is always in motion, switching positions and feinting. He is training by dancing to the rhythm of music in the *Roda* (Circle of practicioners) against a partner who is as restless as he is. The basic *Capoeira* moving stance is the '*Ginga*', from which nearly any move can become a going down to the ground by using feet, hands, head and shoulders as anchors or pivots. The interested reader is invited to research *Capoeira* moves for his own practice. We shall limit ourselves to illustrating a basic switch from *Ginga* to a lowering evasion (*Negativa*), presented in the next Drawings. This is really only the shadow of the tip of the iceberg, but not the subject of this book.

A basic Capoeira move getting you to the ground

- **Twist Down Descent**. Here come three classic evading steps common to many Arts that are worth drilling and that will take you down safely. The Photos show how to simply twist while bending the knees for a *Spin-back Descent*. The practical use of these important maneuvers is explained in our book about *Essential Kicks*.

The Twist-Down Drill

- **Goose Step Descent**. This is a great drill for strength and situational kicking. Refer to *Essential Kicks*. The technique is good to come up or to go down, as illustrated by the Photos.

The Goose Step Drill

-      **Cross-step Evading-out Descent**. This is a classic evading step of some *Kung Fu* styles; a great drill and a surprising technique to get out of a center-line thrust. From the end-position, you can either go to the ground or spring back up.

Step out of the center-line and cross-kneel down

b. Ground Movement

As mentioned, some ground movements are partly descent-to-the-ground moves described in the previous section. The list below in not exhaustive, as you can basically move as simply or as acrobatically as you want; but it presents the most commonly used moves. All are great stamina-builders and should be drilled often, for example as competitive races with partners in the dojo.
Here come these promised 'Ground Steps':

-      **The Knee Walk**. See Figure. This is the traditional way the Japanese used to move in kneeling position, sometimes called 'Samurai Walk'. This great exercise is common in *Aikido* and in traditional *Ju-Jitsu* styles; it is often drilled as a warm-up or a strength-building move. It is an important part of the classic forms of techniques in which one or both protagonists are sitting on their knees (*Suwari Waza*). You simply use one knee, or the front knee as an anchor to pivot with your hips ninety degrees; then repeat on the other side.

The Knee Walk: pivoting on your knees

- **The Knee Step**. See next Figure. In this method, you step forward with one leg, or the back leg if you are in movement-, and then you lower the knee straight forward to the ground while pulling the other knee. Repeat. This feels more natural to Occidental trainees and it is a very good drill, but better executed on a mat. You should drill for form first, but then later for speed (*fast*) or for stamina (*until exhausted*).

The Knee Step method, a good exercise

- **The Crab Walk**. See Figure. This is a very important exercise, statically reminding of *Capoeira* transitional moves. This is an explosive way to move fast, and in a position from which it is easy to kick. This <u>must-do drill</u> is also a great way to build strength and stamina. Remember, though, that your groin is quite unprotected and that you should *always be on the move*.

The unorthodox Crab Walk

- **The Monkey Walk**. See coming Figure. This great callisthenic is a simple and classic way to move on the floor, which you are touching with hands and feet only (not with the knees!). It is, by the way, typical of the 'Monkey styles' of *Kung-Fu*. It allows for easy transitions and changes of direction, as well as for standing up. Continuous practice will help build your core and leg muscles! [The version *with no-hands* is called "Duck Walking", -basically walking in squat position. It is also a great strength-building drill, but with less relevance to ground moving for fighting; it was an ubiquitous strength exercise when I started Judo fifty years ago.]

The simple and natural Monkey Walk

- **The Front and Back Rolls**. Both those moves have been described in the '*Going-to-the-ground*' section above. You simply start the roll from a kneeling position and finish it on the ground as well (lying in guard or kneeling). Many examples will be presented in the applications further in the book.

-    **The Side Shoulder Roll** (*Sokuho Kaiten – Nin Jitsu*). See Figure below. This is simply a shortened Front Roll or a kind of Side Roll (presented below), and this, executed from a kneeling position. The Illustration is clearer than a thousand words; just notice that you can emphasize the "side" or the "front" rolling according to the circumstances.

The Side Shoulder Roll: a hybrid between Front- and Side-Roll

-    **The Side Roll**. See next Figure. Lying on your back, you simply roll a full 360 turn sideways, a bit like a turtle. This move should be practiced for speed *with legs bent and with legs straightened*. It is a fast and easy evasive move, but it should be drilled seriously and not taken for granted. Sometimes, speed is of the essence.

The Side Roll: fast and easy

-    **The Buttock Walk**. See coming Figure. This is an exercise we have all done at some point, whether in games or in training. Using only our buttocks, -one cheek at a time-, to go forward or backward is (1) a great stamina builder, (2) a fantastic exercise for the abdominal belt and (3) an effective situational drill for ground movement. Of course, you are not going to run away from your opponent "buttock-walk-style"; but this is a great transitional move between many others. As a drill, it is easy to present to the students as a race (forwards and backwards) to forge Dojo camaraderie while motivating by competition.

Move forward and backward by using your buttocks exclusively

-    **The Feet-based Buttock Pivot**. See the Figure at the top of next page. On the ground, you do not go back and forth in a straight line, not ever! You must keep on the move and constantly change angles and direction. The *Buttock Pivots* are only one of the ways to change direction, together with the Rolls already covered and other trivial body movements...

➡

... This method uses the feet, in a sitting position, to pivot around your center axis; and your buttocks are the point of contact of this axis and the ground. This is, again, a transitional move, from which you can roll, walk, lie in guard, and more... For stamina and familiarization, drill full turns in both directions, as fast as possible.

Pivot on your buttocks by using your feet only

- **The Hand-based Buttock Pivot**: See coming Figure. This method uses the hands on the ground to propel your body in the buttock pivot; and you need to lift your legs to make this possible. The raised legs make it a nice abdominal drill as well: execute full turns in both directions, as fast as possible.

Lift your feet and pivot smoothly on your glutes, using your hands only

- **The Humpty-Dumpty Pivot**. See next Figure. The "Humpty-Dumpty" move is *very useful* in ground movement: rolling back gives you the necessary range for a powerful forward momentum. The resulting forward momentum can be used to kick, to pivot, to stand up or even to jump up. In the *Humpty-Dumpty Pivot*, you lift your legs and roll back on your shoulders, but you do not complete the roll; with the stored energy you roll forcefully forward *while pivoting on your back*. Keep moving in the new direction you are now facing.

The Humpty-Dumpty Pivot

- **The Hops**. Of course, you can hop from a kneeling position; you can hop in several directions; you can hop *long* (first Figures at the top of next page) or you can hop *high* while kicking (second Figure, next page). This is trivial and logical, but it should certainly be mentioned for completeness. Practical examples will be given along the book. You can of course do several hops in series; and you can also simply stand up and jump,...Everything goes.

➤

Long Hop

From kneeling directly to Flying Front Kick

- **The Knee-to-knee Pivot**. See Illustrations. This is a transitional pivot from which you keep moving smoothly by extending the leg, by rolling, or anything else. From a one-knee-up/one-knee-down sitting position, you pivot fully while lifting the down knee and lowering the other knee. A great drill and a move to be used to connect other ground moves.

The transitional Knee-to-knee Pivot

- **The Extended-leg Walk**. See Drawings. This is more sophisticated and requires more flexibility, and it is therefore and good exercise. It is also a very good situational drill giving you the feeling of ground movement principles. From a kneeling position, you extend one leg and "hook" the ground with your heel. Pull yourself forward by bending this leg and repeat on the other side.

The challenging Extended-leg Walk

- **The Leg-sweep Walk**. See Figure *at the top of next page*. This is another challenging and sophisticated drill in which you use, again, an extended leg to pull yourself forward on the ground; but this time, you bring the rear leg forward *in an arc reminiscent of the wide Kung Fu Leg Sweep* (Sometimes called 'Iron Broom').

The difficult Leg-sweep Walk

Standing back up

As already mentioned: **Do not attempt to stand up while in the fighting range!** While standing up, you are at your most vulnerable. Only stand up *when totally out of range of your opponent*: Should he rush you as you start standing up, you should have time to complete your move and get into a full-fledged fighting stance with guard up and forward-focused fighting spirit (*Zanchin*).

Herebelow are a few of the best ways to stand up; and the list is certainly not exhaustive. These are also great strengthening exercises, and they'll prepare you for an automatic and fast standing recovery when needed. Practice by repeating the Drills at least 10 times in a row. A great strength-building drill is kicking immediately after the stand-up, go back down and repeat until exhausted!
Standing-up moves are strongly related to some ground moves and getting-to-the ground ones: practice all Drills with an open mind and in series, by easing from one to another. Afterwards, we shall recommend that they be bundled together for drilling with smooth transitions into a long uninterrupted exercise, going up, down, back, forward,...

- **The Front Roll Stand-up**. Refer to the Drawings. The Roll is identical to the "*Going to the ground*" one. Simple. Rolls must be drilled from the ground in all ground positions (lying, sitting, kneeling), and they must be drilled from standing, all the way to ground positions or back to standing. Front Rolls must be drilled for both height and/or length of the jump.

The Front Roll Stand-up

Sensei Sidney Faiga, *founder of the Shay-Heun School, in a 'kicking' high front Roll – 1950ies*

- **The Back Roll Stand-up**. See the explanatory Figures below. It is similar to the previously presented Back Rolls. The Back Roll has the advantage of taking you *away* from the opponent (if you are facing him, of course...).

The Back Roll Stand-up

- **The "Humpty Dumpty" Stand-up**. See Illustrations. The Humpty-Dumpty move was presented earlier in *Ground Moves*. As it uses a balancing move to create momentum, it is of great use to stand up fast. You gather energy by rolling back, and then roll forward all the way up. The regular rolling variation is presented in the first set of Drawings; the more energetic, spectacular and acrobatic "kicking-out" version is presented in the next set at the top of next page.

Humpty-Dumpty rolling Stand-up

Humpty-Dumpty jumping Stand-up

- **The One-leg-sit Stand-up**. Illustrated below. This is a very simple and natural stand-up, which makes it even more important to practice and drill *with focus and concentration*.

Drill for speed and for achieving an immediate strong guard position. The Stand-up can be preceded by a Humpty-Dumpty move.

The natural One-leg-sit Stand-up

- **The Knee-stance Stand-up**. See Illustrations. This is also a very natural stand-up: you first get into a *Knee Stance*, and then straighten the rear leg into a full standing guard. The advantage of this stand-up is that you are in focused guard all the way up. This Stand-up is worth drilling a lot: not only is it a good strengthening exercise, but its simplicity should not lure you into neglecting it. By drilling, you will improve speed much more than commonly expected, while building powerful legs.... Yes! I know it is boring.... But important.

Get in Knee Stance first, then stand up with concentration

- **The Knees-straightening Stand-up**. See Figure. This is trivial, but should be drilled all the same for speed, flexibility and strength. You simply lift your knees from the ground into kneeling position, and straighten your knees. You can also jump from sitting on your knees into kneeling, and then straighten.

Simply straighten your knees

- **The Hand-assisted Stand up**. As illustrated. Using one hand to help you stand up is also trivial and natural. The advantage of this method is that you pull your legs rearwards and stand up away from the opponent. The use of the hand helps for a fast stand-up. This one is quite important, although not sexy, and should be seriously drilled for speed, explosiveness and smoothness of execution.

The simple but important Hand-assisted Stand-up

- **The Both-hands-assisted Stand-up**. See Drawings. This stand-up is the same as the previous one, but uses *both* hands to help; comments and key points are identical.

The Both-hands-assisted Stand-up

Now that we have reviewed how to move on the floor and how to stand back up, we can start the description of the main *Ground Kicks*. Please note that some other Ground Kicks will be described in a future book about *Joint Kicks* that is in preparation, as the author believes that their 'joint kick' aspect is more relevant than their "ground" basis. Please also note that Ground Kicks description will start from an array of positions: Some will be described from a Cross-legged Sitting Position, others from a Ground Guard or sitting on the floor. We shall even sometimes describe the Kicks delivered from sitting on a chair, as it is relevant and a great kicking drill. As mentioned, ground-fighting is exclusively dynamic: there is no lying down immobile and waiting! **You must move constantly**, switching positions and range all the time. And so should you train. Always move and kick! Kick going down, kick between ground moves, and kick going back up

Kick before going down to the ground; it is safer

Crab-walk, kick towards groin, roll back fast into stand-up, immediately kick

These sections about movement on, to and from the ground should be concluded with a **general comment**. The ability to control ground movement can be greatly enhanced by the assiduous practice of ***Yoga Series*** of the type encountered in *Vinyasa* and *Ashtanga Yoga*. The transitions between poses and groups of poses in different planes are akin to ground movement and done in a controlled and economical way, albeit while requiring *flexibility* and high *core strength*. The serious drilling of these series will help develop these qualities, while heightening situational awareness and instinctive ground movement. All this, of course, will be an additional benefit to all other physical and mental improvements that Yoga practice can bring. The practice of Yoga is warmly recommended to all Martial Artists, and to the kick-lovers in particular.

Training

Generating power from the ground is not easy and you will have to train hard. If you want to become an effective ground kicker, you will have to drill for power, especially by hitting heavy *Bags* whether hanging bag, standing bag, bag held by a partner, bag hold by you on the ground in grappling moves, or bag lying on the ground beside you. You will have to kick the *Medicine Ball* fast, hard and far. You should also kick the *old tire*, and kick it as hard as possible from the most awkward of positions, and so learning to develop power from "down under".

Drilling Ground Kicks for power on bags, tires and medicine balls

The development of general **explosive** power is best achieved by the systematic and combined training in both **Plyometrics and Intense Stretching**. The progress that can be achieved by a regular regimen of these combined drills is short of amazing. The reader is invited to refer to our 'Plyo-Flex' reference book.

Hard training is the only way you will be able to translate the standing technique into a worthwhile Ground Kick. Ground Kicks are inherently weaker than standing kicks and need a lot of work, -general and specific-, to become effective.

The good news, though, is that working on improving your Ground Kicks will do much to improve your corresponding regular standing kicks and your general kicking proficiency. The rewards for training hard on ground kicking will follow fast: better stamina, improved general kicking proficiency and a surprisingly effective and deceptive weapon in your arsenal.

It is also important to remember that training ***ground movement*** is key to ground fighting proficiency. Unfortunately, it can sometimes look boring and reward-less to the novice fighter. But the trainee should regularly drill the particular moves and then free-roam on the mat: getting down, moving around, standing up, and then down again. He should do so slowly but with concentration and focus at the beginning; then he should start increasing speed while maintaining the smooth transition between moves. It is recommended to drill free ground-moving in group, so that each participant moves on his own but makes sure he does not bump into another trainee. This is both strength-building and entertaining. An even more fun way to train is playing Ground Soccer with a few students, moving on the Ground and kicking ball towards the other team's goal. Drilling Ground Movement is less interesting than kicking, **BUT** it is extremely important and surprisingly rewarding.

Lastly, the serious ground kicker must work on his **core muscles** for better ground proficiency. This seems trivial, but many trainees prefer to go directly to sexy kicking, (again) and tend to underestimate the importance of core muscle-building. The core musculature is more difficult to train because unresponsive to the traditional large callisthenic movements and the traditional moves of outside muscles' body-building. The best way to develop them is *isometric training*, which basically means with constant muscle length. The five most important exercises for the ground fighter are illustrated below. They are, not surprisingly, *Yoga Poses* to hold for as long as possible, starting from a few seconds and then gradually increasing to several minutes. This may seem easy and boring; it is, in fact, difficult and **extremely beneficial.** These poses are: the Three Planks and the Two Bridges. Do them, preferably every other day for a few minutes each.

The Two Bridge Poses: *Bridge (SiraSetu Bandhasanasana) and Wheel Pose (Urdhva Dhanurasana)*

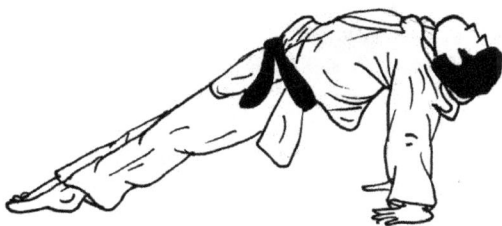

The Three Plank Poses: *High Plank (AdhoMukha Dandasana), Side plank (Vasisthasana) and Upward Plank (Purvottanasana)"]*

Ground Twin Back Kick by Roy Faige

Nothing will work unless you do.
~Maya Angelou

THE KICKS

**Nothing gives one person so much advantage over another as to remain always cool and unruffled under all circumstances.
~Thomas Jefferson**

1.   THE GROUND FRONT KICK

General

The *Ground Front Kick* is probably the simplest of all Ground Kicks: it is fast and easy to deliver. It requires your facing the opponent though, which is not always an enviable position. Please note that it is a great Kick to deliver from the 'Crab Walk position', and it is often so done in *Capoeira* practice. Drill this Kick a lot, from all Ground Positions, and use it automatically if you get involuntarily to the floor. The *Drop Front Kick* has been presented in detail in our work about *Essential Kicks*; it is basically sitting down into the Ground Front Kick: kicking *while* going down.

➡

The classic full penetrating Ground Front Kick

... In this section, we shall present in detail the many possible ways to execute a *Ground Front Kick*: front/rear leg, jumping, assisted and more. This is to show the reader the many possible ground-specific variations that will be applicable to the other Ground Kicks as well. It would be tedious and unnecessary to repeat all these specific variations in full detail for the following Ground Kicks, as the idea and principles stay the same; we shall go through all now, and sprinkle the rest of the book with different examples for the other Ground Kicks.

It should be noted that the Front Kick is a basic Kick which standing version has also many possible standing variations; our previous book about *Essential Kicks* does comprise a full chapter about Front Kicks only. All these variations of the basic Front Kick are applicable to Ground Front Kicks in their own different Ground-specific version. Therefore, the specific Ground variation can also be: penetrating, or upward, or heel, or side, or tilted-heel, or inward-tilted,...and more. It will be left to the reader to experiment these "version within versions" as he becomes more proficient.

Description

The *Ground Front Kicks* are all based on the basic standing Front Kick's development principle, in which you lift the knee high before extending the leg into the target with a hip push; and then retract the leg forcefully as soon as having connected a few inches into the target. The mastery of the Standing Kick is a must to fully understand the biomechanics behind a powerful Front Kick from any position. Drill the basic Kick often and seriously: the basics will always be the basis of your progress (pun intended).

The Figures below and the Photos at the top of next page illustrate the orthodox delivery from an 'Extended-legs sitting-on-the-floor' position: Chamber a regular Front Kick and use one foot and both hands to start lifting your hips from the floor. Kick simultaneously with the forward/upward hip thrust. Chamber back! This is the classic full delivery of the Kick, using maximum power from the body. The hip thrust makes it a full Penetrating Front Kick that you can deliver at any height according to the circumstances: the knee or the groin of a standing opponent, or the face or solar plexus of an opponent on the ground with you.

The basic full Ground Front Kick – Front View

The full Penetrating Ground Front Kick – Side View

Key Points

- Just like for the Essential Standing Front Kick, the *hip thrust* and the Kick are simultaneous, and they reach their full range together for maximum power delivery.
- Remember that the more and the stronger your 'anchors' to the ground (hands and foot), the more powerful your Kick will be.
- Always *chamber back* fast.
- One Ground kick is rarely enough: *keep kicking*.

Variations

The *Ground Front Kick* cannot always be executed in its pure full-hipped form. The Drawings below and the Photos at the top of next page show a "lighter" version, -from a 'Lying-in-guard' position-, in which the hip thrust is replaced by a small hip forward move on the ground. The Kick illustrated is also a more "upward" version of the kick, aiming at hitting diagonally from below, to connect with a groin or a chin for example.

Upward regular Front Ground Kick from lying position

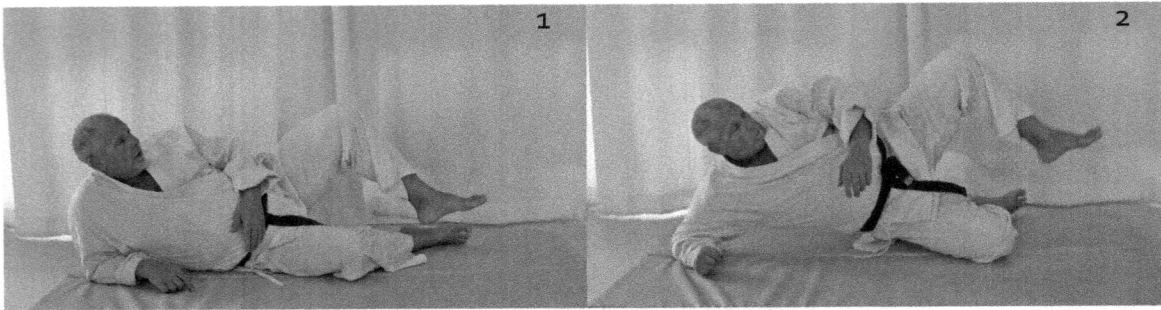

Ground Front Kick; the hip crawl is clear on these pictures

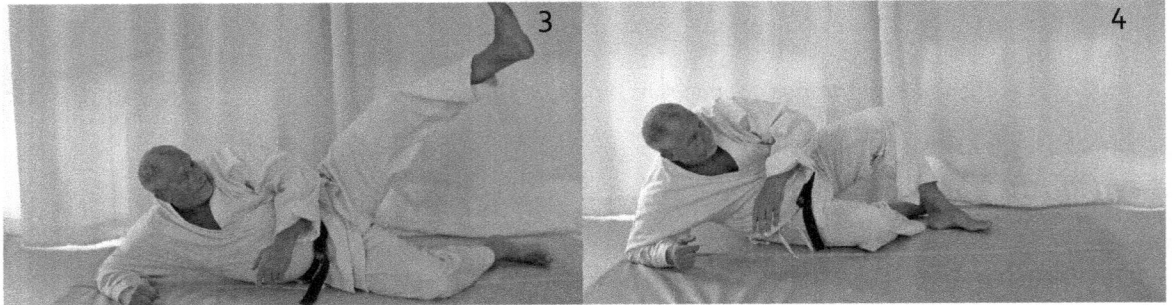

As every novice trainee knows, the basic Standing Front Kick can be delivered either with the front leg, or with the rear leg. There is a parallel to that in ground-kicking: front-leg kicking would be the use of the leg *that is upward in near-chambered position*. The previous example would be such a "front-leg" Kick, usually less powerful than the alternative; but, like its standing counterpart, also faster. The next Figures show another regular *Front Ground Kick*; this time, the purpose is to underline the **"Rear-leg-version" of the kick.** The "Rear-leg" version requiring a body twist, it is inherently more powerful than the "front-leg" version. It is still less powerful than the orthodox full-hipped penetrating version though, and you also need to know that you will finish in opposite stance. Please note that all these distinctions and variations will apply to other Ground Kicks as well, as will be described further in the text.

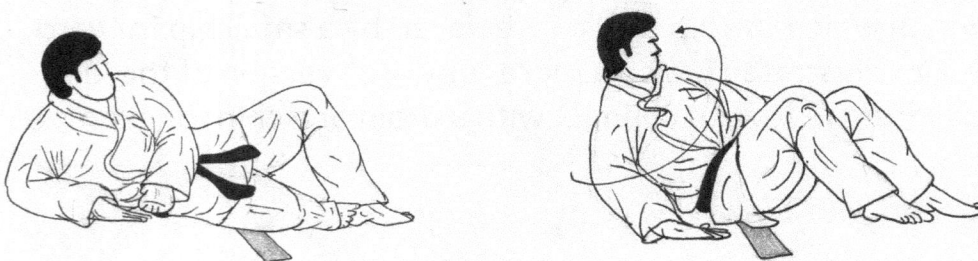

The "rear-leg-version" of the regular Ground Front Kick from lying-down position

An important variation of all Ground Kicks is the **Pressing** or **Assisted** version of the Kicks. We shall refer to those kicks as *Pressing Kicks* in the remainder of this book, although many other names and denominations are in use. This is simply the Kick delivered *while the non-kicking leg is "pressing" upon the opponent and using him as an anchor.* This 'Pressing' usually immobilizes the limb or limbs of the opponent while providing a step on which to push and engage the hips. Many practical examples will be presented in the course of this work, and drilling these *Pressing Kicks* will be done on a chair, a lying bag, a stool, an aerobic step, a tire; anything that gives you the relevant height. In practice the anchor point can be the knee or the thigh of a standing opponent; it can also be a leg or the body of a grounded opponent. The coming Photos illustrate the drilling of one possible *Pressing Ground Front Kick*; but many other variations are possible. The following Figures will then show a typical application of the **Press**, which is an important concept of Ground-fighting.

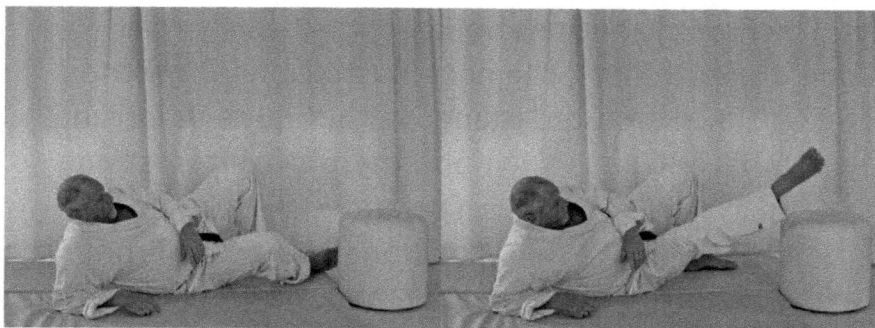

The Pressing Ground Front Kick

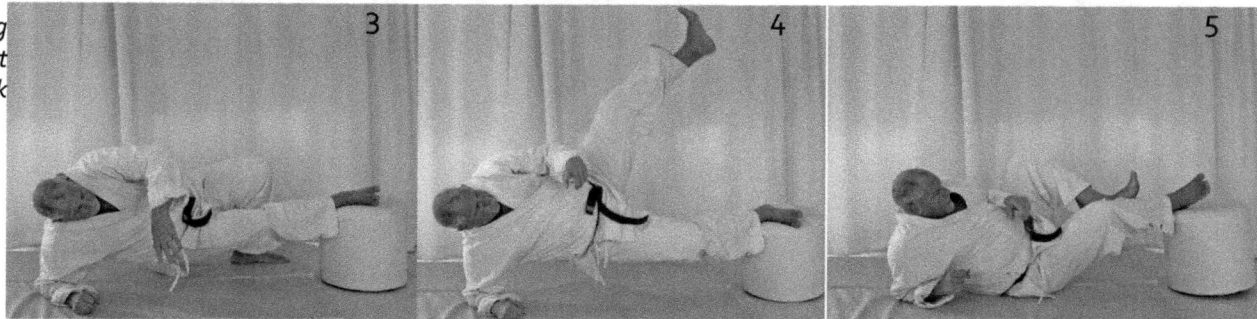

Press the opponent knee down to neutralize both legs and immobilize him; and then, front-kick

Most *Ground Kicks* also allow themselves **Jumping versions** of various types. The Photos at the top of next page do illustrate one possible *Jumping Ground Front Kick*; there are many more, particularly after momentum-building ground moves like the Front Roll.

➡

The Jumping Ground Roundhouse Kick

Many *Ground Kicks* also lend themselves to a **Spin-back version**. Just like for the basic standing Spin-back Kicks, it will be more the realm of Circular Kicks like the Roundhouses, Hooks and Crescents. The Front Kick does not lend itself easily to a spin-back, especially not a ground one. Nevertheless, the next Illustrations show the *Spin-back version of the Ground Front Kick*, a convoluted maneuver but quite surprising and therefore interesting. The end-kick is, again, a diagonally Upward Front Kick, and the whole exercise is a great drill for overall ground proficiency.

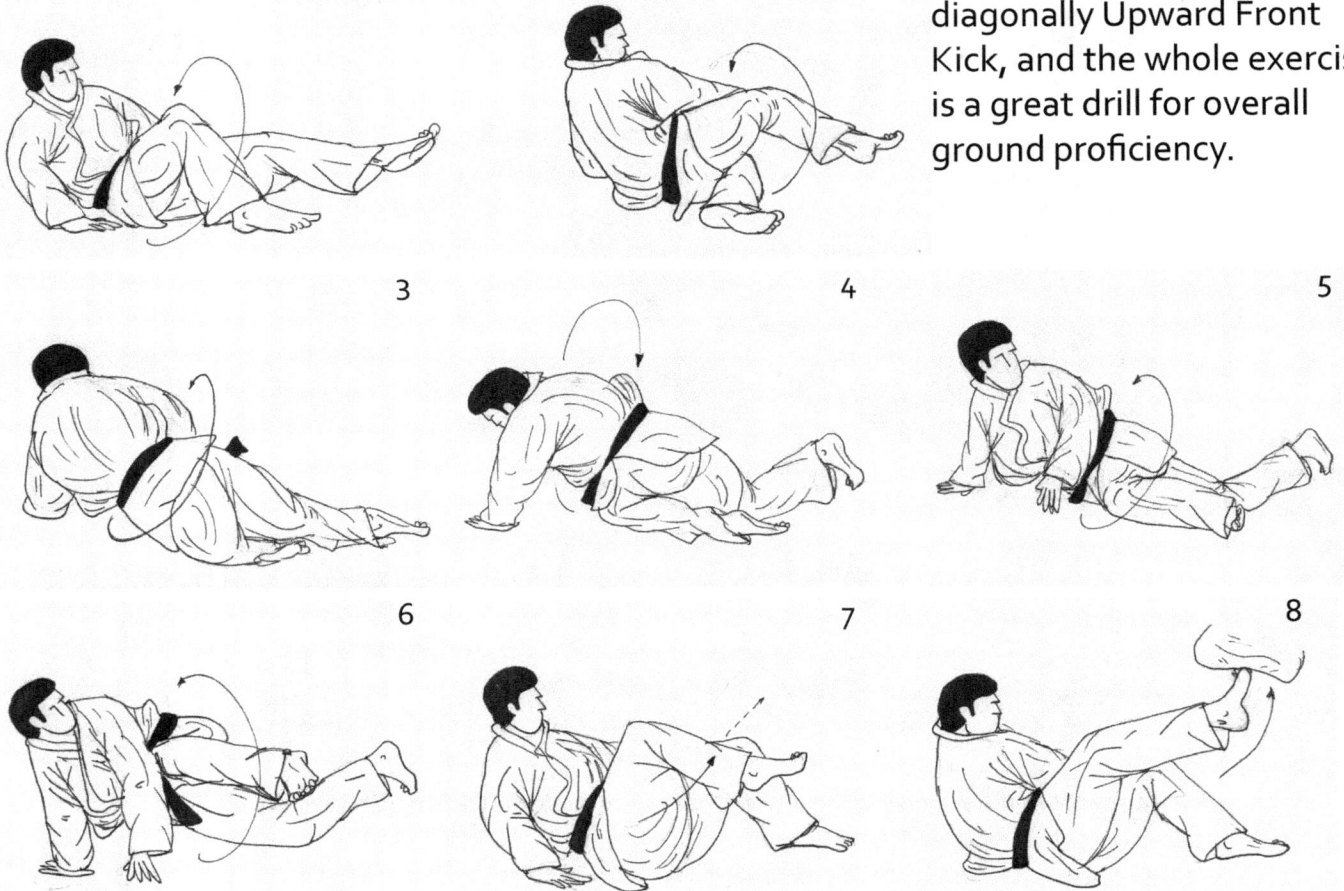

3

4

5

6

7

8

The Ground Spin-back Front Kick

Front-kicking from sitting on your knees (**Zeiza**) or from the **Quadruped position** is quite straightforward. Like most simple things though, it is very efficient, and should be drilled thoroughly, both for kicking proficiency and *as a great way to stand back up*. A great classical exercise is presented in the Illustrations at the top of next page; this is the typical Japanese 'sitting-on-your-knees-technique' against a standing assailant (*Hanmi-handachi Waza*), remnant of Samurai times but very good for martial proficiency. In the example, you evade a straight Heel Front Kick to the face by bending sideways at the last moment, while catching the kicking leg from below. You then immediately kick the offered groin and let your kicking foot land forcefully in a Stomp Kick on the top of the assailant's standing foot. Keep your foot on top of his while pushing him back: the fall will damage his ankle joint (**CAUTION**: In practice, release the stomp before pushing!)

Ground Front Kick from sitting on your knees

Ground Front Kick from all-fours and all the way to stand-up guard

A traditional Tai-Jitsu series with a Ground groin Front Kick from sitting on your knees

A great momentum builder for many *Ground Kicks*, but especially for a fully-hipped Front Kick, is the **Humpty-Dumpty** move previously described in Ground Movement. You roll back and *come back forward forcefully, kicking out before your lower back touches the floor in order to engage the hips into a forward thrust*. This is a very powerful variation of the Penetrating Ground Front Kick. The same effect could be achieved at the end of a full Forward Roll, and it is the reason why Ground Movements must be drilled thoroughly and must become innate and automatic. Further examples of Ground Kicks at the end of a Forward Roll will be presented later in the text.

The powerful Humpty-Dumpty Penetrating Ground Front Kick

Chair Drills

Kicking from sitting on a chair has a lot in common with Ground-kicking: the Kicks are different from the standing ones, because the position limits the muscles that can be used for the specific Kicks. In fact, the *Chair Kicks* are quite similar in execution to the corresponding *Ground Kicks*. That is why we shall present a few examples. *Chair Kicks* are important as drills for muscle-building and for kicking spatial-awareness. But they also certainly have fighting relevance, both for self-defense applications and for general kicking proficiency. One should also remember that a training chair can be a surrogate for a bar, a desk, a table or a parked car. And one should also remember that the same chair can be grabbed after the Kick has been delivered to be used as a poking weapon...

➡

... The next Photos illustrate the same distinction for Chair Kicks that we made for Ground Kicks between the *regular* Front Kick and the *fully-hipped Penetrating version*.

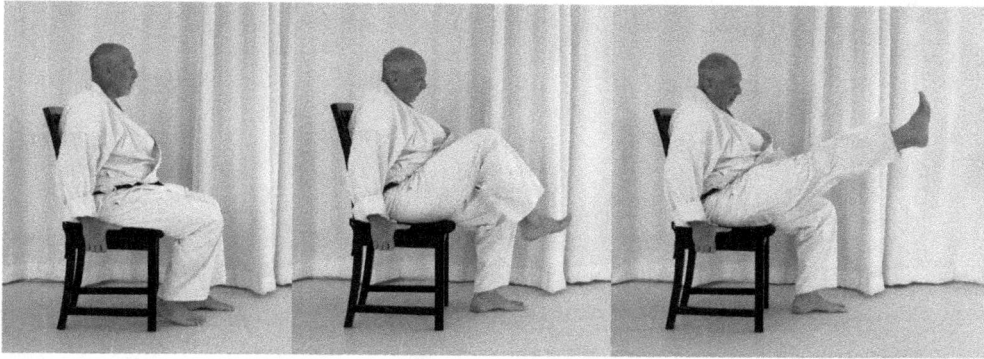

The regular Chair Front Kick

The full-powered Penetrating Chair Front Kick

The reader is now invited to compare this to the **Stand-up-then-kick**-version in the following Photos:

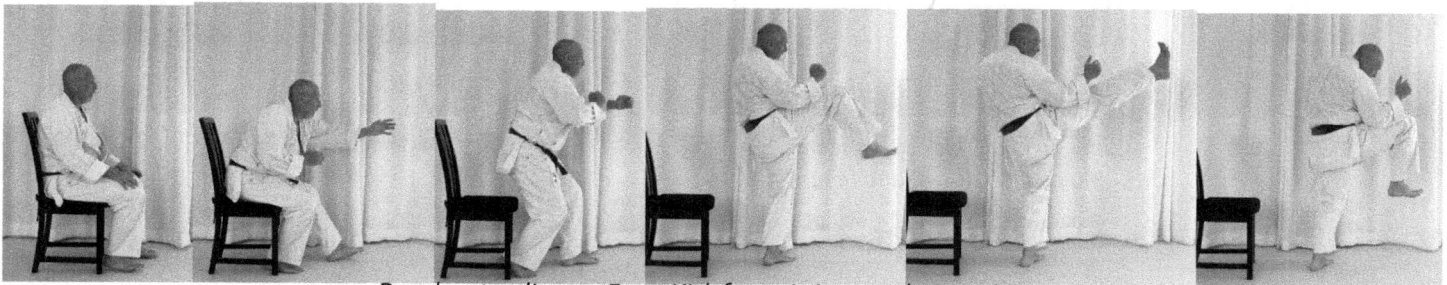

Regular standing-up Front Kick from sitting-on-chair position

As mentioned, a chair is a great training aid; we present here a few possible general drills to illustrate the point. More can be found in our previous books about *Essential Kicks* and about Plyo-Flex training. The Photos will be found at the top of next page.

→

Stand up, pivot, kick over the chair; sit and repeat

Climb on chair, kick over second chair, climb down, and repeat

Targets

Preferably: Shins, knees and groin.
Sometimes: The solar plexus or ribs.
The head and the face if your opponent bends or dives down towards you.

Possible Ground Front kick targets: Groin, Solar Plexus, Chin, Knee

Typical Applications

The *Penetrating Ground Front Kick* should be used against a standing opponent

approaching to attack, <u>as soon as he gets in range</u>. In this example, you aim for the groin, and follow up with an Upward version to the chin as he bends over.

Ground Front Kicks in series against a standing opponent

As mentioned, we do not present the *Drop Kick* variations as Ground Kicks per se in this book. The basic Drop Kicks have been presented in detail in our previous book about *Essential Kicks*. We shall simply illustrate the **Drop Front Kick** at the end of this section for completeness and reference only. But…

➡

...the following Figures do not show a pure Drop Front Kick, **but a very close cousin**. It gives an example of how to react if you fall involuntarily to the floor. In this instance, you lose your balance because you have over-evaded a jab backwards: at this stage, it is much safer to let yourself fall totally than to stumble or to try to redress, and then get punched! As soon as you reach the floor, do kick with a hip thrust, as if rebounding, preferably to the groin of the forward-driven opponent. This would be something like an "involuntary full-hipped Penetrating Drop Front Kick".

Evade a too-close-jab by sitting down and ground-kicking

In the same spirit, the classic *Aiki-Jitsu* technique presented below could be classified as something *between* a Ground Kick and a Drop Kick; it is also a reminder of the wholeness of Martial Arts. As your opponent attacks with a rushing and fully-committed overhead strike (*Shomen Uchi*), you go towards him while evading down and outside. In a classic *Aiki-Jitsu* use of the opponent's own momentum, you catch his striking arm and pull it forward and down under the 'breaking down the open door'-principle. You will help the throwing of your assailant by **kicking** is rear knee up.

A Ground Upward Front Kick in Aiki-Jitsu's **Kokyu Ashi Nage**

Specific training

- Drill the *basic standing* Front Kicks as the principles must be respected when executing from the ground. It is imperative to have really mastered the basic versions in order to be able to develop power from the floor. It is recommended to drill all the variations of the Standing Kick as presented in our book about *Essential Kicks*; they are all relevant to ground-kicking.
- *Crab-walk* forward, kick, crab-walk back. Repeat (See Figure).
- Kick a *heavy bag or a tire* held on the floor by a partner. Alternate kicking legs and drill for power (see Illustration below). It may look simple, but developing power from Ground Kicks requires serious training; the results are spectacular and rewarding, but they do not come by themselves.
- Start the Kick from *other ground positions*, like the previously presented Humpty Dumpty version. Switch positions fast & then kick. Repeat.

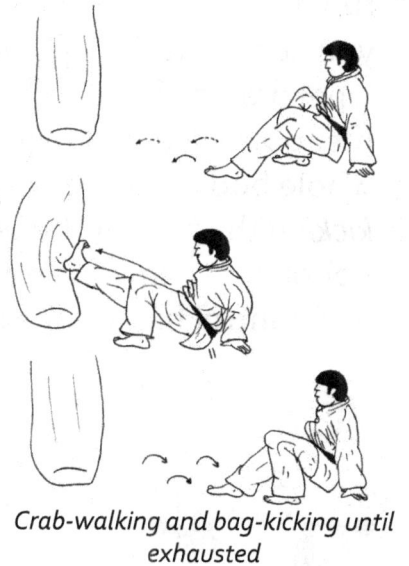

Crab-walking and bag-kicking until exhausted

- Drill seriously the *Chair Kicks* presented above. Interestingly, those are one of the best ways to drill the leg muscles for Ground Kicks; it neutralizes most of the body muscles usually used and it forces you to concentrate on the leg movement alone.

Developing power on targets like tires and heavy bags

Self-defense

Remember that this is a fast and 'easy' Kick; use it in ground fighting as soon as possible in any situation. The Figure shows the use of the Kick *as soon as* your opponent sets up an Ankle Lock. *Do not push* but **kick** his gluteal muscle or his kidneys with the heel. Simultaneously, point the caught foot and try to slide-pull it out of your opponent's grip. Repeat the kicking if necessary, and keep pulling your feet out.

The Ground Heel Front Kick in an ankle lock escape

The example below will illustrate an important point: you can deliberately go down in order to execute a *Standing-up Kick*, if it is to your advantage. In this specific instance, the going-down helps you setting up a painful Wrist-Lock, while the standing up gives you additional kick power. What is not to like? This is an advanced variation of a classic lapel grab defense, common in *Krav Maga*, *Ju Jitsu*, *Aikido* and more. But in this case you first go back and down on one knee for extra power in setting the wrist-lock. Using the whole body can even cause a serious joint dislocation. You can then *stand back up while kicking* the face of the bent-over assailant. This is a typical **Standing-up Front Kick**. The opponent is now at your mercy. You could for example keep pivoting into an Arm-Lock and control him on the ground.

Go down then stand up with a Front Kick!

The next drawings show an *offensive* use of the Kick in a triple-whammy *combination*. Crab-walk offensively towards a standing assailant; do not wait for him to come to you, but surprise him by coming on to him aggressively. Kick his forward knee powerfully *as soon as in range*, preferably with an Outward-tilted Heel version of the Ground Front Kick; that should stop him. Follow-up immediately with an Upward Ground Front Kick to the groin, preferably with the same leg. As the pain causes him to bend down, do front-ground-kick his chin. <u>Remember that, in ground-kicking, lowering the leg will not give you more power for the following Kick</u>; it is therefore best to kick in series with the same leg by just chambering back each time; this will allow for speed without concomitant loss of power.

Confront a standing assailant with an offensive triple Ground Front Kick

In the next example, you front-kick the plexus of a standing opponent leaning forwards to punch you down. Having stopped him and stunned him, you catch his ankle while passing your kicking leg between his own legs and while pulling yourself in. All the while, you are kicking him again with the other foot. You can even catch his wrist if you can: Kicking while holding him gives you much more power. You can then follow up with a classical BJJ Leg-lock Takedown. The purpose of this example is to illustrate how important ground-kicking is for set-ups, even if you are a good grappler and think you do not need it. The number of grappling techniques available after a Ground Kick is limitless; this one is simply an example among many.

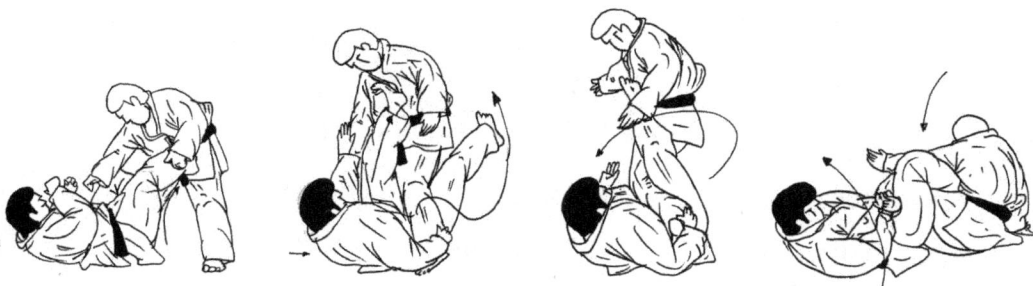

Two Ground Front Kicks to set up a leg-lock submission

And the next Figures show a **Pressing** (*Assisted*) variant of the Kick, and delivered directly from a "Shell" protective position, in which you are lying on the floor without hand support. In this case, you wait until your opponent comes close, and then "explode" into the Kick. You lift your hips from the floor by using your shoulders and elbows, and then you kick. If possible, as illustrated, you place your non-kicking foot on his knee for further support, for what becomes an Assisted version. In all cases, kick up with maximum hip power.

Assisted Ground Front Kick with no hand support

The next Figure shows in turn the technical delivery of the **orthodox** Kick version without hand support: you push up the hips *together with the development of the Kick*, using your shoulders and your neck as support while "bridging" on one leg. This quite a powerful kick, and also an important drill for core muscle building.

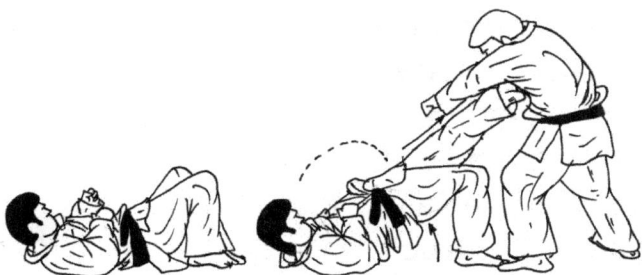

The no-hand-support "bridge" Ground Front Kick

The variation illustrated in the coming Drawings bundles both previous versions together in one sophisticated variation: a 'No-hand-support and Assisted' Ground Front Kick. You use as supports: his hip for your non-kicking leg, and the ground for your shoulders and elbows. In the ground fight of this example, you have your opponent between your legs, - in the BJJ "guard"-. You place one foot on his hip and push him (or yourself) away. You have so made room for the Front Kick with the other leg, delivered with a hip lift and a thrust. Fast and powerful. If successful, this is a mean kick.

The Assisted No-hand-support "bridging" Ground Front Kick

The next Photo shows the very simple but devastating use of the Kick against a standing assailant trying to come <u>over</u> you. Wait for the last possible moment before kicking. The reader should note that this *Upward Ground Chin Kick* is so dangerous that it is forbidden by the rules of the UFC and of most MMA bouts.

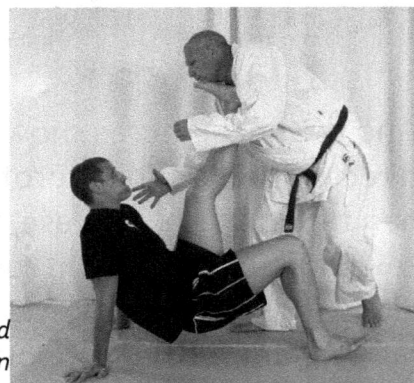

The dangerous Upward Ground Front Kick to the chin

The same Kick can be used as a *Groin Kick*, should an assailant standing in front you be stupid enough to lift his leg for stomping you. See Photos.

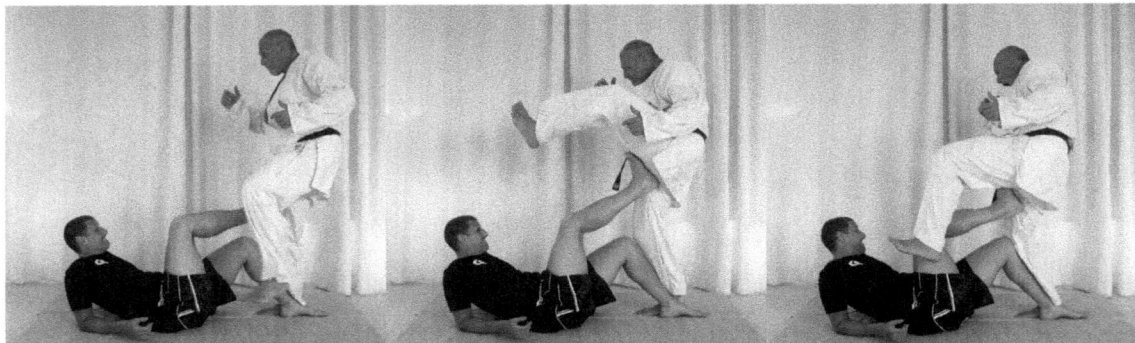

Upward groin Ground Front Kick against stomping assailant

And the Figures at the top of next page show a way to cope with a stomping/punching opponent at a later stage of the attacks, should you have missed the first opportunity (as illustrated above). As your assailant stomps, you try to smother the kick into your forearms while kicking up in his groin. If his punch is already on the way, block it too into your protecting forearms. Tough it all up! But after the painful kick/punch, catch his ankles with your hands, kick him in the groin and lift him up with your foot still in his groin area; push him up and back. Ouch!   ➤

Smother overhead attacks and then upward-front-kick the groin; follow up by catching his ankles

And the next Photos show the **Overhead** version of the Kick, to be delivered to an assailant *behind* you (On your "head" side). More will be told about this important Kick later in the text, but, -being bio-mechanically a typical Front Kick-, it was important to mention it here.

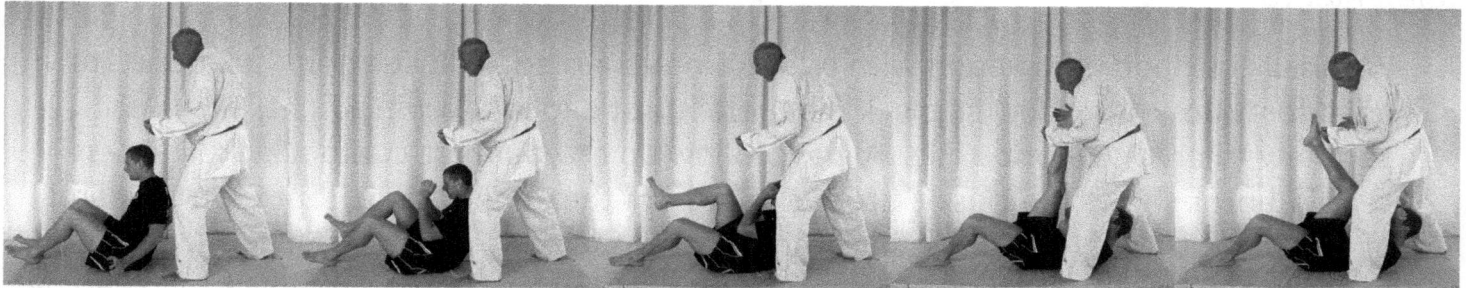
The Overhead Ground Front kick

The coming Drawings show an application of this *Overhead* version of the Kick. In this example, you are threatened from behind while sitting on the floor. Grab the assailant's wrist (or wrists) while dropping to the floor and do front-kick <u>overhead</u> into his face. Keep kicking until he is subdued.

The Overhead Ground Front Kick from cross-legged sitting position

And if we have already presented here the *Overhead* version of the Ground Front Kick, the coming Illustrations will present a classical application at the end of a *rolling escape from an Arm-lock*. The Drawings at the top of next page show how your opponent has caught you in a Side Arm-lock and how you roll forward as soon as possible to escape the lock (before it is set). After the stop-on-the-floor-roll (*Mae Ukemi - Judo*), you'll find yourself in perfect position for the Kick. It could be that your kick trajectory will have to be diagonal as per your respective positions, but the principles stay obviously the same.

➡️

Roll to escape lock, stop on the floor, roll-back into the Overhead Ground Front Kick

*Roll forward to evade typical Aikijitsu **Ik-kyo** Arm-lock, let leg rebound into Overhead Front Kick*

We shall conclude this section with two examples aimed at illustrating the important need for **follow-up** kicks. One kick is generally not enough to win a fight, and it is certainly truer for Ground Kicks. Always follow up on your first-contact kick. The first set of Photos shows the classic Ground version of the Penetrating Front Stop Kick and of the Chin Upward Front Kicks in combination, as already presented. The second set, of Figures this time, illustrates the natural flow of a *Ground Front Groin Kick* followed by a *Ground Roundhouse Kick*, and then capped by a *Ground Back Kick*.

Ground Double Front Kick

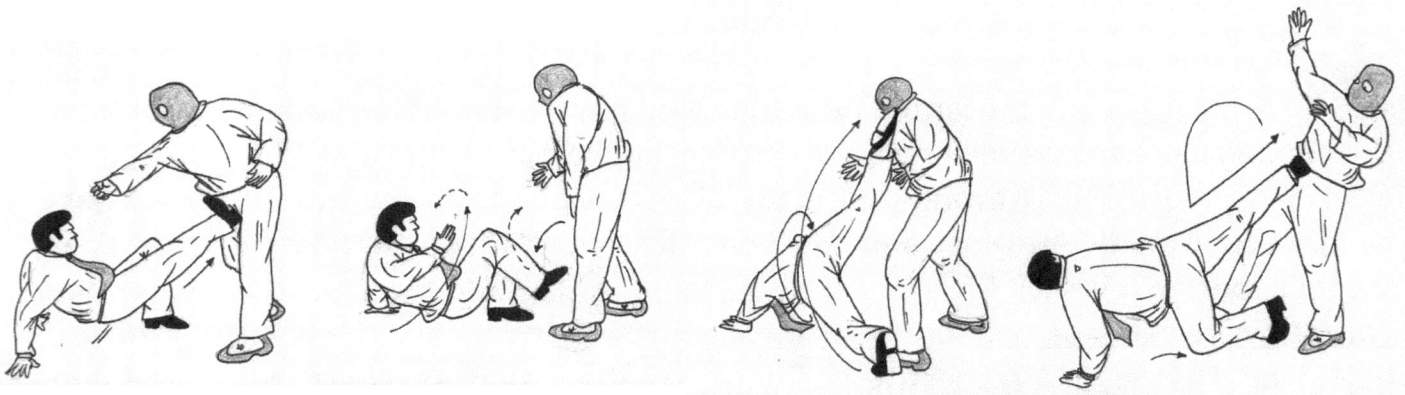

Triple combination of Ground Kicks

Illustrative Photos

The Essential standing Penetrating Front Kick

The basic Upward Front Kick

The classic Essential Drop Front Kick, close relative of the Ground Front Kick

An unorthodox Descent into the Ground Front Kick

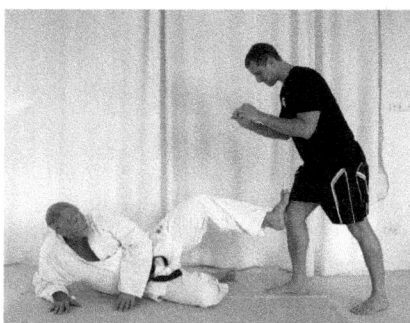

Ground Side-Front Stop Kick to the knee

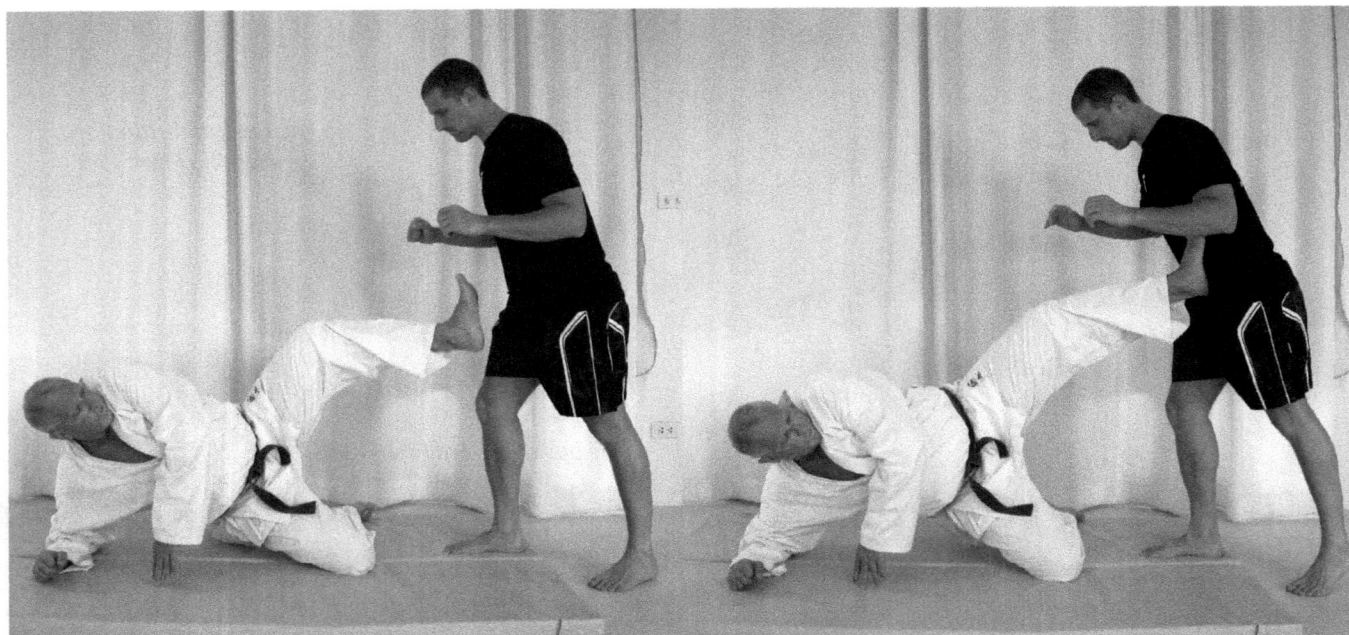

The Side-Front version of the Ground Front Kick

Evasive Ground Descent – Ziv Faige

Ever tried. Ever failed. No matter. Try Again. Fail again. Fail better.
~Samuel Beckett

2. THE GROUND TWIN FRONT KICK

General

This *Simultaneous Double Ground Front Kick* is much less powerful than the single one, because it lacks the anchoring support of one leg and the possibility of the anchored hip thrust. It is a nice kick, though, when it makes use of the forward momentum of the opponent; but it is not really a very suitable *Attack Kick*. Accordingly, it lends itself very naturally to the classic follow-up with the famous Judo Wheel Throw (*Tomoe Nage*) because aiming at an opponent into forward momentum. The Kick can be performed hitting with both feet at the same level, or hitting simultaneously at different levels (like groin and knee for example).

As mentioned in the previous section, Ground Kicks are relevant to kicks executed with the assistance of a table, a chair, a bar or a similar prop. The adjacent Photo illustrates the use of the Twin Front Kick when backed against the front of a car.

The standing Assisted version of the Ground Twin Front Kick

Description

This Kick is, again, a very close relative of the *Essential Drop Twin Front Kick* presented in previous volumes, and that is also illustrated at the end of the section.

The underlying principles stay the same as for the standing Front Kicks or as for the single Ground Front Kicks.

The Figure below illustrates the delivery of this Ground Kick from a regular relaxed extended-legs sitting position. You lean back on your buttocks and place your weight on your hands behind you, while bending both legs in classic Front Kick chamber. Kick with both legs simultaneously at groin level, and chamber back.

The classic Ground Twin Front Kick

Key Points

- *Time your Kick* against the forward momentum of your opponent, in such a way that you kick a few inches into the target at full extension.
- *Chamber back* forcefully and always follow up.
- Drill the kick against targets to learn to develop power as much as possible; *drill 'exploding' into the kick with everything you have.*

Targets

- First and foremost: The *groin*, as this is not a very powerful kick.
- Also the *ribs* and *solar plexus*, if your opponent bends down towards you.
- The *knee* as a secondary target, if you kick simultaneously at two levels.

Typical Applications

The Illustrations below show a common use of the Kick with its classic follow-up: As your opponent bends down over you (lying on the floor) and punches you, twin-kick his midsection and grab his arm(s) or sleeve(s). Follow up naturally with the classic (Sacrifice) Wheel Throw.

Ground Twin Front Kick followed by Wheel Throw

And the next Figure shows the **Two-levels** kicking application of the Kick: As your opponent walks towards you, you stop him by simultaneously kicking *his front knee, and his groin*. Follow up.

The Split two-level Ground Twin Front Kick

Specific Training

Practice power and timing for the Kick by stop-kicking a *heavy bag, at groin level*; the bag should be <u>swung forcefully</u> at you by a partner. This is the most relevant drill to actual effective use.

Self defense

The next Illustrations show how to entice your assailant to lunge towards you, and this by throwing a long but half-baked regular Ground Front Kick *as a trap*. As you chamber back slowly, let him follow confidently your retraction into attacking you. Then, twin-kick him explosively in the groin. You could follow up with a Ground Roundhouse Kick, as presented later in this book.

Lure your standing opponent into a Ground Twin groin Front Kick

The coming Drawings will show a dangerous version of the Kick in which you hold the assailant's ankles while twin-kicking. Not only is the kicks' impact multiplied by the fact that the opponent is held in place, but the subsequent fall is a nasty one. This is an appropriate move when an assailant is standing over you as you fully lie on your back. Remember that this is a **Kick** first and foremost; the Takedown is a by-product. Do not push, but do kick hard.

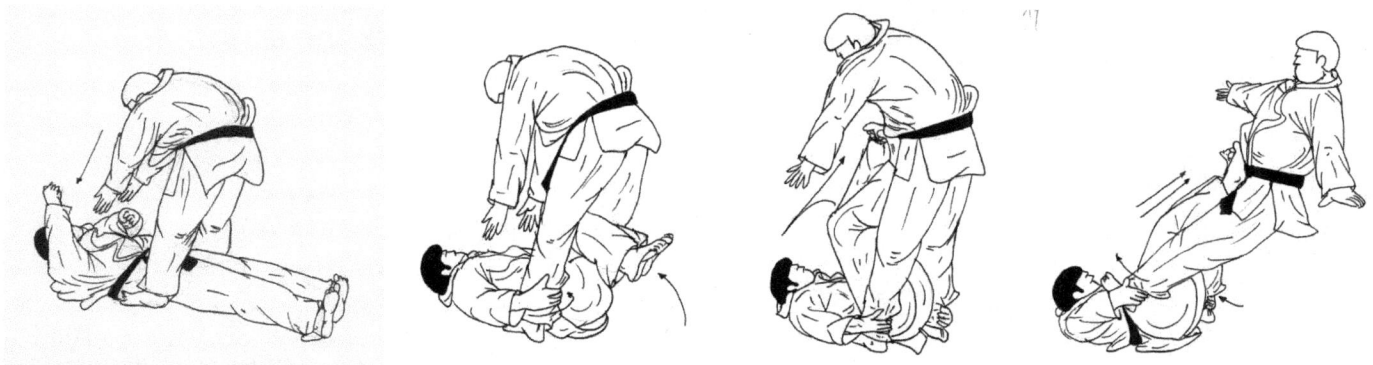

The nasty Ankles-held Ground Twin Front Kick

Self defense (Continued)

And if we are already dealing with Take-downs, here is the kicking version of the now famous *Wheel Throw*. Unlike in previous examples, -in which the classic 'Tomoe Nage' Throw follows the Twin Kick-, we present here the version in which the Kick *is* the Take-down. The Throw does not follow the kick but *is* the Kick.

The nuance is real and the 'Kick' part must be emphasized. This is again an appropriate technique against an assailant standing over you and reaching out, as you are lying on your back. You will need to grab both his wrists to execute the technique. You will then twin-kick forcefully as you pull him forward over your head.

Wrist-held Ground Twin Front Kick Takedown

To conclude, we shall present a *Drop* version of the Kick and its possible follow-up, in order to underline again the fact that Ground Kicks rarely suffice by themselves and usually require serious following-up. The *Drop Twin Front Kick* is an Essential Kick covered in our previous book; it is, of course, simply a Ground Kick following an appropriate Descent to the floor. In our example illustrated by the next Figures, you evade a twin chest push (or maybe a second one following a first push by said assailant) by falling down directly into shell position. Your assailant will push hard into the void. Twin-kick into your tumbling-forward assailant and follow up, for example by scissor-kicking one of his legs: Hook-kick the ankle and Roundhouse-kick the knee.

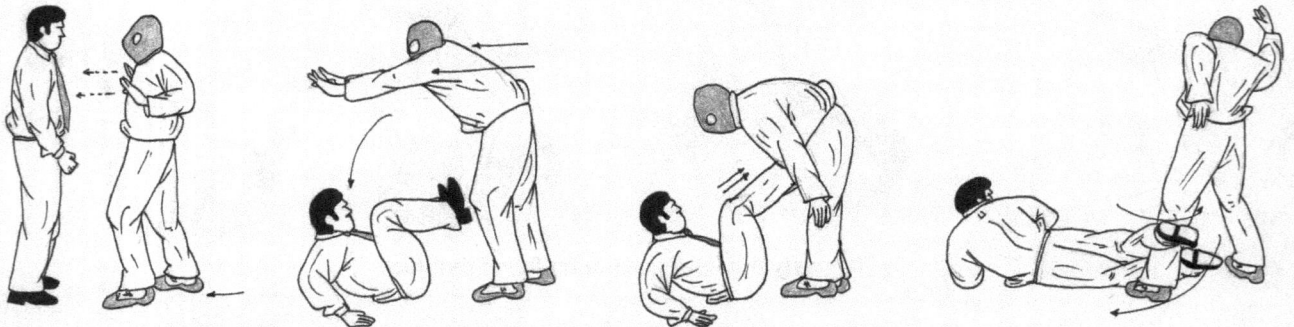

Application of the Drop Twin Front Kick and follow-up

Illustrative Photos

The Drop Twin Front Kick

Ground Twin Front Kick to the groin

Ground Twin Front Kick to the knee

The Flying version of the Twin Front Kick

3.   THE DROP PULL-IN FRONT KICK

General

This is a very effective kick, especially for real-world use: It is a Ground Front Kick to the face or upper torso of the opponent, delivered *while you pull him in towards the Kick*. It is more generally used in its Drop Kick version, in which you use your body weight to pull the opponent in by his arms or sleeves. This gives a tremendous momentum adding to the opposite energy of the Kick itself.

The Kick can also be delivered from the ground as a regular Ground Kick, provided you succeed in catching your opponents' arms or sleeves. It is not a basic Kick, and therefore we did not present it as a Drop Front Kick variation in our book about *Essential Kicks*. It could have been classified as a "Suicide" Kick, as you usually would drop to the floor voluntarily, but we chose to present it as a Ground Kick because it is both easy and relatively safe to execute.

On top of the fantastic power achieved by kicking towards a target you are pulling in, the Kick has the advantage of neutralizing the blocking options of your opponent. In short, this technique, very typical of Indonesian *Penchak Silat* styles, is an extremely punishing move. It is very natural and very easy to execute, but it needs a certain set-up in which you get control of the opponent's arms. If you can get there, the success is a no-brainer. This mean maneuver is definitely worth drilling for instinctive use in a self-defense situation.

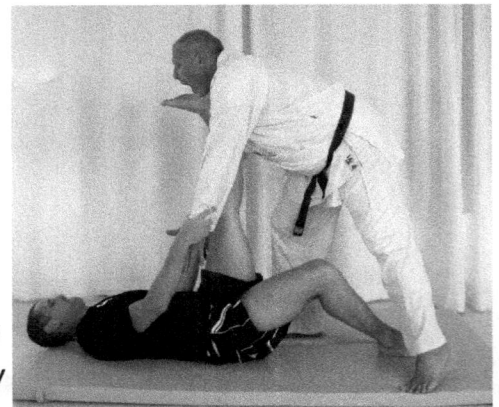
The Ground Pull-in Front Kick

Description

The Illustrations below show the Drop-delivery of the Kick. Once you have caught your opponent's wrists, let yourself fall back in place, *not away but down*, while chambering a Front Kick. Pull on his arms while kicking up, aiming for the chin. **<u>Be very careful in practice! This is an extremely dangerous technique.</u>**

The classic Drop Pull-in Front Kick

Key Points

- Let yourself *get down explosively*: the fall will be softened by your holding the opponent's arms.
- The key of success is into *the strength of your grip*: do not let go, whether you hold his wrists or sleeves.
- Make sure to *fall back in place*, just before or between his legs, and do not attempt to pull him forward by falling backwards.
- *Synchronize* the arm-pull and the Kick.

Targets

Preferably the *chin*.
Also the face, throat and sternum.
In specific applications, the shoulder is a worthy target as well.

Typical Applications

The technique is quite straightforward once you have achieved control of your opponent's arms. The natural follow-up would be, again, Judo's *Wheel Throw*. As illustrated in the adjacent Figures, you retract the leg after kicking his chin *while pulling yourself up slightly*. You then kick his belly and throw him over.

The classic follow-up to the Drop Pull-in front Kick

Should you fumble during the execution of the Kick, do not give up. Kick the opponent's midsection and smoothly follow up with a "save". In the example illustrated below, you hook your non-kicking leg behind his knee to pull yourself and catch his ankle with your hand. Pull his ankle while pushing with your foot still stuck in his midsection. This should take him down for more ground fighting.

Save a missed kick by redirecting to the belly and switching to a takedown

The *Drop Pull-in Front Kick* is an ideal maneuver for a good grappler to get on the ground. It will give him a great guard set-up and an opponent stunned by a very dangerous Kick. The Drawing illustrates one follow-up technique among many, a classic Arm-lock achieved after having pushed the opponent's hip with the non-kicking leg.

A classic arm-lock set-up by the Drop Pull-in Front Kick

Specific Training

- Drill the Kick alone, *shadow-kicking*.
- Drill the other classic *Ground Front Kicks*.
- As mentioned, this is a very effective and important Kick. But the only real specific training possible is very carefully *with a protected partner*. **This Kick is potentially lethal and extreme caution must be exercised when drilling with a partner.**

Self defense

As mentioned, the key to this Kick is the grabbing of your opponent's wrists, arms or sleeves. Many Arts have refined to an extreme the control of the opponent's hands; *Wing Chung Kung Fu* and *Penchak Silat* come to mind. From this "sticky hands" practice will come many ways to come into control of an assailant's arms. You could also simply go for a double wrist grab, or a double block turning into a double grab. The possibilities are infinite.

But the next Figures do show the most natural application of the maneuver: a Release against a double choke attempt from the front. You simply block and grab the arms extending towards you (*Or you break the hold and catch the wrists*), and then you fall back to deliver the Kick. The follow-up presented in the example is especially interesting and it is easy to execute if you have stunned the assailant. Keep hold of his wrists, encircle his arm with your kicking leg and hook the foot into his groin. In this arm-locking position, scissor his front leg and roll to take him down. Keep control of his locked arm into your leg to control and hit him if necessary.

Grab of assailant's wrists extending in a choke attempt, Drop Pull-in Front Kick, Arm-locking follow-up

Another good set-up for this wrist-grabbing Kick would be the Clinch. The coming Illustrations show the use of the Kick from such a clinching position: Soften him up with a *Knee Kick & Stomp*, then switch your grabs appropriately and fall back into the Kick. You can then release his sleeves and follow him with a fully-hipped Ground Front Kick to the groin from the other leg. You could keep coming after him with further Ground Kicks to the knee, if so you fancied.

The Drop Pull-in front Kick is very suitable to get out of a Clinch

The next Figures show a **Ground One-hand Pull-in** variation; this is not a Drop Kick but a Ground Kick special version. You lie on your back with your assailant kneeling on your side, attempting to catch you and punch you. Tighten your neck muscles, catch one of his wrists, and use the other hand to attack his face and. By doing so, you jam any incoming attack; you can use a Palm Strike to his chin or a finger jab towards his eyes. Immediately roll towards him, placing your close knee under his controlled arm and strengthening your hold of his wrist with your other hand (the one that delivered the head strike). Push his body away with your knee while pulling his arm in, and deliver a full-powered stomp-type Ground Front Kick to his face, *while pulling on his arm*. Keep his arm straight, as your kicking leg passes in front of his face to pull him down into a classical arm lock (*Ude Hishigi Juji Gatame – Judo*). Lift your hips and press wrist down for arm-locking.

One-hand Pull-in Ground Front Kick turning into classic Juji Gatame Arm-lock

A great way to close off this section after the previous example is to show a close relative of the ***Pull-in Front Kick*** in the *Juji Gatame* Arm-lock set-up. This is a Kick that should help keep the opponent 'softened' for a better arm-bar control, or that could cap the hurting of the joint with a dangerous head kick… ➡

...Practice with extreme caution. Note that, in our example, the non-kicking leg envelops the arm for better control during the kicking; this is a dynamic variation of the classic arm-lock to allow for the Kick without losing your position.

Juji Gatame variation and dangerous Ground Pull-in Front Kick

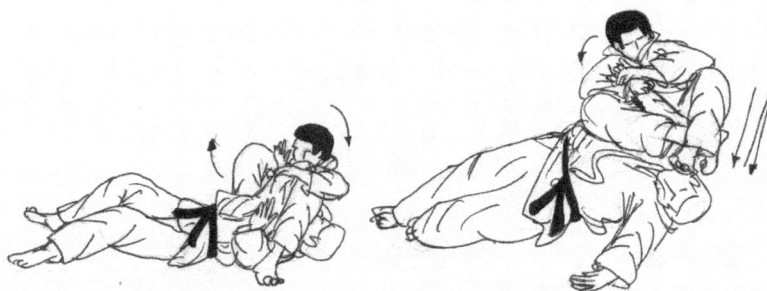

4. THE GROUND SIDE KICK

General

This is a versatile Ground Kick, easy to deliver from many ground positions, and with many variations, a few of which will be presented below. It is a must-practice Kick, to be used automatically if you fall sideways to the floor. It is also a useful Kick from which it is relatively easy to get back up on your feet. The Kick relies on having two hands and one knee on the floor, and it uses the hip thrust to generate power, just like with the standing version. Unfortunately, the power achievable by the *Ground Side Kick* is still very far from that of the standing version, and it must be drilled seriously for power optimization. The reader is also invited to refer to the *Essential Drop Side Kick* described in detail in previous work.

Ground Side Kicks

The Jumping version of the Ground Side Kick

Interestingly, *Capoeira* sports an important variation of the Side Kick where you place both hands on the floor, and that is either somewhat of a Drop Kick or somewhat of a Ground Kick that is delivered from the floor up (*Escorão* or *Coice de Mula*).

Jumping to the ground: The 'Suicide' Drop Side Kick

Jumping from the ground: The Jumping Ground Side Kick

Description

The next Photos show the **light-and-low** version of the Kick; there is not much hip thrust, although the floor leg pulls the body forward during delivery. This Kick aims at the knee of a standing opponent or at a grounded opponent, but not much higher.

The low Ground Side Kick

The next Photos illustrate the orthodox **fully-hipped version** of the Kick, delivered higher. This is a more powerful kick where the arms lift the body up for more hip thrust.

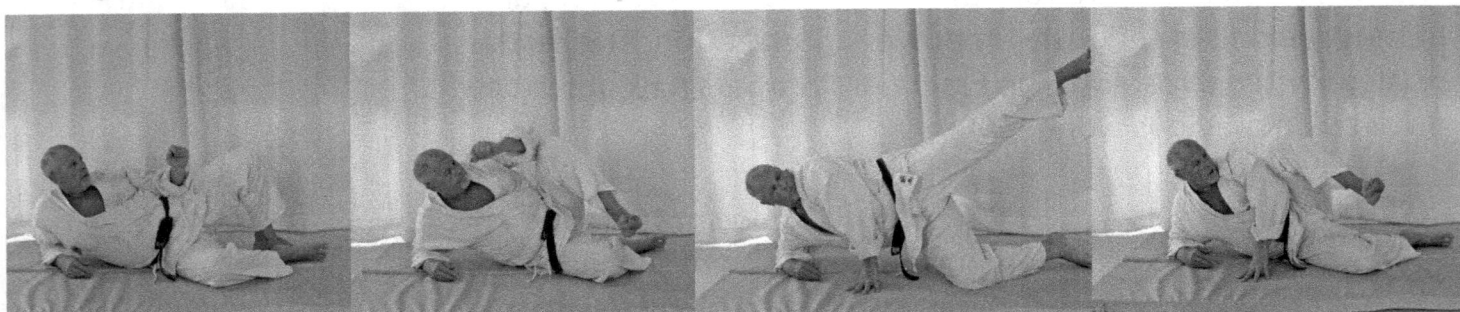

The classic fully-hipped Ground Side Kick

The adjacent Figure shows the delivery **starting from an extended-legs sitting position** on the floor. Pivot on your side and place both hands on the ground, while getting up on your knee. Chamber the upper leg and kick with maximum hip thrust. Connect with the arch of the foot, the heel or the knife edge of the foot, like for any Side Kick. Chamber back.

The Drawings *at the top of next page* illustrate the **Pressing/Assisted version** that we have already met in the context of the Ground Front Kick. The Illustrations show clearly how this variation allows both for extra high support and for the neutralization of the opponent's own legs. The drilling of the Kick is presented in the subsequent Photos.

Ground Side Kick from extended-leg sitting

The use of the Assisted Ground Side Kick

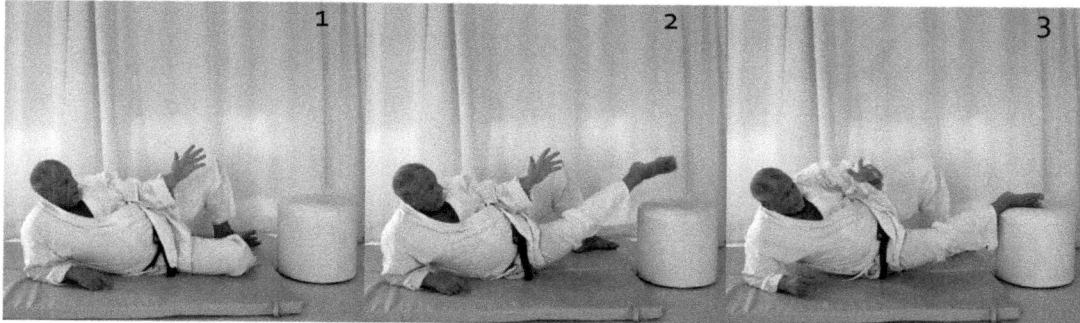

1   2   3

Training for the Assisted Ground Side Kick

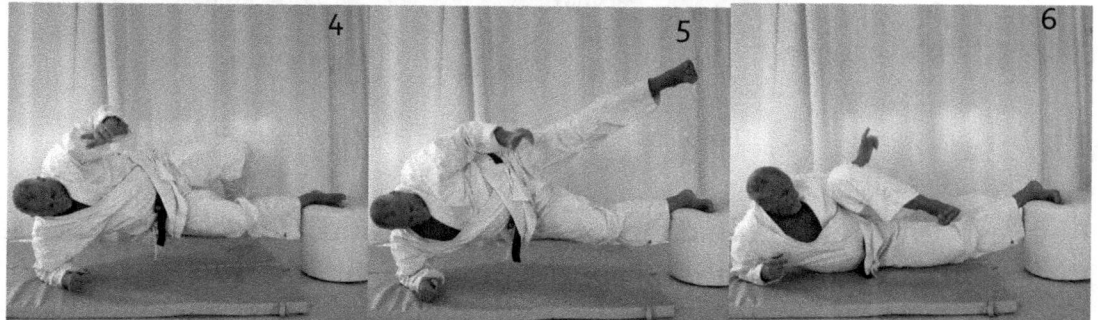

4   5   6

The **Jumping version** of the Ground Side Kick can be executed with one or two hands on the floor as illustrated below.

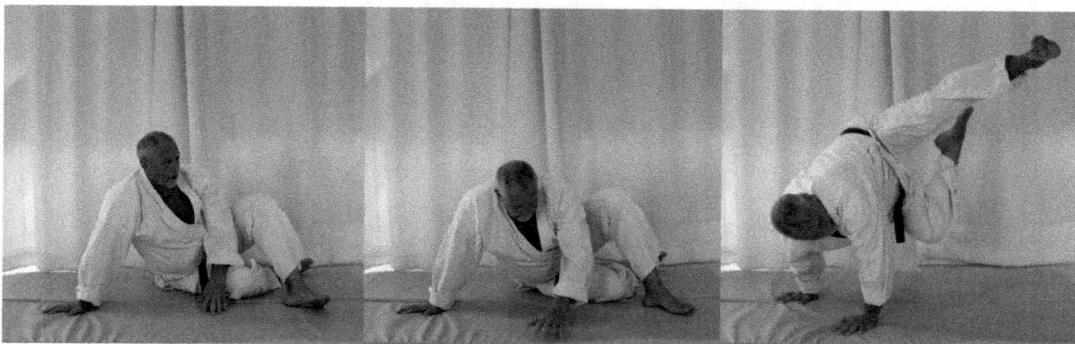

The Jumping Ground Side Kick – two hands

The Jumping Ground Side Kick – one hand

Jumping Ground Kicks are all the more relevant if momentum can be added. The best way to do so is the use of a preceding Front Roll. The *Front Roll*, as explained in the Introduction, can start on the ground or even from a standing position. The next Figures illustrate the Rolling-to-Jumping Ground Side Kick, a surprising Kick and a fantastic drill. The preceding Roll helps to jump and to surprise, and the key is the *hand push* at the end of the roll to propel you **_forward_** (not up!).

The surprising and far-reaching Roll to Jumping Ground Side Kick

As a last reminder of the concept of **Rear-leg** and **Front-leg** differentiation for Ground Kicks, we shall present the Ground Side Kick versions, just like we did for the Ground Front Kick. The rear-leg version will always be slower but more powerful because of the extra momentum.

The **Front-leg** *Ground Side Kick*

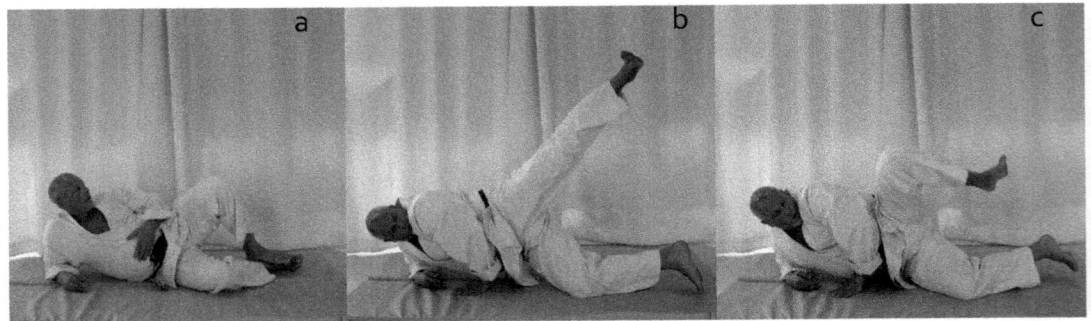

The **Rear-leg** *Ground Side Kick*

There are two basic ways to deliver the Ground Side Kick from a **quadruped position**, -on all fours-: **1.** directly to the side or **2.** after a 90 degrees pivot for more hip thrust. Both are important drills for muscle building and for overall kicking proficiency.

1

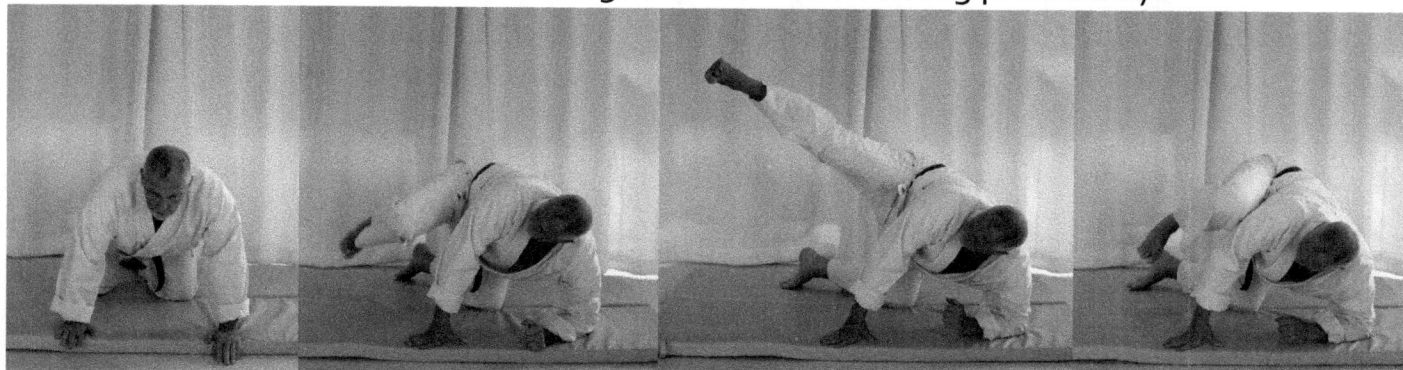

On your hands and knees, direct Ground Side Kick to the side

2

On your hands and knees, pivot and execute Ground Side Kick forwards

In the spirit of showing all possible Ground Kicks variations, we shall present also the exotic **Climbing version** of the Ground Side Kick. This is like a supersized Assisted Kick, using the opponent's body to kick high. This is spectacular, interesting and a good drill; but unnecessary as an effective technique in the author's eyes: the groin and knees are much closer, are easy to attack and are more effective targets. We do strive to be complete though, and also admit that it could be justifiable in certain circumstances or as a "toying" maneuver in the case of a great difference in proficiency between the protagonists.

The spectacular Climbing Ground Side Kick

Chair Kicks

Just like for the Ground Front Kick, we shall present a few *Chair Kicks* for completeness. The reader is invited to research his own variations and drills.

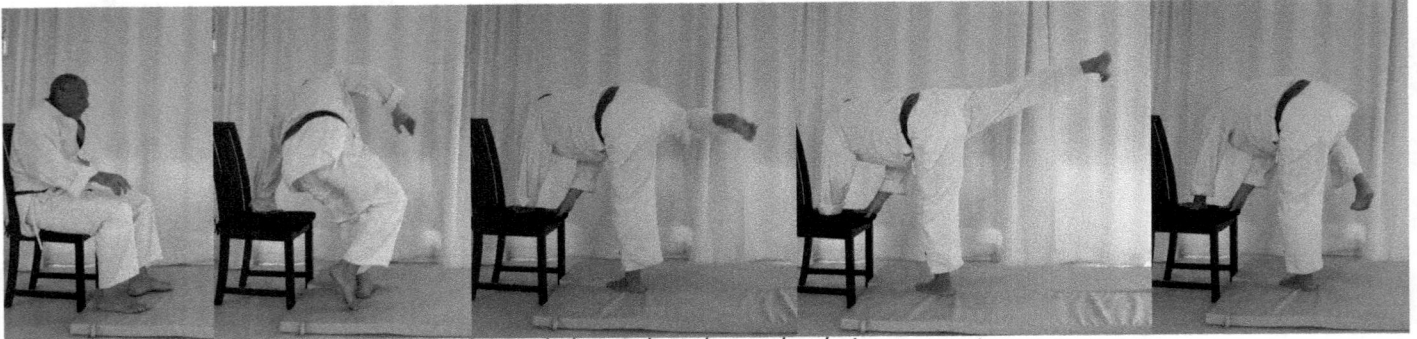

The forward Chair Side Kick; use the chair as support

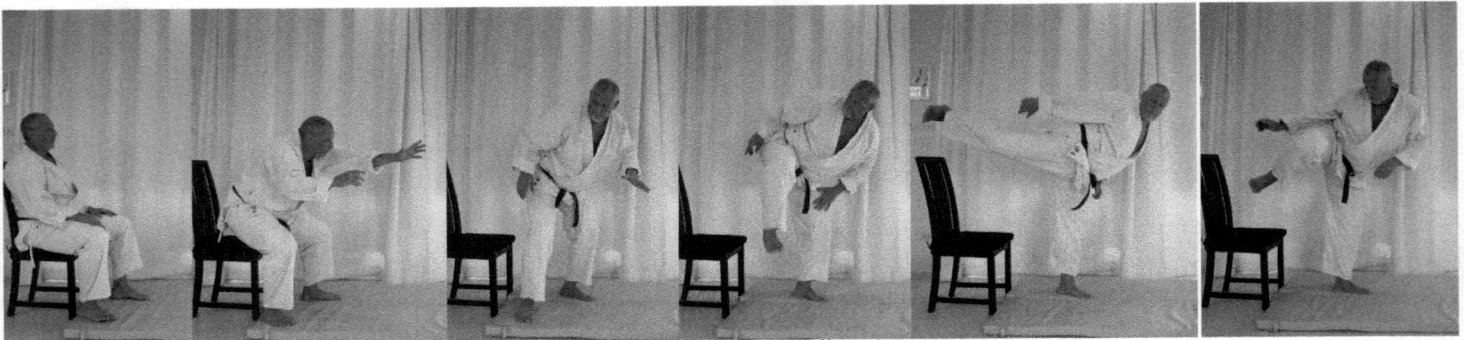

The backwards Chair Side Kick Drill; a great exercise

Key Points

- *Push the hips* into the kick as much as possible.
- Always *chamber back* immediately and forcefully.

Targets

Usually: the groin, the knee, the shin, the solar plexus and the ribs.

Typical Applications

As shown in the Photos at the top of next page, the *Ground Side Kick* is ideal as a **Stop Kick** against a standing opponent coming towards you as you lie on the floor. The example shows a *high* Stop Kick, but you could just as well, or even preferably, kick at shin level (as illustrated in the following set of Photos). ➤

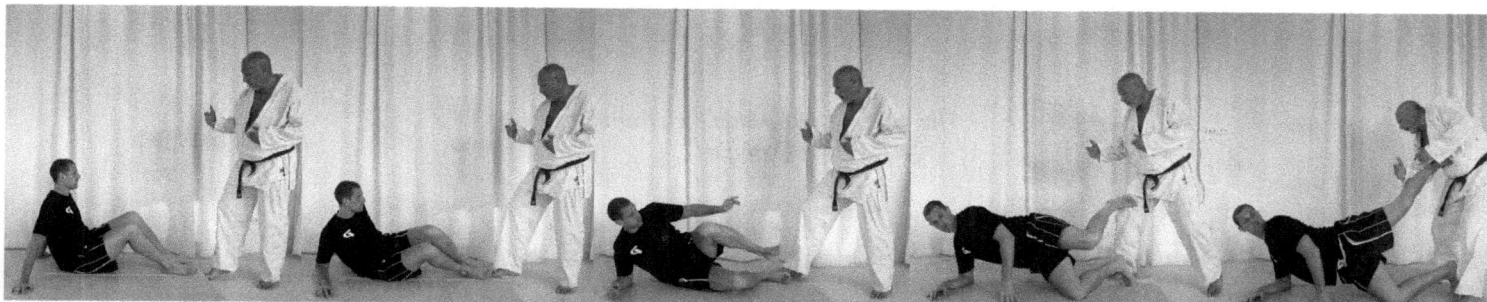
Stop an incoming standing opponent

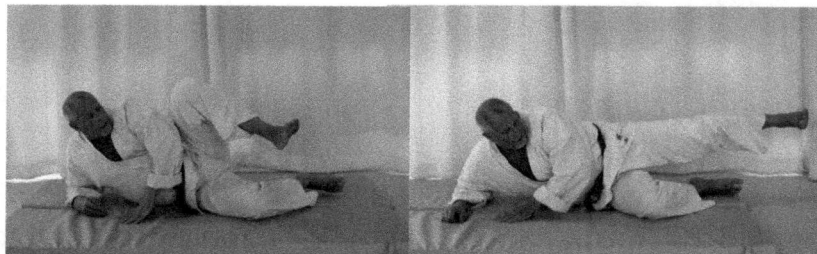
But the Ground Side Kick is best delivered at the opponent's shin level

The Ground Side Kick, whether as an Offensive Kick or as a Stop Kick, is a great **combination opener**. It lends itself to a multitude of follow-ups. The next Photos show the Ground Side Kick *as a set-up* for a full powered Ground Roundhouse Kick.

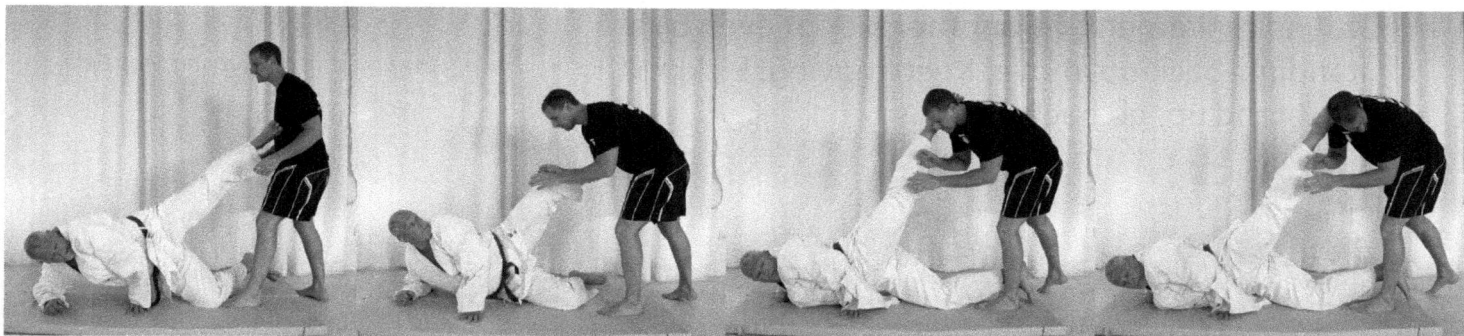
Ground Side Kick followed by Ground Roundhouse Kick

The Figures below and the Photos at the top of next page show a very close relation to this Kick: The **Suicide Drop Side Kick**, or *Flying Drop Side Kick*. This is not fully a Ground Kick, but it is very close and an extremely useful technique to master. As you are attacked, you let yourself drop backwards to the floor on your hands, with the legs already airborne in chambered position; a little bit like a Flying Kick. This is either a very fast evasion or an exotic Stop Kick; both of them always surprising. Kick as soon as your hands reach the floor and land in "Ground Guard". You could immediately follow up with a classic Ground Side Kick as you already are in cocked position for delivery.

'Suicide' Drop Side Kick, immediately followed by Ground Side Kick

The 'Suicide' Drop Side Kick from different angles

Specific Training

- Kick a *heavy bag swung at you* by a partner (See Illustration). Make sure you kick and retract: make it a kick and **not a push**.

- Practice *from various starting Ground Positions*; or even from a standing position as illustrated in the Figures below. The Kick should be followed by a Ground movement, by another kick or even by a 'standing-back-up' move. Keep moving: kick, roll, kick, stand up, go back down,…

Drilling the power of the Ground Stop Side Kick

A great drill: Twist-down Spin-back into the Ground Side Kick, keep moving

Self defense

The Photos at the top of next page show a technique akin to an *Offensive Drop Side Kick*: You use a fast back-fist to provoke a punching counter that you will evade by going down to the floor for a Ground Side Kick.

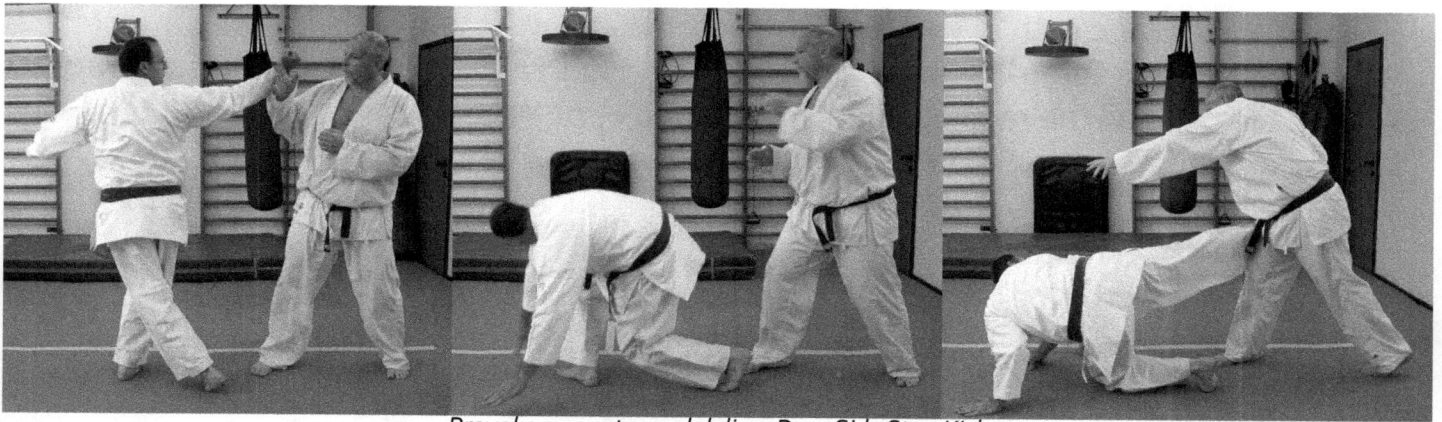

Provoke a counter and deliver Drop Side Stop Kick

The next Drawings show how great this Kick is as a natural follow-up of the Ground (or Drop) Front Kick: Evade a stick attack with a *Drop Front Kick* to the groin. Pivot while chambering back and follow up immediately with a *Ground Side Kick* to the throat as he bends up from the groin pain. You can follow up with another Ground Side Kick, to the knee, to send him safely away; all kicks are executed with the same leg.

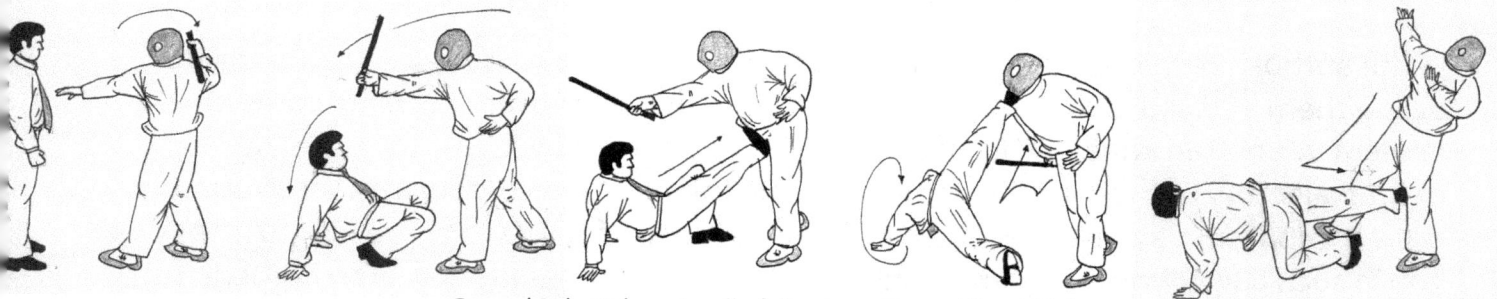

Ground Side Kicks naturally following a Ground Front Kick

The coming Figures show a short & easy version of the Kick against a close assailant. As you are downed, you let your assailant step close to you and you get your feet in between his to then *forcefully open his legs*. Immediately, in one smooth move, you will side-kick up into his groin. Instead of chambering back, you will then push him up and away.

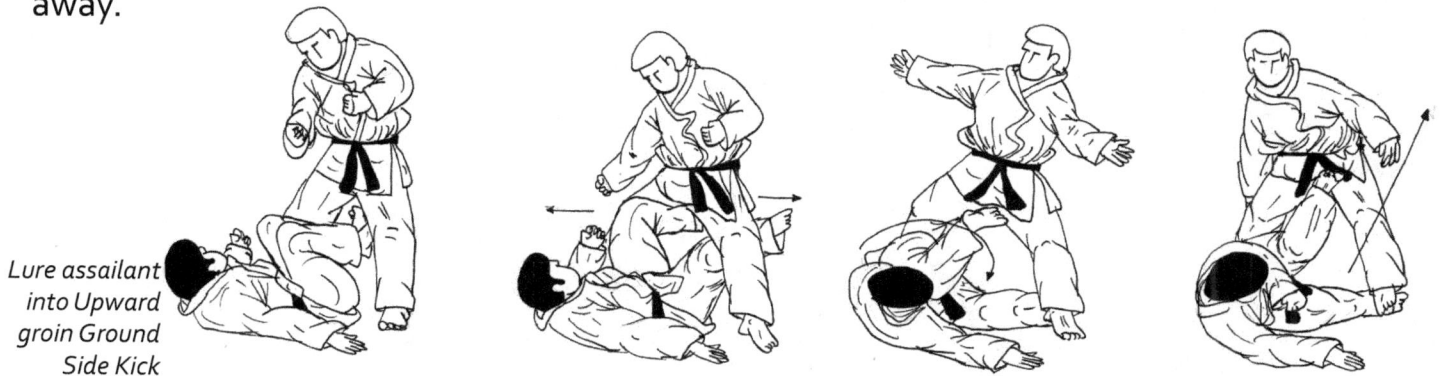

Lure assailant into Upward groin Ground Side Kick

THE GROUND SIDE KICK   83

There was a time in the Seventies when groin kicks were allowed in semi-contact karate tournaments in some US States. And typically the Drop Side Kick was all the rage against high-kicking opponents. Similarly, the Ground Side Kick can be of great help if you are being kicked while lying on the ground. The Photo shows an attack of the standing leg of the assailant: you do not wait for the kick but you go towards the attacker in 'Stop Kick-mode'.

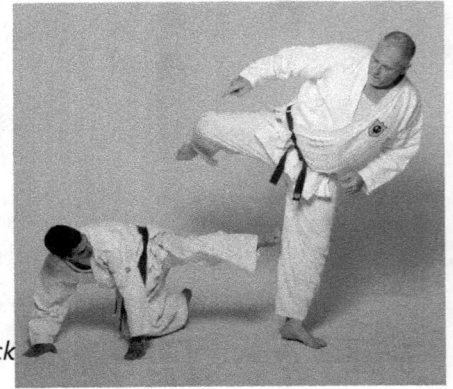

Offensive Ground Side Stop Kick

Of course, you can also side-kick his chambering in typical 'Stop Kick' fashion. The reader is invited to refer to our previous book about *Stop Kicks* for the general principles behind the different types of stop-kicking.

Ground Side Stop Kick to the shin or knee of a chambering kick

In the author's opinion, the best way to deal with kicks when you lie on the floor is to evade them and cause the opponent to lose his balance by over-reaching. You should present your lifted knee as a juicy target to lure him into a kick, just to move the leg out of his trajectory at the last minute. Kicking the thighs of an opponent on the ground is pretty common and natural; it should be no problem for you to cause him to attack you in such a way. You can then let the knee down and let his kick fly over. Immediately deliver a Roundhouse Kick to the back of his kicking leg to push him even further in his own momentum. The Roundhouse can chamber back naturally into a Side Kick chamber. The *Ground Side Kick* to the back of his knee should both hurt him and push him away.

Evade opponent's kick to the presented knee and use his momentum to attack his kicking leg

3

4

5

Another way to deal with such a kicking attack to your thighs would be a **Leading Kick** of yours around his kicking leg, encircling it and accelerating its momentum over your body. Your opponent will finish even more off-balance. You then can deliver the same *Ground Side Kick* to the back of his knee. The Leading Kick is a kind of *Ground Crescent Block Kick*, surprisingly efficient in use, but requiring good timing.

Ground Side Kick to rear knee after Ground Crescent leading Block Kick

By now, the experienced artist could be surprised not to have met the Ground Side Kick to the opponent's knee with checked ankle, as illustrated in the Figure. This classic knee attack, very typical of Old Ju-Jitsu (*Kanihasami*) and of East Asian fighting styles, is simply a Side Kick to the front knee, while hooking and pulling on the ankle from behind. The reason we have not presented this Scissor Kick is that it belongs more, -in our eyes-, to the *Joint Kicks* category than to the simple Ground Kicks. This is of course debatable. But in any case, the author is preparing a forthcoming book entirely focusing on **Joint Kicks**.

The Checked-ankle Knee-breaking Ground Side Kick, a Joint Kick

Illustrative Photos

The Essential standing Penetrating Side Kick

The Essential standing Upward Side Kick

The basic Jumping Side Kick

The low Stomp Side Kick

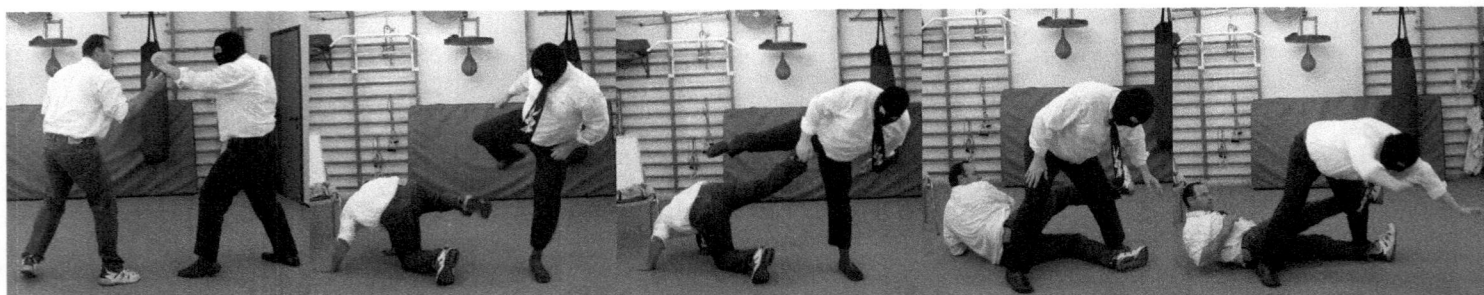

An application of the Essential Drop Side Stop Kick

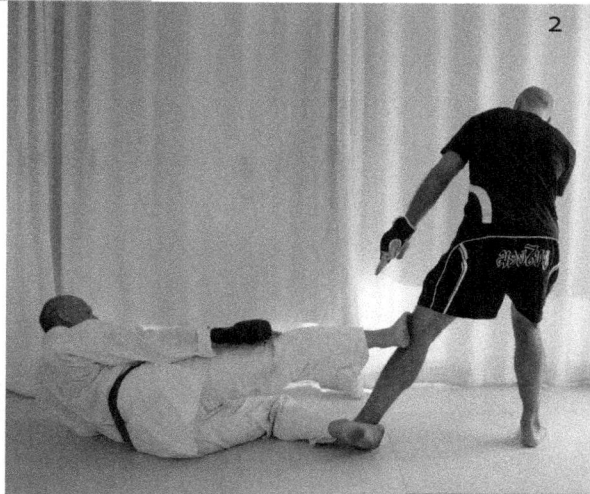

The ankle-checked Ground Side Kick
to the knee

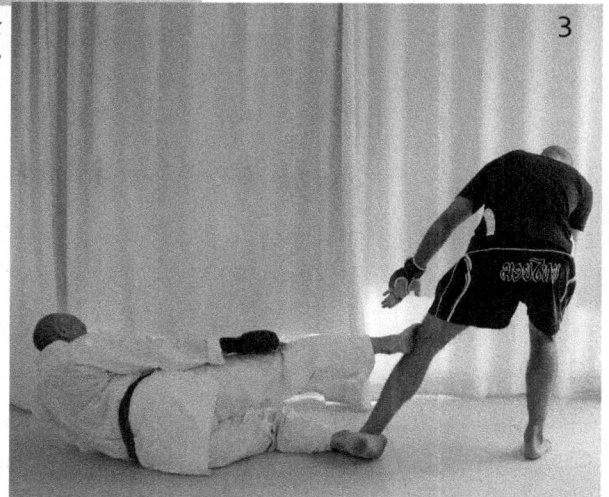

Luck is where opportunity meets preparation.
~Seneca

5. THE GROUND ROUNDHOUSE KICK

General

The Ground Roundhouse Kick is a very fast and versatile Kick. It is surprisingly powerful because of the natural body 'twists and moves' that are impossible with straight Ground Kicks. You generally can kick very much *through* the target with strong momentum, rather than chamber back like in standing Roundhouse Kicks (although 'whipping' versions to sensitive targets like the groin are as effective). Moreover, speed and accuracy make it a fearsome weapon. It can be used very fast and quite easily from all positions, and it can be highly undetectable during most of its trajectory. It will always

The Ground Roundhouse Kick

Chambering the Ground Roundhouse Kick

need to be followed up, but it is certainly a great combination opener.

Drilling the Ground Roundhouse is also a great work-out for the perfection of the standing Roundhouse Kick and for general kicking proficiency. For this reason only, it should be part of the training of any kicking Artist.

It is interesting to note that the Ground Roundhouse Kick is the only Ground Kick appearing in traditional *Shotokan Karate* forms (Kata); Shotokan being a very parsimonious style in sophisticated kicks. An excerpt of *Unsu Kata* is illustrated in the Drawings coming at the top of next page. Finding this kick in battlefield-oriented classic Japanese Karate speaks volumes of the importance of this Kick.

Applied Ground Roundhouse Kicks

➡️

Excerpt of Unsu Shotokanryu Kata with Ground Roundhouse Kicks in series

Description

The basic Drop Roundhouse Kick is a very important kick described in detail in our previous book about *Essential Kicks*. It was an important technique of Old *Aikijitsu* (*Musoken*) and of *Ninjitsu*, because of its efficacy and its surprise-effect. It is, in fact, a very close relative of the classic Ground Roundhouse Kicks and some variations will be presented throughout the text.

The basic *Ground Roundhouse Kick* is presented in the next Photos. It is quite straightforward; you just have to decide, according to the circumstances, how much you do want or need to commit to the kick: from a 'chambering back' version, all the way to kicking fully-through with momentum-rolling on the floor.

The basic Ground Roundhouse Kick

Already at this stage of the basic *Ground Roundhouse*, one can find **three** general versions to drill, *based on the trajectory of the kick*: it can travel upwards, downwards or in parallel to the ground. Each of those versions has its applications and preferred conditions in which to be used. The reader should note that the diagonal downward Roundhouse illustrated here is **not** the full Ground Downward Roundhouse Kick which will be presented later in the text.

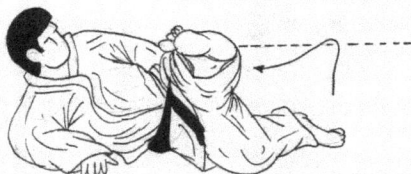

Classic **Horizontal** *Ground Roundhouse Kick*

Diagonal **Upward** *Ground Roundhouse Kick*

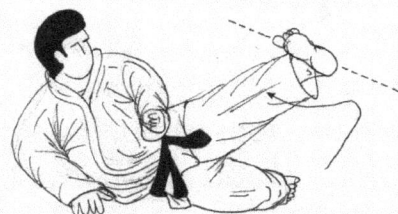

Diagonal **Downward** *Ground Roundhouse Kick*

The Ground Roundhouse being based on body-twisting movements, it is a kick easily deliverable from many various starting positions. It should be understood that the move from the starting position usually involves some pivoting *that can be harnessed for more centrifugal power to be added to the kick*. The next Figures show the delivery of the Kick from the trivial *extended-legs sitting position*: Pivot onto your hands and knee, just like for the basic Ground Side Kick. Then, chamber, **but use the pivot to boost the kick's momentum**. The version illustrated is a "Whipping" Kick based on a fast and powerful chamber back and a return to the starting position. According to the circumstances, it could become: **1**. a "kick-through" version ending with no chamber-back roll, or: **2**. a follow-up Ground Hook Kick in the reverse direction. ➤

Chamber-back Ground Roundhouse Kick from the extended-legs sitting position

Likewise, the next Photos illustrate the *Ground Roundhouse* delivered from an 'Indian' leg-crossed sitting position, but again in a "**whipping**" chamber-back version.

The chamber-back Ground Roundhouse Kick from cross-legged sitting

The coming Figures, in turn, show the delivery of the '**rear-leg**' version of the *Ground Roundhouse Kick* from either regular ground sitting, or by going through a squatting position: Squat, pivot sideways (as in knee guard posture), and then deliver the Kick while twisting towards the floor. This is a more difficult but *more powerful* execution of the Ground Roundhouse.

The Rear-leg Ground Roundhouse Kick from squat sit

The Drawings at the top of next page show the traditional Ground Roundhouse Kick delivered, -mostly as a Stop Kick-, from a traditional Japanese *Zeiza* kneeling position: Sitting on your knees and heels, you let yourself fall back and sideways to free the leg delivering the Kick. Should you have more timing to deal with the incoming opponent, you could go for the more powerful delivery with hand support, as illustrated in subsequent Photos. ➤

Falling Ground Roundhouse Kick from sitting on your knees

*The classic chamber-back Ground Roundhouse from **Zeiza** position*

We have now clearly established that the *Ground Roundhouse* can be delivered from many a starting position. The reader is invited to explore further and to drill other starting positions, especially the ones he fancies or finds himself easily in. The Kick lends itself to many ground moves and many ground starting positions; this includes going-back up (See first set of Photos) or going-down to the ground (See second set of Photos). The reader is urged to drill constant movement, on the ground as well as up and down, while smoothly inserting kicks in the routine.

The Essential Kneeling-up Roundhouse Kick

The Essential Drop 'Rear-leg' Roundhouse Kick

We can now go through a few more examples of basic variations for the *Ground Roundhouse*.

Kicking ***from the quadruped position*** should now be trivial for the reader; it can be done "lightly" just by using the leg (See first set of Photos) or with more power generated by some body movement (See second set of Photos). Both versions are important exercises that should be drilled thoroughly for muscle conditioning and for general proficiency.

The classic Ground Roundhouse Drill from all-fours position...

...and the more powerful Twist-down Ground Roundhouse from quadruped position

The Pressing/Assisted version of the Kick is based on the same principles already encountered with previous Ground Kicks. The trainee should just remember that the idea behind the *Assisted versions* is either to use the opponent's body to climb and kick higher, or to neutralize his limbs while kicking (or both!). The Drawings at the top of next page illustrate the <u>basic Assisted Ground Roundhouse</u> drilled by using old tires. The Photos then illustrate the more powerful version <u>with additional hand support</u>. And finally, the <u>climbing application</u> of the Assisted Ground Roundhouse Kick is illustrated by the subsequent Figures. *Climbing Kicks* are sophisticated techniques, often a bit over the top for regular fighting or free-fighting; they are great drills, though, for overall kicking mastery and could be useful is some circumstances for expert Artists against unmatched opponents.

➡

The easy version of the Assisted Ground Roundhouse Kick

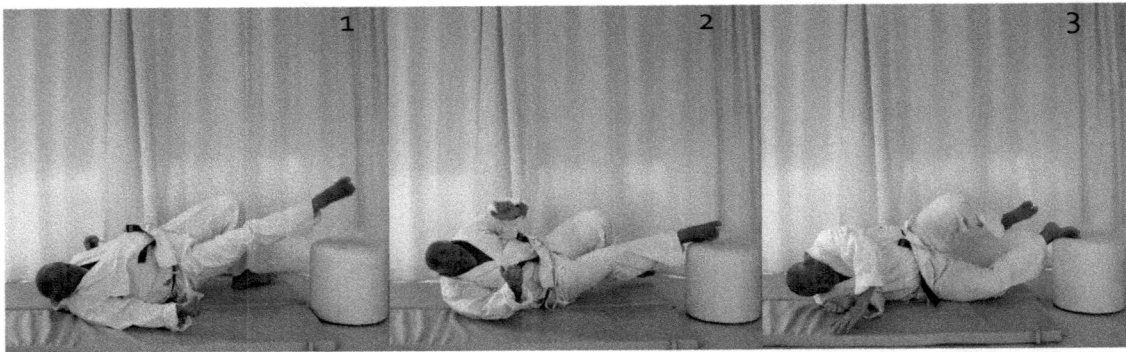

The hand-supported Assisted Ground Roundhouse Kick drill

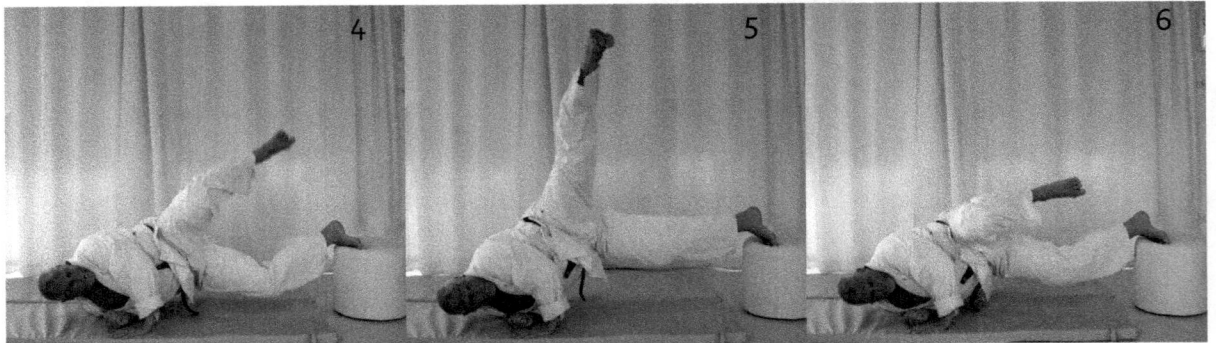

The climbing version of the Assisted Ground Roundhouse Kick

The **close** Climbing Ground Roundhouse kick

The **Jumping** Ground Roundhouse is a very important kick to drill: It is very efficient, surprising and powerful; and it also allows to kick all the way to a stand-up position if so required. Practice this Kick even if it is not your cup of tea: it will improve your stamina and your situational kicking awareness.

The Rear-leg Ground Jumping Roundhouse kick, all the way to stand-up

Chair Kicks

Roundhouse Kicks around a **chair** are very much in the spirit of what we have already seen with Front- and Side-Chair Kicks. The reader is invited to refer to these sections and design his own variations and drills. We shall just present an important general drill that will do wonder for overall stamina and for the power of all Roundhouse Kicks; it is extracted from our previous book (Plyo-Flex) for Explosive Kicking Power Development. Drill on both sides, each time without stopping until fully exhausted.
See Photos at the top of next page.

➤

Plyo-Flex chair drill for a more powerful Roundhouse

Key Points

- The power of the kick comes *from speed and from body twist*. If the situation requires chambering back, then the speed of the chamber-back is also, -and even especially-, important; the muscles must therefore be kept relaxed. If you kick through, keep moving: roll (First set of Photos) or twist back in Ground Hook Kick (Second set of Photos, at the top of next page).
- Use the momentum of the *body pivot* to give the kick power.
- You must be *accurate* to be effective; and you must always follow up after a Ground Roundhouse.

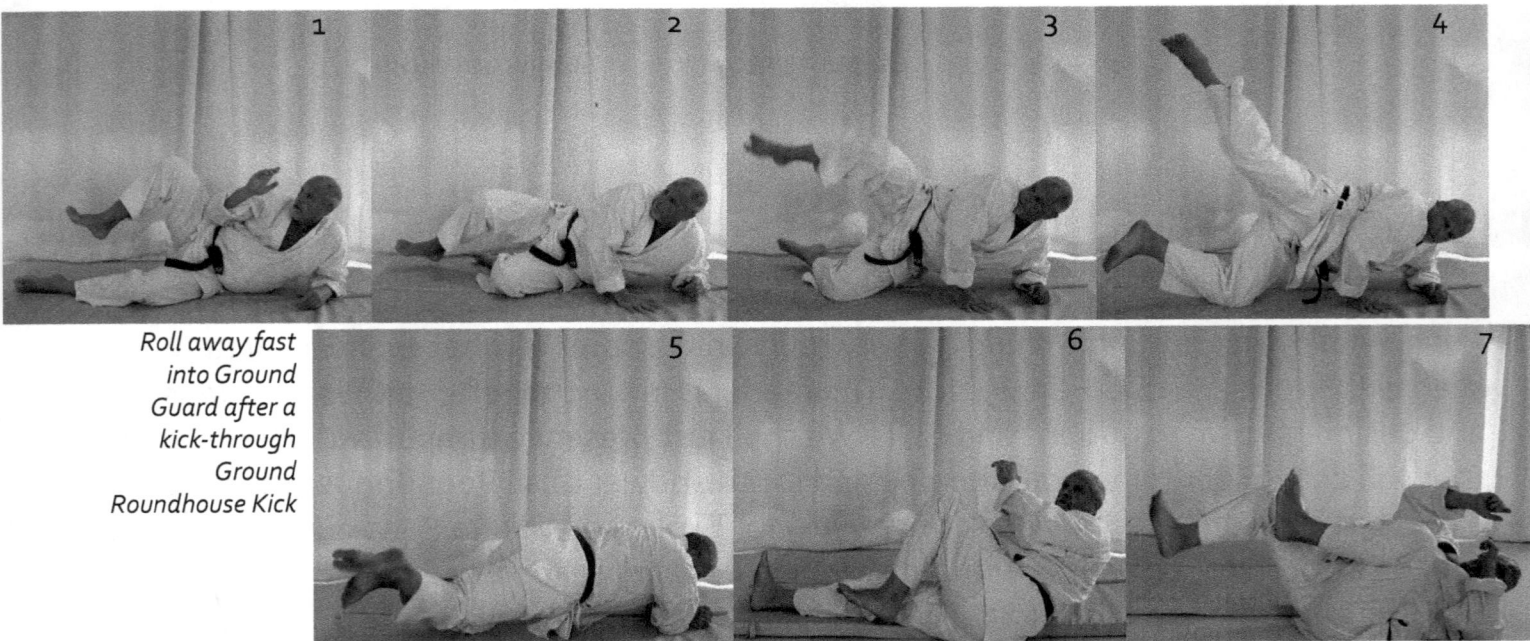

Roll away fast into Ground Guard after a kick-through Ground Roundhouse Kick

➤

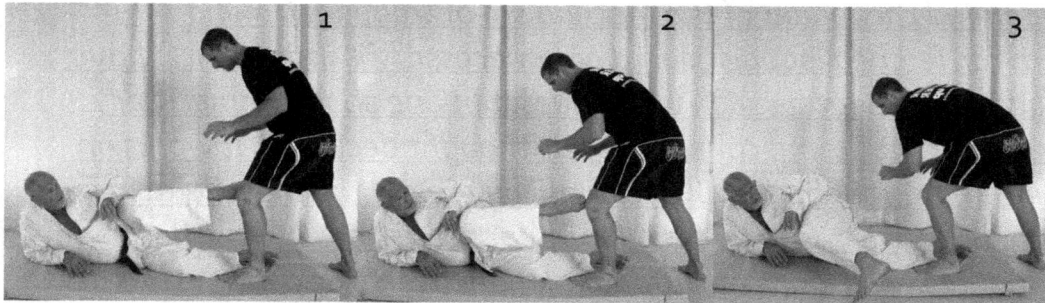

Twist-back Ground Hook Kick after a kick-through Ground Roundhouse Kick

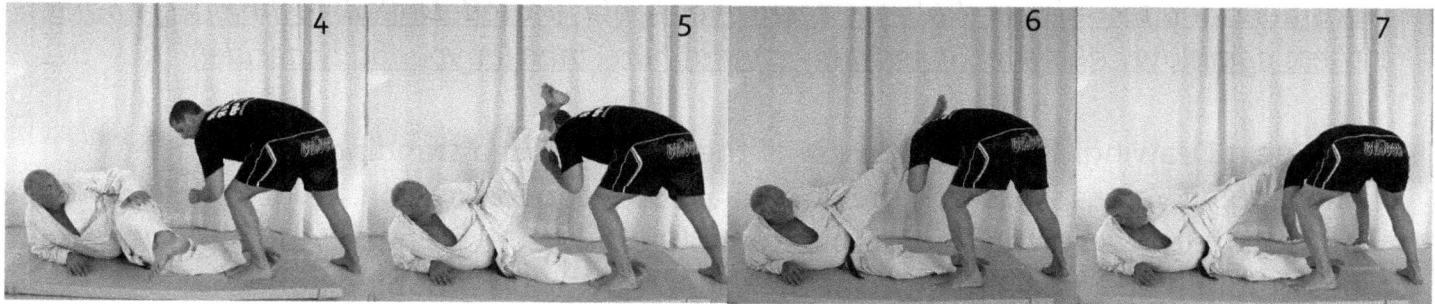

Targets

Preferably the *groin* and *knees*.
When possible, the *head*.
The ribs and thighs are also valuable targets, but should be hit with the ball of the foot.

Typical Applications

Figure 10.5.92 shows what the author considers the most important application of this Kick: When thrown to the floor, use the momentum of your fall and extend the pivot immediately into a *Ground Roundhouse Kick*; then always do follow up. This should be drilled to become automatic when you are thrown down, in order to foil or hinder any subsequent technique planned by your opponent. This is a technique I drilled often and thoroughly during my tournament career, as, back then, karate sweeps immediately followed by a punch or kick where all the rage and great points gatherers; it was important to be able to react instinctively if taken down to negate the success of an opponent's sweep.

When swept to the ground, smoothly blend into a Ground Roundhouse Kick

Here is the time again to remind the reader of the mechanism of training. Drilling techniques that may seem far-fetched, sophisticated or unnecessary is important! I have sometimes been challenged for presenting such techniques, but one should remember that the body in fighting mode is not using conscious well-thought decisions; it works on adrenaline, instinct and intuition. Your body will automatically select the most suitable technique for the situation, provided it is to be found in your unconscious mind. That is why it is important to drill continuously all kinds of situational maneuvers, kicks from strange positions and techniques that may seem over-sophisticated. Drill all techniques, and drill them again over and over, it certainly cannot hurt; then let your body decide!

The next Drawings illustrate the use of the Kick against a standing opponent challenging you as you sit on the floor in a cross-legged position. Pivot with your whole body to deliver an orthodox Ground Roundhouse Kick to his head. And if the opponent has grabbed you, pull him down at the same time by his grabbing hand.

Ground Roundhouse Kick application from cross-legged sit

The next Figures show a traditional application of the Kick as a *Stop Kick* from sitting on your knees and heels in classic *Zeiza* position. Your standing opponent attacks you with a full-stepped lunge punch; you evade by falling to the side while delivering the Roundhouse Kick as described above, to his groin. As he reels from the Groin Kick, you can follow up with a Ground Side Kick to the back of his forward knee. Sit up and grab the back of his shoulders to pull him powerfully down to the floor for further ground-fighting.

Evading Ground Roundhouse Kick to the groin from a traditional Zeiza sitting position

Specific Training

- Work a *low hanging heavy bag* from all possible starting positions; work for speed and power. Kick from all possible ground movements; go up and down and insert kicks between positions.
- Have a partner *swinging a heavy bag* at you, and time-kick it from a given position.
- Drill being taken down and *flowing into the Kick*, as described on the previous page.
- The *kick-through* version of the kick needs to be drilled on a focus pad or target; not on a bag (See Figure)

Drill the kick-through version on a focus pad

Self defense

The *groin* should always be your first target for the Roundhouse against a standing assailant. In the example below, you can follow up with a Twin Ground Back Kick.

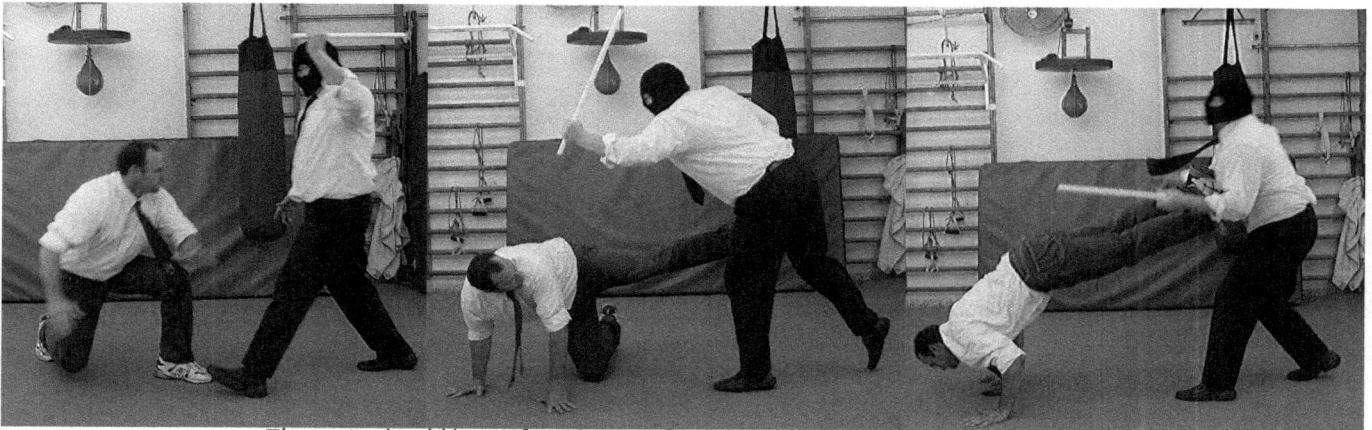

The groin should be preferred target for the real-life Ground Roundhouse Kick

The next set of Drawings shows a more traditional ground-fighting application: an **Evading Kick** from *Zeiza* classic sitting (as presented before). Follow up.

Evading Ground Roundhouse from sitting on knees and heels

The coming Figures show a "*Kung Fu's Iron Broom*" version of the Kick: a kick-through low Roundhouse Kick to the lower leg which purpose is to take the opponent down. The reader is also invited to notice the illustrated *starting position*, typical of Indonesian styles and sometimes named Swastika Ground Position (See the legs' position! **Note: This refers to the Buddhist Indo European symbol, of course, and not the cursed nazi icon**). Let your Kick start *after* you start pivoting, -just like for a Straight-leg Roundhouse-, and kick forcefully *through* your assailant's ankle to bring him down. Use the momentum of this full-powered Kick to roll and come back with the other leg in a Ground Downward Heel Kick (*Axe Kick*) to the groin, body or head of the taken-down adversary. Notice that the Axe Kick comes with the additional power of Humpty-Dumpty-like move (with added scissoring).

Ground 'Iron Broom' and Axe Kick combination

And the next Drawings show the use of the Kick after you have let your assailant come close to attack you on the floor. You basically kick him in the head from a grappling guard, as he gets between your legs.

Ground Roundhouse Kick from grappling guard

The following Illustrations show another example of '*kick-when-taken-down*'. As your opponent succeeds in setting up his Inner Reap Throw (*O Uchi Gari – Judo*), you suddenly throw yourself to the floor instead of resisting further. You then use the momentum and the body pivot to deliver a powerful 'suicidal' Roundhouse Kick to his head. If possible, keep hold of his sleeve or arm.

Kick automatically if taken down, use the momentum of the throw for body twist power

Stripping Kicks are kicks delivered to an opponent's arms when they are holding one of your limbs, generally the ankle. By kicking the arm holding your limb, you should be able to break the hold and be released, hence the "stripping" kick name. The coming Figures show such a Stripping application of the *Ground Roundhouse Kick*. Please refer to my monologue above about the importance of drilling techniques in order to make them automatic. The Stripping Ground Roundhouse should become instinctive, should your assailant succeed in grabbing your foot and twist it outwards to force you to roll on the ground. This Twisting Leg-lock can be very painful if jerky: do not resist but roll with the twist to deliver a powerful kick-through Roundhouse Kick to his elbow joint. Keep rolling a full turn as both the Kick and the unexpected momentum of your roll will set you free. Take up the Ground Guard position and be ready for a Ground Front Kick, should he be in range. The **Stripping Roundhouse** is an aggressive technique delivered *with the intent of hurting his elbow joint*. It is an important maneuver that should be drilled into your unconscious fighting intuition.

Stripping Ground Roundhouse Kick against Ankle Twist

And the next Illustrations show what to do if the previous technique fails, and they show a naturally-flowing *Ground Spin-back Hook Kick* follow-up. If your Stripping Kick has missed for one reason or another, let yourself strongly fall on the floor while pulling your legs forward and down. Pull yourself forward on the ground by using your hands and start pivoting. If needed and possible, you should push yourself away from him with your free leg as well, pushing on the ground or on his thigh or body. As you free yourself, keep pivoting smoothly into the Ground Roundhouse Kick. Pursue the circular motion to deliver the Spin-back Ground Hook Kick. This maneuver is easier and more natural that may seem at first glance. It also should be used in any ground situation in which you have your back to the opponent.

Applied Roundhouse/Spin-back Hook Kick Ground Combination

I have been criticized in the past for advising to go to the ground in Self-Defense situations. I stand by my opinion that a ground-moving adversary is very dangerous and difficult to handle. Drilling the coming exercise should give you the right feeling of being down against a standing assailant: His groin is dangerously close to you, dangerous... to him! In the example illustrated below, you stop an incoming assailant by punching towards his groin. Pivot back down smoothly for a Front-leg Ground Roundhouse to his groin, with the additional advantage of removing your upper body from his reach. Keep rolling for a Scissor Kick of his front leg to take him down.

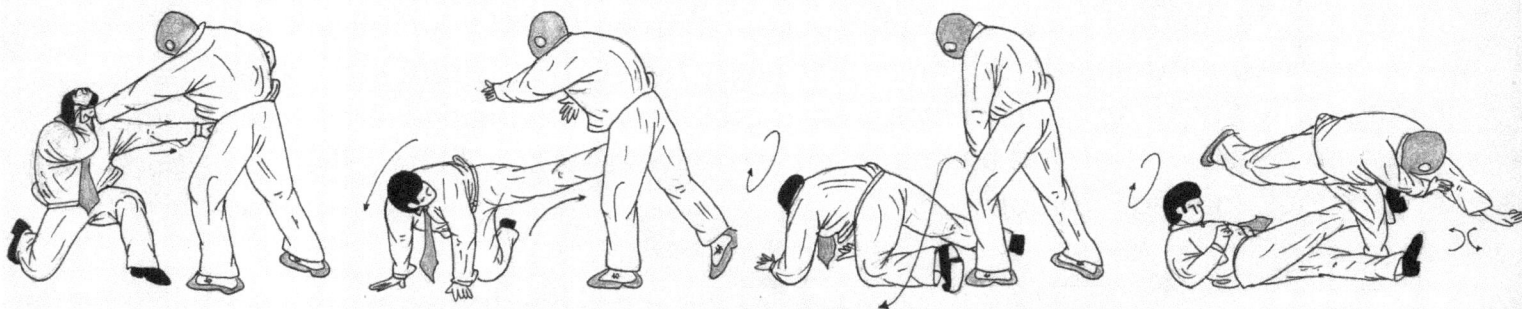

Applied Front-leg groin Ground Roundhouse rolling into leg Scissor Kick

Illustrative Photos

The Essential standing classic Full Roundhouse Kick

The Essential standing Small Roundhouse Kick

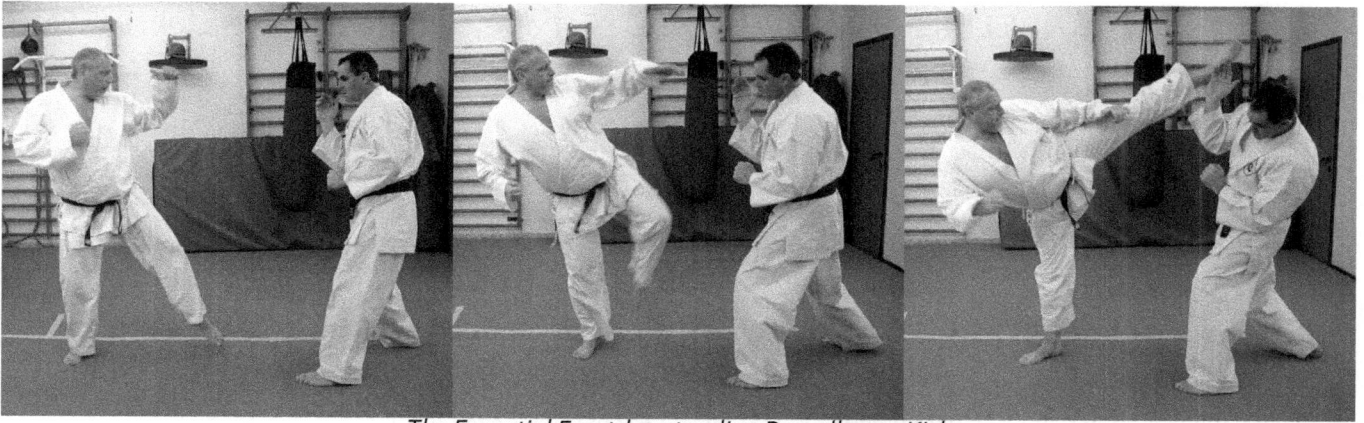
The Essential Front-leg standing Roundhouse Kick

The Essential Drop Roundhouse Kick

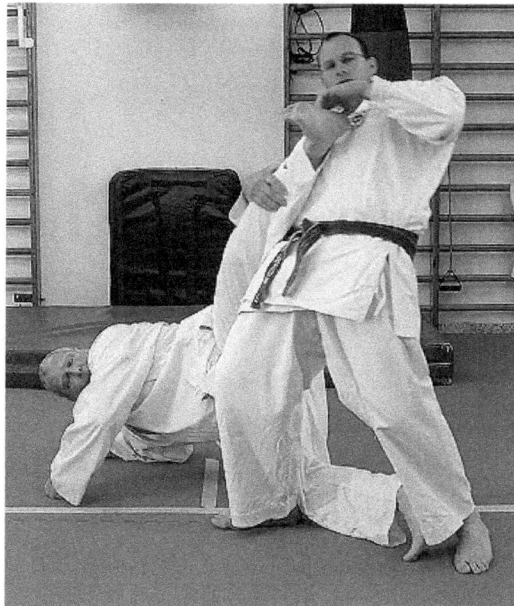
Spin-back Ground Hook Kick

It's not the size of the dog in the fight, it's the size of the fight in the dog.
~Mark Twain

6. THE KNEELING-UP ROUNDHOUSE KICK AND CLOSE RELATIVES

General

This is the Ground version of the basic Kneeling-up Roundhouse Kick described in our previous book about *Essential Kicks*. In the traditional Essential version of the Roundhouse, you do kneel down to escape or befuddle your opponent, and then you pop up to deliver the Kick. But the Kicks presented briefly in this section do *start from the ground up* and simply ignore the preceding kneeling-down part. This Kick is presented here for the sake of completeness; the reader is invited to consult our previous work for more detail. The reader should also take into account that all the principles involved in the execution of this Kick are applicable to other "Raising" Kicks, especially the Kneeling-up Side Kick. We shall also include in this section other Kicks delivered while standing up, regardless of the initial position.

The orthodox basic starting position is the *Crouching Cross-legged Stance*, very common in Indonesian and Southern Chinese styles. It is a surprising maneuver, but one should remember that this is a Classic Kick to use only if you are well trained and proficient: you are always more vulnerable *while* standing up.

It is, in any case, this Kick is above all a great strengthening exercise and a fantastic drill for versatility and for overall kicking proficiency.

Description

The basic *Kneeling-up Roundhouse Kick* is illustrated in the first Figures at the top of next page: from a sitting cross-legged stance, you will stand up *by using the legs exclusively*; no help from the hands. The upper leg lifts into chambered position while the lower leg pushes the whole body weight. Kick *as soon as standing*. And always follow up. Please take particular notice of the starting position: the Cross-legged Ground Stance common in East Asian Arts and also illustrated on next page.

The execution of the raising maneuver is also important: the next Drawings will show the progression from the Sitting Stance to the standing Universal Chambering Position from which the kick will be delivered. [*The reader is here reminded that the Universal Chamber is a deceptive position from which either a Side Kick, or a Roundhouse Kick, or even a Hook Kick can be delivered. For more about Universal Chambering Kicks, the reader is invited to refer to our previous book about Essential Kicks.*] ➡

The Kneeling-up Roundhouse Kick

One of Silat's Crossed-legs
Sitting Stances

Stand up into Universal Chamber position and kick!

Key Points

- Keep your *guard up* while in standing-up mode: you are vulnerable.
- Stand up *directly into chambered position*, and there hence smoothly and seamlessly into the kick.
- This is not an especially powerful move, so it must be *followed up*.

Targets

This is not a very powerful kick, as the upward momentum does not contribute much to the kick's energy. Therefore, targets must be *vital points*: groin, knee, face, throat, solar plexus, or kidneys.

Typical Applications

This 'Kneeling-up Kicks' section is all about: simply kicking while standing-up. The coming Figures illustrate the delivery of the **rear-leg version** of the Kick from a *Side One-knee Stance*. This is already a more powerful version than the classic Kick. Kick as soon as the opponent comes in range.

The Kneeling-up Roundhouse Kick from one-knee-on-the-floor position

And the next Illustrations show a Standing-up Kick from *conventional relaxed sitting-on-the-floor*. In this example, the opponent is further misdirected by your forward hand deceivingly held high, all the while your Roundhouse Kick is delivered at groin level.

Kneeling-up groin Roundhouse Kick from common floor sitting position

The most useful application though, will be the *Standing-up Kick executed smoothly just after a Ground Kick*; this is also the best way to stand back up if so desired. Once you have scored with a Ground Kick, your opponent will be either hurt or flustered; you can use this time-out to continue smoothly with a Kneeling-up Kick. If you are successful, you will be back safely on your feet after having kicked him twice. For this reason the drills like the one presented in the Drawings at the top of next page are of great importance: deliver a Ground Kick from which you uninterruptedly start a Kneeling-up Kick. Vary the Ground Kick and Kneeling-up Kick types, and practice with focus. ➤

Kneeling-up
Roundhouse Kick
executed seamlessly
after a Ground
Roundhouse Kick —
An important drill

Specific Training

The reader is invited to consult our previous books for more about *Kneeling-up Kicks* training and similar drills.

All the kicks described above, and below, are in fact excellent drills by themselves; they will help become proficient in all Standing-up Kicks, but they will also: develop power and stamina, improve kicking situational awareness, sharpen the corresponding standing kicks and give the fighter more ground-fighting confidence.

All the kicks delivered while standing-up and all similar drills are relevant to these goals.

The classic warming up "**Kneel and Kick**" drill is probably the best-known, the simplest and the most effective; it is illustrated here in Photos for the Side Kick, though as relevant for the Roundhouse, the Front and all other basic Kicks.

The kneeling to Standing-up Side Kick Drill — repeat until exhausted

Another common drill, also illustrated for the Side Kick version, is kicking from and back to the Crossed-leg Sitting Stance: Stand up and kick with the rear leg, then go back down to stance with the kicking leg in front. You can so progress in the Dojo, alternating kicking legs until exhausted.

Walking and side-kicking in low Cross-legged Stance

Drilling kicks on stairs, as presented in our previous book about **Plyo-Flex** Training, can be of great help to improve explosiveness in Kicks. Some drills are particularly close to Ground Kicking or to Kneeling-up Kicking. As a general comment, Plyometrics and Flexibility training are highly recommended to the aspiring expert kicker.

Stair-drilling the Roundhouse Kick, a Plyo-Flex exercise

Another exercise to strengthen the muscles involved in Roundhouse-kicking in general, but that is highly recommended for the ground-kicker is presented in the next Photos. This drill engages some hip muscles that are difficult to solicit and is extremely beneficial to kicking performance. Execute in series until exhausted, switch legs, repeat.

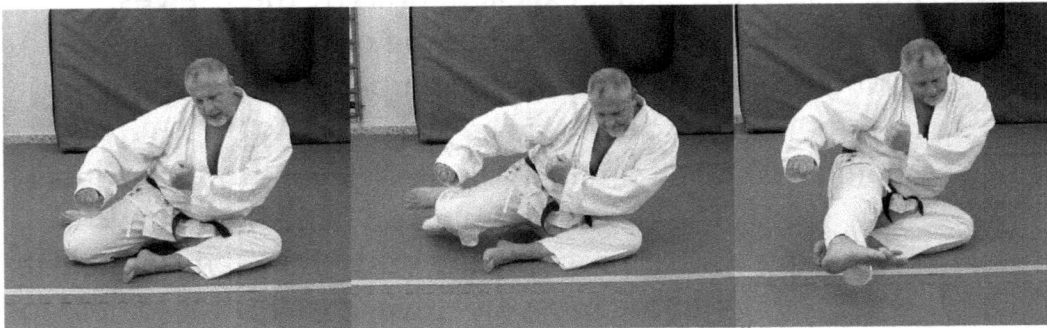

Ground Roundhouse Strengthening Drill

Self defense

The Illustrations at the top of next page show the use of the Kick when attacked while sitting cross-legged on the floor, Indian-style. Back-fist the assailant's close groin as he approaches or as he tries to punch you. Stand up while chambering your front-leg Roundhouse Kick. Aim for his groin again if he steps back, as he should naturally do. But, should he still be presenting his back to the Kick, you should then preferably aim for his knee (though kidneys or even neck are worthy targets too). In any case, keep the pressure and follow up, for instance as illustrated.

➡

1 2 3

From crossed-legs sitting, the groin is an easy punching target; use the opportunity for a following Kneeling-up Roundhouse Kick

4 5 6

The coming Figures show a *Kneeling-up Side Kick*, after the blocking grab of a punch from a standing assailant. The evasive leaning and the hand on the floor will help you give an extra boost to the standing-up move. Moreover, your catching the attacking wrist will help keep the opponent in range for the more powerful Side Kick.

A Kneeling-up Side Kick in context

The Drawings at the top of next page show, in turn, a Kneeling-up Roundhouse Kick from the same starting position as before. But this time, you surprise the menacingly approaching opponent with the ground version of a *Spin-back Back-fist Strike* to the groin; the groin of these standing assailants is invitingly so close... (*Remember that when you are the one standing over a downed opponent!*) You then stand up while chambering the Roundhouse Kick. Should the range justify it, you can hop during delivery of the Kick. Follow up.

➡️

THE KNEELING-UP ROUNDHOUSE KICK

Kneeling-up Roundhouse Kick after a sneaky Ground Spin-back Groin Back-fist strike

7. THE GROUND HOOK KICK

General

Just like the corresponding *Essential Drop Hook Kick* presented in earlier books, the **Ground Hook Kick** is sneaky and often surprising, but it is not a very powerful Kick by itself. It requires getting into position to allow for some twisting momentum during the delivery of the Kick, so as to allow the use of the hips and the participation of the whole body. It is why it is more a natural follow-up to the Ground Roundhouse Kick, as we have already seen; and more example will be presented. This is also why the Ground Hook Kick is most used in its Spin-back form which will be presented separately in another section. All in all, the reader should just remember that the Ground Hook is a great Kick when inserted into a dynamic situation that allow its potential to be realized. We shall present several examples in the text.

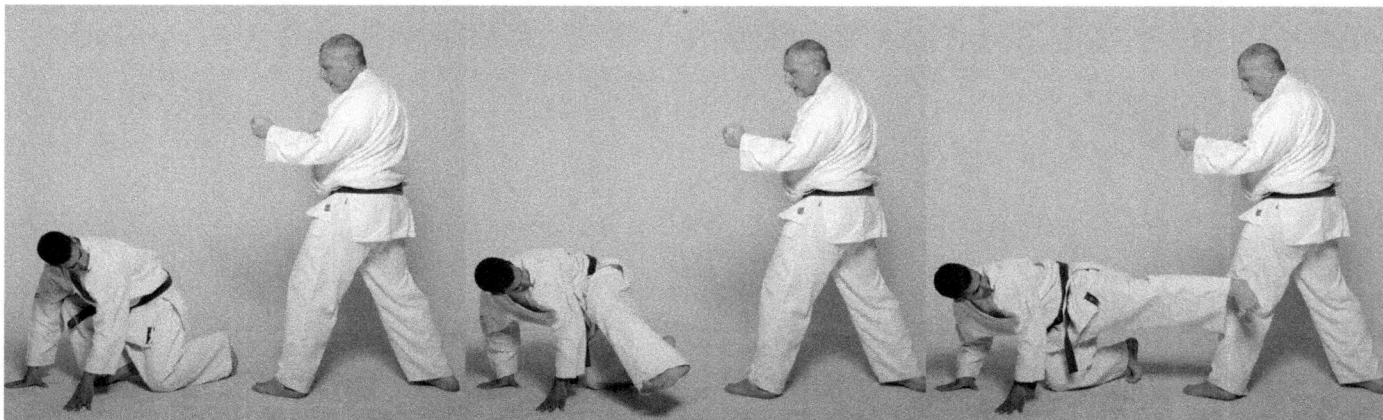

A Ground Hook Kick to the knee

Description

The Drawings at the top of next page illustrate the basic delivery from a *crossed-legged lying position*. It is the best way to understand the biomechanics of the Kick. As mentioned, the **Ground Hook Kick** is to be used in a dynamic situation, and any movement bringing you to this particular set-up begs for a Hook Kick follow-up.

➡

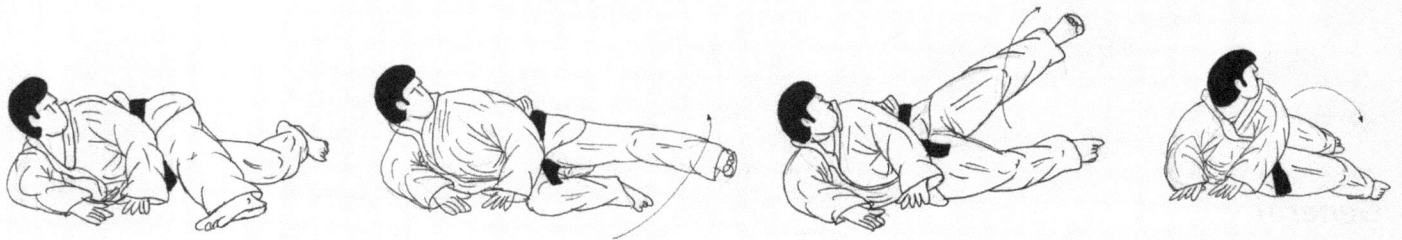

The basic Ground Hook Kick

Of course, you can get into the previous starting position directly from any other ground position and with the sole purpose of delivering the Hook Kick. The Photos below show the full delivery from the basic lying Ground Position: reach the starting crossed-legs position and kick! Simple.

The fully-powered Ground Hook Kick from lying-down position

The next Illustrations show the delivery of the Kick from the normal relaxed extended-legs sitting position. You pivot to one side onto your hands and one knee, then pivot back all the way with the *Ground Hook Kick*. The principle is the same as for the basic version, but the kicking leg should 'rebound' forcefully on the floor for a more powerful Kick; think of an elastic band or a coil.

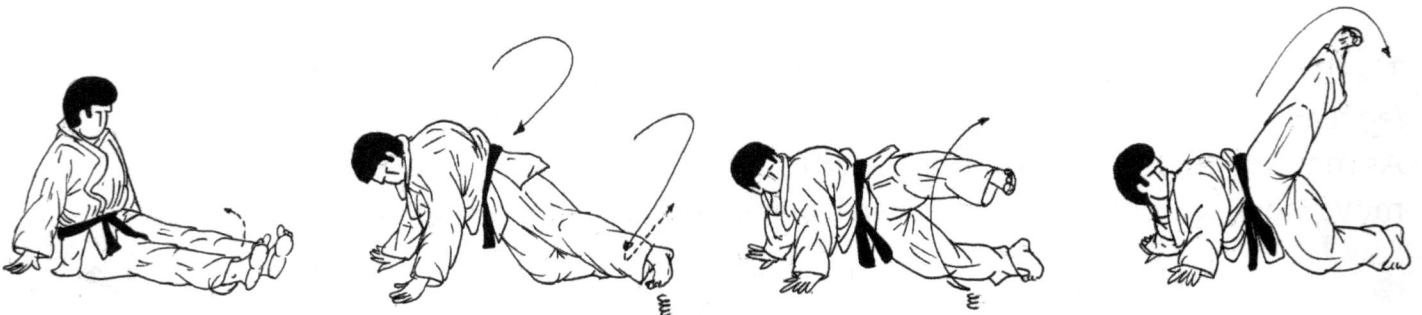

Starting the Ground Hook Kick from normal floor sitting position

Key Points

- You need to go all the way to one side, and then pivot back to allow for enough length of trajectory and therefore for enough acceleration. *Kick with the hips*, not the leg.
- If possible, always "*hook*" into the kick at impact, as for the Essential Hooked Hook Kick. From the ground, it will give you a much helpful 'zing'.
- Aim for a specific '*soft*' *target* like the groin, the knee, the throat, the face,...
- Always *follow-up*; this is not the most powerful of kicks. Examples will be given.

Targets

Aim for the *head, neck, groin or knee*.

Ground Hook Kick, respectively hitting the hip at groin level, and targeting the back of the neck

Typical Applications

The next Photos show the self-explanatory delivery from the **all-fours position**.

The Ground Hook Kick from quadruped position

The next Figures illustrate the meaning of "sneaky" for a Kick: This is simply the delivery of the classic Kick, as your opponent bends down towards you. You just have to make sure he bends towards you. It should not be too difficult: from the "guard" position, you roll to one side, and then pivot back unexpectedly into the Kick. You should look as if you roll in fear of being hit, and then send the Hook Kick from your opponent's blind side. A bit of acting is required to lure him in. Follow up; a Ground Roundhouse would flow in very naturally for instance.

Surprise an opponent bending over you in order to punch you... with a Ground Hook Kick

And the next Illustrations show the logical use of the Kick as a follow-up to the Ground Roundhouse Kick. This has been mentioned already in the section about *The Ground Roundhouse Kick* and has been illustrated by Photos. In the coming Drawings you deliver the Roundhouse to the assailant's *groin* as he steps in menacingly and then follow up naturally by rolling back into the Ground Hook Kick as he bends over in pain. These kind of drills are important to condition your body to always naturally hook-kick after a Ground Roundhouse.

A Ground Hook Kick smoothly following a groin Roundhouse

As mentioned, the *Ground Hook Kick* is a Kick to execute mainly in dynamic situations that will help give it the needed momentum for efficacy. The next Figures show a "sweep" application of the Kick, delivered as a surprise move after luring an opponent to counterattack. From a standing opposite stance, you deliver an Essential full-powered rear-leg Crescent Kick into your opponent's front arm, preferably as he is on the verge of jabbing. Kick *through* very powerfully until you land on one knee after a full half-circle. As your opponent lunges forward to attack you in your seemingly bad ground-reaching position, you kick back with the same leg while leaning on your hands. This powerful Ground Hook Kick to the side knee of his forward leg will have him fall down. You can follow up with a Ground Downward Roundhouse Kick (Presented further in the text) to his face. Please note that, although close, this is not a Drop Kick: you go down at the end of your Crescent Kick and stop for a millisecond to lure him into starting a small lunge towards you: this would be more of a Feint Kick. The whole story of seeing you suddenly go down and kick will certainly disconcert your opponent and give you an unsuspected advantage.

Ground Hook Kick to the knee from dynamic kneeling position

Specific Training

- Lie down *below* a hanging heavy bag and practice the Kick for **power** from all possible ground positions (See Figure).
- Practice the drills and combinations presented on a *heavy bag*.
- Drill the combinations presented with a focus pad hold by a partner; kick *fast and through*.

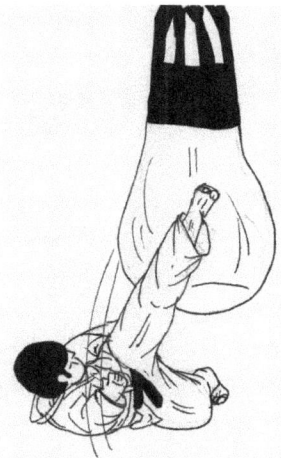

Drill for power on the heavy bag; drill from below the bag

Self defense

The next Drawings will illustrate a variation of the Kick that very close to the *Essential Spin-back Drop Hook Kick* described in previous books. In this example, it can still be considered a Ground Kick as you land down first, then kick, but the nuance is light. A fully continuous move would be a Spin-back Drop Kick, no doubt. As mentioned, the Ground Hook Kick is valid nearly exclusively in *dynamic* set-ups; so distinctions are difficult. Here is one, and the slight interruption, in order to make this a Kick and not a sweep, makes all the small difference. The combination will also introduce the all-important Ground Axe Kick to be described later in the text.

Both protagonists are standing. Attack your assailant with a full-powered *Straight-leg Roundhouse Sweep Kick* (as presented in detail in our previous book about *Low Kicks*). This important Low Kick variation ought to at least place him off-balance on one leg. Keep the spinning momentum to lower the leg, while dropping on the knee of the leg which executed the first kick. This gets you in ground position to launch a low Spin-back Hook Kick. You will be hitting the knee or the calf of his standing leg **with a kick-mindset**, not a sweep. You can then Downward-heel-kick him (*Ground Axe Kick*) as he lands on the floor.

Ground Hook Kick to the knee after Spin-down

Illustrative Photos

Standing Essential rear-leg Hook Kick

Another example of standing Essential rear-leg Hook Kick

The extra hooking effect at the end of the Hook Kick

The standing Essential **front-leg** Hopping Hook Kick

The Drop Hook Kick

A Ground Hook Kick to the hip joint

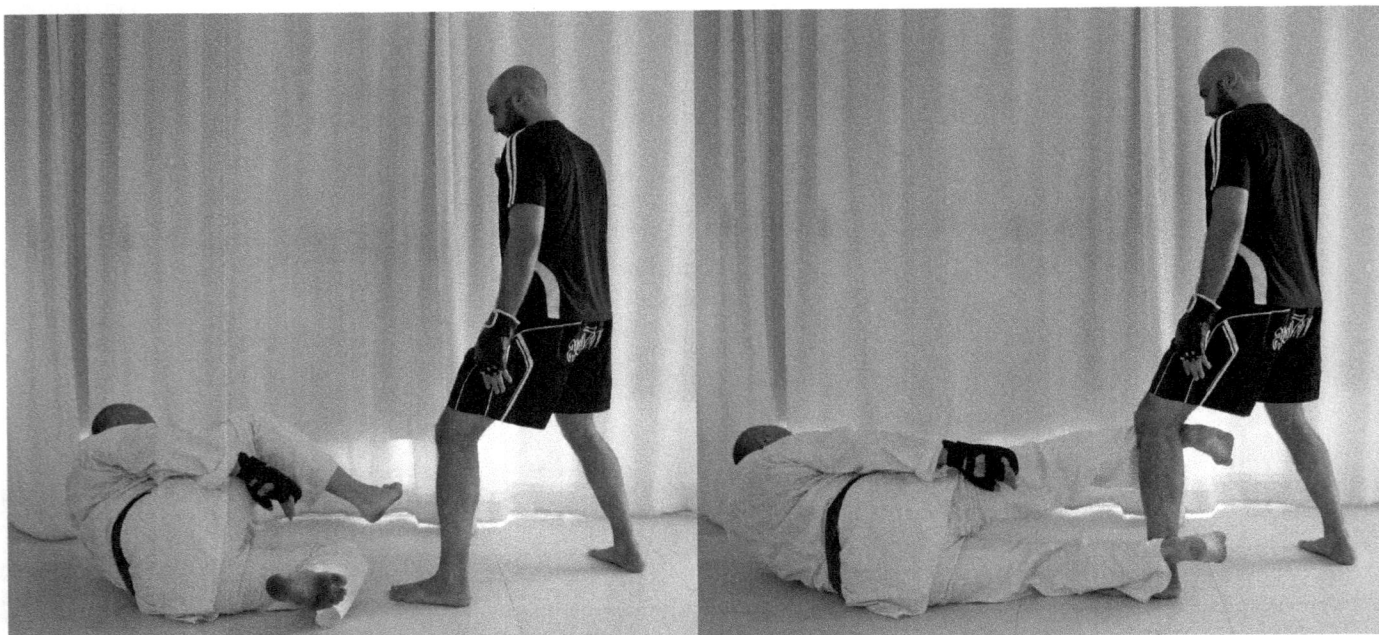

Ground Hook Kick to the knee with checked ankle: a version of the Ground Scissor Kick

He who knows when he can fight and when he cannot, will be victorious.
~Sun Tzu

8. THE GROUND DOWNWARD ROUNDHOUSE KICK

General

In the section about the basic Ground Roundhouse Kick, we have presented the diagonal downward variation of the Kick. The **Ground Downward Roundhouse Kick** presented now is simply this version, _but taken all the way to a nearly fully-vertical downward trajectory_. This is a very important Kick for the aspiring ground-fighter. It is the Kick to use if your opponent is also on the floor near you, or if you succeed in felling him near you, or if he bends or crouches towards you. This is also a great Kick to use to keep the opponent at a distance, as it is often done in _Capoeira_ (and we shall present this fantastic Capoeira version of the Kick in the text). Just like the Essential standing version of the Downward Roundhouse Kick, it is always a surprising Kick because of the direction it comes from and because of its inherent speed. It can also pack some serious power because of the weight of the leg itself adding itself to the momentum.

The Ground Downward Roundhouse to your side

Description

Just like all previous Ground Roundhouse Kicks and other Ground Kicks, this one can be delivered from nearly all starting positions. The coming Illustrations show how to deliver the Kick from the classic extended-legs sitting floor position: Pivot to find yourself on your hands and one foot (or knee). But this time, you pivot all the way until you find yourself with your back towards the opponent. You have of course chambered during the pivot and immediately kick vertically downwards.

Ground Downward Roundhouse from regular sitting on the floor, legs extended

One of the most naturally flowing deliveries of this surprising Kick will be from a *Roll-back move*. The Figures at the top of next page illustrate how you roll back from a sitting position into the required chamber set-up, and then kick down, with the added momentum of the roll.

➤

The Roll-back Downward Roundhouse Kick

Another set-up very much attuned to the *Downward Roundhouse* delivery is the interesting **Climbing version**. The reader will remember that Climbing Kicks are Assisted Kicks executed from very close, which allows to place the assisting leg high onto the opponent's body in order to kick him in the higher gates. It is probably a Kick too sophisticated for casual use by most, but it is still an interesting technique and a good drill for situational kicking awareness. The Drawings do illustrate the maneuver clearly; go and drill it. Enjoy the work on this version, even if you will never use it yourself.

The Climbing Ground Downward Roundhouse Kick

It is clear to the experienced Artist that the Ground Downward Roundhouse Kick can be delivered from most ground positions in all variations described previously for the regular Ground Roundhouse and other Ground kicks already covered. The reader is invited to start drilling the regular Ground Roundhouse variations and applications already described above, but in their "downward" version as well.

Key Points

- The "feel" of the kick is that of a *Roundhouse Kick*, just like for the classic standing Downward Roundhouse Kick: You deliver a Roundhouse, but its trajectory becomes downwards because you turn the hips until you are with your back to the target.
- Kick *through* into the target, before you chamber back.
- Always *follow up*.

THE GROUND DOWNWARD ROUNDHOUSE KICK   121

Targets

This is not a full-powered kick and it must attack vital points: the head, throat, the back of the neck, the solar plexus, the groin, the knee and the kidneys. The list is limited by the fact that the Kick strikes from above; it will obviously be a factor of the respective position of the protagonists.

Typical Applications

Ground Kicks and Near-ground Kicks are obviously the specialty of the Art of *Capoeira*. The next Illustrations show an interesting Capoeira variation (*Passa Pescoço*) in which you use your head and two hands on the floor for a Downward Roundhouse-type of Overhead Kick. You start from a kneeling position and lean sideways onto your head and hands. Lift the leg high and kick down while lifting the other leg. This very effective and surprising Kick is also a fantastic drill to execute as slowly as possible for quasi-isometric training. Even if you do not execute this Kick in its perfect Capoeira form, it is still a very important maneuver for your arsenal. Adapt it to your own style and morphology, and your own Art will be richer for it.

A Capoeira variation on the theme of the Ground Downward Roundhouse

The next Drawings, at the top of next page, illustrate a small variation of this Kick, seen from a rear view. This one starts from a *Ginga* position, keeps a foot on the floor all the time and ends up standing (*Martelo de Chão*). The foot travels a full half circle towards its target with all the body weight and its twisting momentum.

Needless to add that *Capoeira* is a great Martial Art to practice for the Universal Kicker. It also will teach you ground movement and sneaky misdirecting fighting tactics.

➤

*Rear view of the **Martelo de Chão**, one of Capoeira's version of the Ground Downward Roundhouse*

This is also, obviously, the Kick of choice if your opponent lies on the ground near you; it should even be unconsciously automatic. The Figures show the application of the Kick after the release from an attempted supine choke. As your opponent straddles you to initiate a choke, grab both his sleeves at triceps level. Pull on one side while pushing on the other, and lift the buttocks in a twisting heave. Everything must be immediate and simultaneous, before the opponent can strengthen his hold. Hit him in the face with a punch or a palm strike as he rolls to the side. Strike him again as he lands and keep the pivoting momentum to deliver the naturally flowing *Downward Roundhouse Kick*. Aim for the head and follow up.

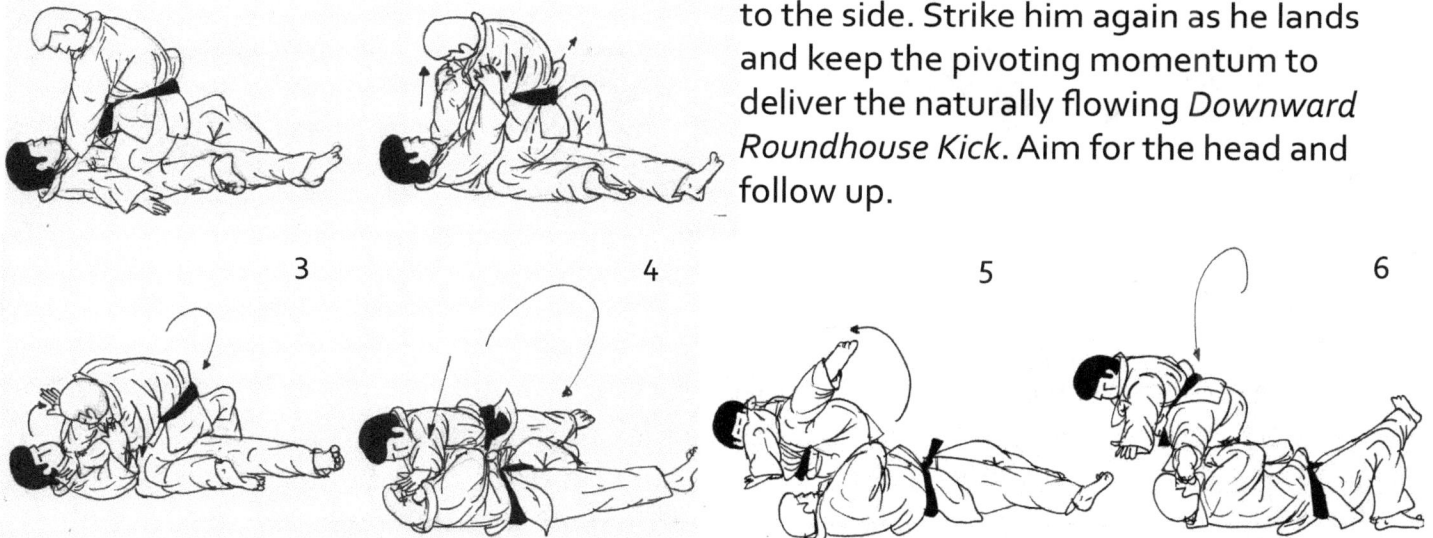

3   4   5   6

Kick your opponent after rolling him to your side

Specific Training

Learning maximum power delivery for this Kick requires serious impact training. Work on a lying heavy bag from all possible ground positions and transitional moves (See Figure P120). And drill the Applications described on the heavy bag.

Self defense

The next Drawings show how this Kick can be the classic defense against the most common of all ground arm-lock techniques, and a darling of MMA bouts: the classic side extended Arm-lock (*Ude hishigi juji gatame – Judo*). As your opponent attempts to pull on your arm to finalize the arm-lock, catch your own hand to resist its straightening. Remember to react fast, before the lock is set. Once set in, the release will be much more difficult. Immediately twist in place to deliver the *Downward Roundhouse Kick* to his face. Repeat until you feel his hold weaken. You can then wrench your wrist out of his grasp and follow up with a Ground Hook Kick, connecting with the heel *into* his head. Repeat if necessary. The reader will remember our previous comment about Roundhouse and Hook being complementary Kicks on the ground: One follows the other naturally, back and forth; this is also true for the Downward Roundhouse.

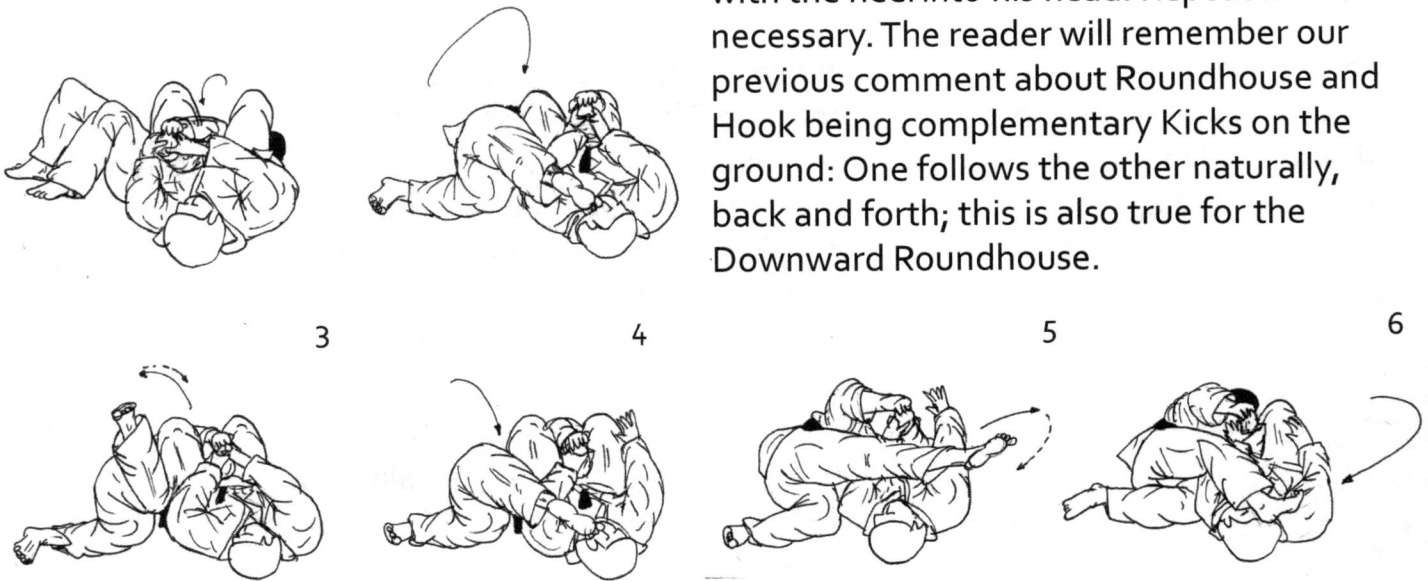

3   4   5   6

The Ground Downward Roundhouse Kick in an arm-lock release

The last example will illustrate a great set-up for the Ground Downward Roundhouse. Start with a 'timing' regular Roundhouse Stop Kick to the *groin* of an approaching standing assailant; you will then attack the back of his neck as he bends over from the groin pain. As illustrated by the Figures at the top of next page, you deliver a Ground Roundhouse Kick to the groin of the menacing assailant as soon as he gets in range. Chamber back and keep pivoting a bit more as he bends over in pain. Deliver the Downward Roundhouse to his exposed neck, while pushing yourself towards him. Chamber back; you can then follow up with a full powered Ground Roundhouse from your other leg, using the full strength of the body twist-back in the opposite direction to crush his forward knee.   ➤

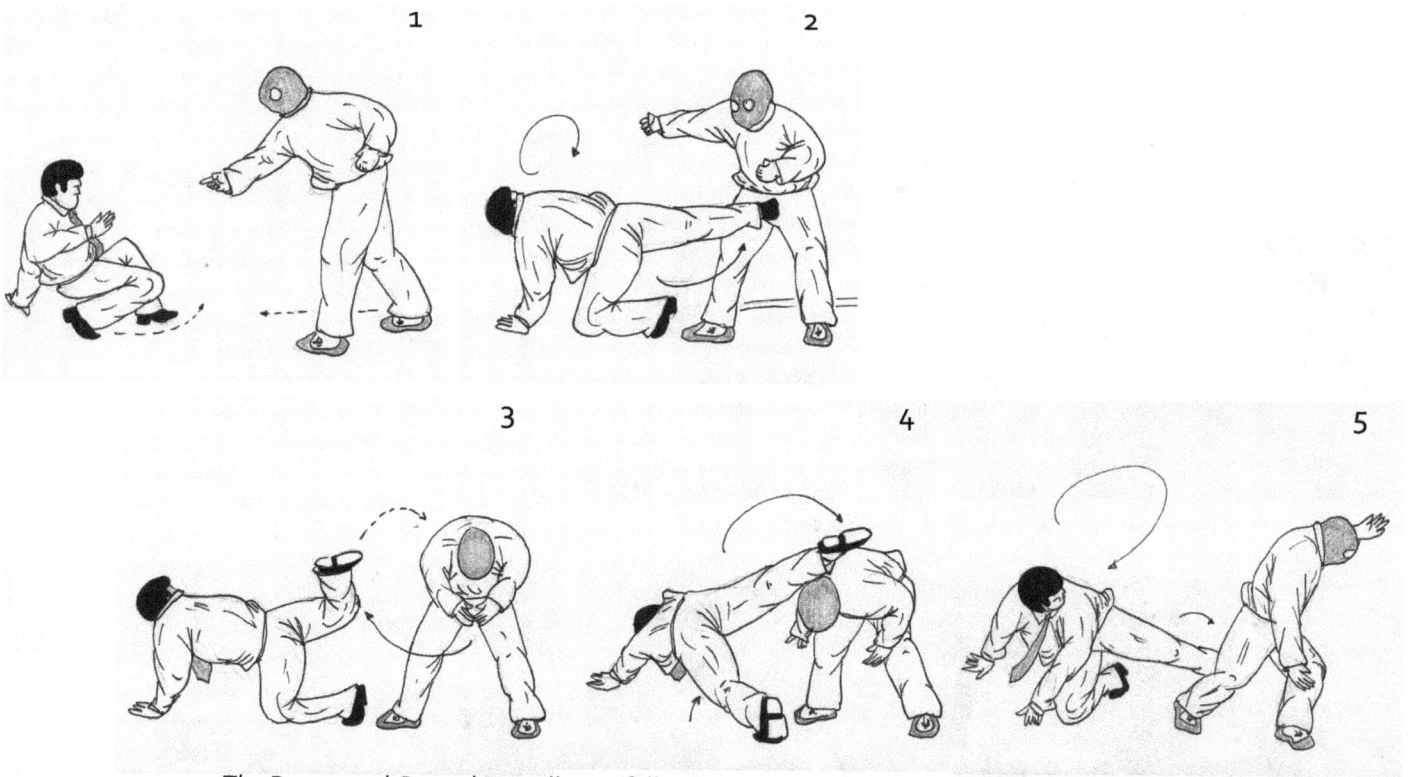

1   2   3   4   5

The Downward Ground Roundhouse following a regular groin Ground Roundhouse Kick

Illustrative Photos

The Essential standing Downward Roundhouse Kick

The classic Hand-on-floor Downward Roundhouse Kick

Drilling the regular standing Downward Roundhouse Kick

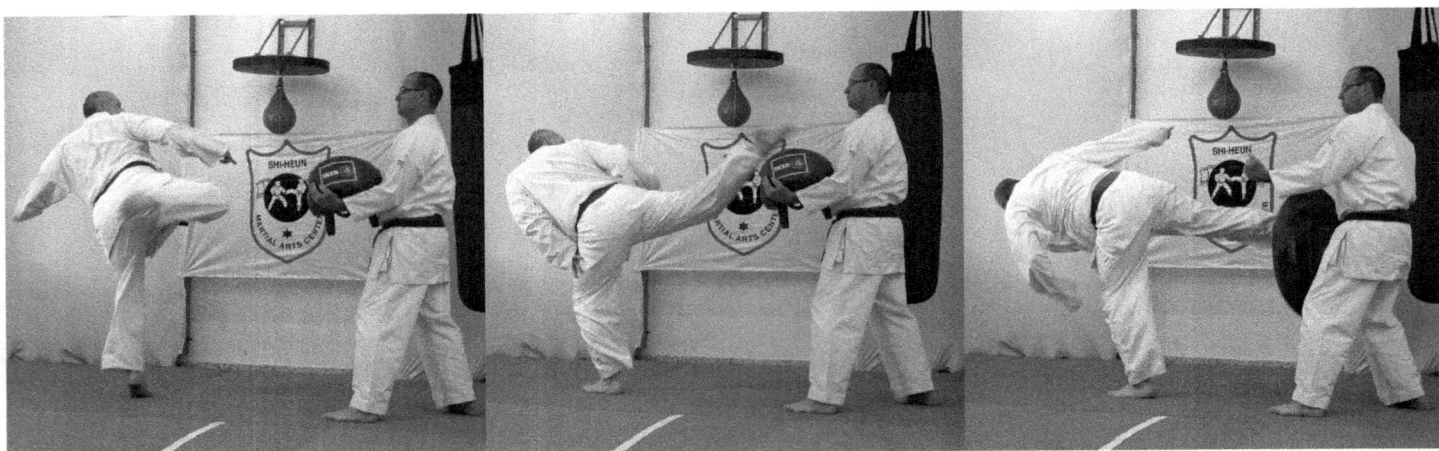

I am not teaching you anything. I just help you to exlplore yourself.
~Bruce Lee

9. THE GROUND SPIN-BACK HOOK KICK

Meia-lua Queda de Rim/ Rasteira Giratoria (Capoeira)

General

This is a very dynamic Kick, involving a lot of body movement. It will never be delivered from a static position, but usually after a Roundhouse Kick or in the midst of a twisting move. As mentioned earlier, it is imperative to be moving a lot when ground-fighting, and this Kick is perfect to insert in-between moves. The *Ground Spin-back Hook* will be very confusing to your opponent, and it will generally be unexpected on the ground. This Kick is also a great way to stand up while kicking,- the safest standing up method. In this case, the Kick could be aimed either at scoring or only at keeping the opponent away.

The Ground Spin-back Hook Kick is very close to the Drop Kick version presented in *Essential Kicks* and which will be briefly hinted at here. In fact, dropping is basically a... (to-the-) Ground move.

Description

The most basic way to train the Ground Spin-back Hook Kick is from the casual Legs-extended sitting-on-the-floor position. The coming Figures show how to simply roll over into the kicking position and to keep twisting. It will immediately be clear that the Kick would be a better fit after a Ground Roundhouse or any other suitable dynamic move, but the static start is a good way to begin drilling the technique.

The basic Ground Spin-back Hook Kick

A more dynamic way to get the Kick rolling is to start from a *basic Kneeling Guard*. The Kick becomes then the "little brother" of the basic Essential Spin-back Hook Kick from the corresponding standing guard. All principles stay the same and this comparison helps understanding the Ground Kick version better. The Drawings show the kneeling spin-back into the Kick. Drill the classic standing Spin-back Hook Kick first, and then use the same feeling to execute the technique from the kneeling guard. You will later proceed to the full Ground technique much more easily.

Ground Spin-back Hook Kick from the Kneeling Guard

An even more dynamic way to execute the Ground Kick is after a *sideways roll-back* from the *Shell Ground Position* or from the *Grappling Ground Guard*; this gives all the momentum needed for a smooth accelerating Hook Kick. The Illustrations show how you roll back and/or sideways, and how,-as soon as on your knees and hands-, you spin back uninterruptedly into the Kick.

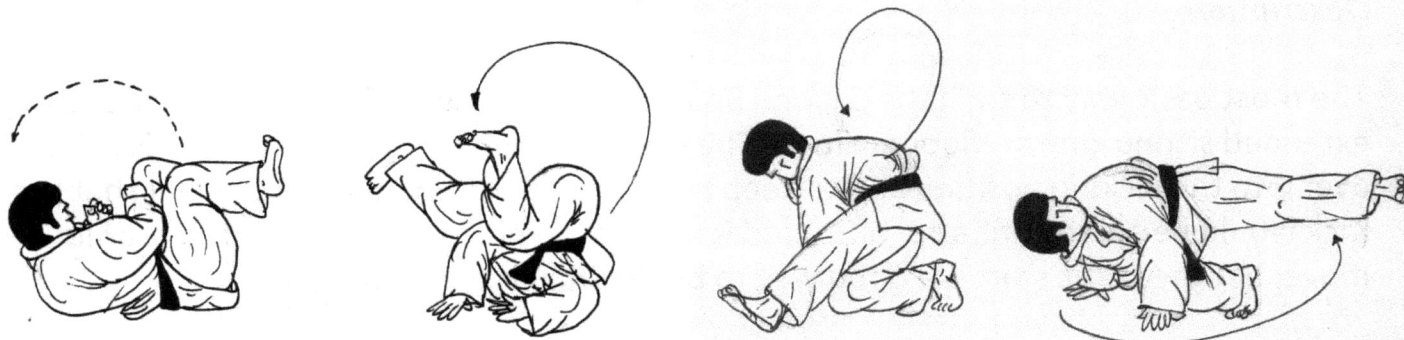

Roll back smoothly into the Ground Spin-back Hook Kick

Key Points

- *It is the momentum of the spin which gives this kick power*: you need to blend the Kick smoothly with the preceding move for an optimal use of the momentum gathered.
- This is exclusively a *committed "kick-through"* Kick; there is no slowing or stopping the momentum at impact.
- Always *follow up*, preferably by keeping the spinning momentum and using it in a following technique.

Targets

Only "soft" targets: the knee, the groin and the head.

Typical Applications

All the common variation types of Ground Kicks are also generally relevant here; even more so if they allow for extra momentum before the kick delivery itself. Refer to previous Ground Kicks variations and apply them to the *Ground Spin-back Hook Kick* as best suited to your temperament and technique. Just as an example, and one among many, the coming Drawings illustrate the drilling for the **Pressing/Assisted version** of the Ground Spin-back Hook Kick. Note that placing your foot on its support (for example onto the lying opponent's legs) and pressing down should be a smooth move that is already part of the Spin-back and gives it some extra speed.

The Assisted Ground Spin-back Roundhouse Kick

In the same spirit, the **Jumping version** of the Kick requires some momentum building that will ultimately add to the kick power: jumping in the air while twisting (as illustrated at the top of next page) definitely packs a strong kick because an airborne twist is unhindered by ground anchors. It is worthwhile reminding the reader that it is important to deliver the whole maneuver smoothly and uninterruptedly. This is a strong and surprising Kick, well worth experimenting with.

➡

The Jumping Ground Spin-back Hook Kick

The next Drawings illustrate how to deliver the Kick **while standing up,** Capoeira-style. *Capoeira* Artists tend to hover around the floor, going up and down and kicking while moving around. The application presented is a *Standing-up Kick,* inspired by the Capoeira version of the Ground Spin-back Hook Kick, and starting from a typical (dynamic) stance. Of course, the Capoeirista will probably follow by going back down for more deceptive kicking maneuvers. This is a great version of the Kick, important to drill both as a kick in itself and as an exercise: Kick and go back down, repeat immediately and without interruption into a constant upward/downward pattern.

The Standing-up version of the Ground Spin-back Hook Kick

And after the Standing-up version, here comes an example of a **'Going-down' version.**
The Photos show a *nearly-Drop version* of the Kick following... (no surprise there!)
a Roundhouse Kick. In this example, the momentum of your standing Essential
Roundhouse Kick helps you spinning as you go simultaneously down. In this example

and because of the way it is ultimately set-up, the Ground Spin-back Hook Kick is also a Takedown; but it is a powerful kick to and through the chest <u>first and foremost</u>. The focus must be on the kicking, not on the takedown that will naturally follow as a result.

Spinning-back downwards after a standing Roundhouse will lend itself naturally to the Hook Kick

We shall now present an application of the "**Assisted**" version of the Kick, but at a
more sophisticated level. The coming Figures show a <u>Double Assisted Ground Spin-
back Hook Kick</u>: the first press will immobilize the opponent's legs and allow to set up
a higher press on the opponent's neck. It so happens that the second press is achieved
by a Roundhouse Kick with no chamber-back (as often mentioned, Roundhouse and
Hook are complementary moves). This is a much simpler maneuver than it may seem
and it is worth drilling. This application is reminiscent of the classic standing version,

where a high *Hooking* Roundhouse Kick becomes a press for a high Drop Spin-Back Hook Kick.

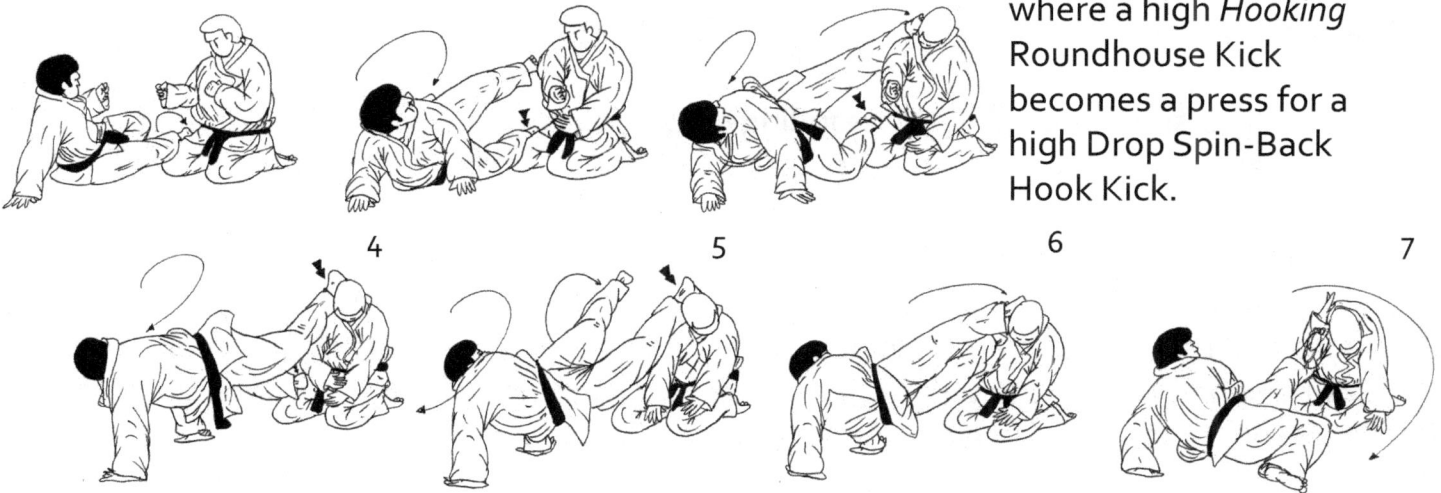

Assisted Ground Spin-back Hook Kick following a Double Press move

The *Spin-back Hook Kick* is, in general, a great **'timing' Stop Kick**. The Ground version is no exception, as illustrated by the coming Figures in an application from a kneeling position. As your standing opponent initiates a Roundhouse Kick towards your relatively low head, you spin back and down into a Ground Spin-back Hook to his open groin; your body stays low to safely keep away from the attacking kick.

The Ground Spin-back Hook Kick as a 'timing' groin Stop Kick

Specific Training

- Drill all versions, including the standing-up version, on the *marked heavy bag* for familiarity, explosiveness and accuracy. Make sure you drill from various starting positions and from dynamic situations. Drill kicking the mark on the bag accurately.
- For speed and power, there is no substitute for kicking a *focus pad* or a focus mat hold by a partner: This is a *kick-through* kick that needs to accelerate all the way into and through the target. Hitting bags and other very "un-giving" targets is detrimental to learning to kick fast and through; doing so could condition your body to wrongly slow the acceleration at impact.

Self defense

The *Ground Spin-back Hook Kick* is especially good as a Takedown Kick against a standing assailant. But two important points are to be kept in mind:(1) start from a dynamic posture and (2) kick with the takedown a natural consequence. We have underlined this many times already, but certainly far from enough. The next Photos show such an example: what may seem like a Scissor Takedown is first and foremost a Ground Spin-back Hook Kick to the groin of the assailant! In this follow-up of an evading Ground Roundhouse, you lower your kicking leg behind the groin-struck assailant while initiating the Spin-back. The Spin-back Hook aims, again, for the groin at full speed and power. The Takedown will be a result of the Kick, but not its primary purpose. When the assailant falls down, grab his leg as clear in last photo and kick his groin again with a powerful Axe Kick (*Not illustrated*).

Groin Ground Spin-back Hook Kick Takedown, naturally following a Roundhouse Kick

The next Illustrations, at the top of next page, show a great use of the Kick (again as a Takedown) in a standing situation against a low-kicking assailant. As your opponent shows he likes to low-kick your outer knee as an attrition tactic, you smother his kicks a few times. You then suddenly evade the next "Low Kick", or smother its impact a lot by bending the target leg while getting down on your knee; *this is also the start of your Spin-back*. This Kneeling Spin-back Evasion is a great move in general, worthwhile drilling for situational reflexes. With one knee and one hand on the floor, you start seamlessly the Hook Kick *through* the knee of his back leg. This is a **Kick** first, and a sweep only after having insured strong impact through the target. As your opponent falls onto the floor, it is a great opportunity to follow up with the Ground Downward Roundhouse Kick already presented.

➤

1 **2** **3**

Going down on your knee to evade a 'Low Kick' can be a great start for the Ground Spin-back Hook kick

4 **5** **6**

And to conclude, we shall present a **Stop-Kick version** of the Kick in a combination that will remind the reader of the close link between Roundhouse and Hook Kicks. But this time, the Roundhouse will follow the Spin-back Hook Kick. As you are kneeling, let your assailant come to you: in order to punch you, he will be have to place himself dangerously in range. As he punches, spin-back down to evade the punch while delivering the Ground Spin-back Hook Kick to his offered head. Keep the spinning momentum for a Ground Roundhouse Kick from the other leg, again to the head. After your Roundhouse Kick has passed *through* his head, you could chamber it to push him away with a Ground Back Kick.

Ground Spin-back Hook Stop Kick against a standing punch, followed by a Ground Roundhouse

3 **4** **5**

The Essential standing Spin-back Hook Kick

The Essential Drop Spin-back Hook Kick as a cutting Stop Kick

Leg-caught Drop Spin-back Hook Kick, a close relative of the Assisted/Pressing Kicks

10.   THE GROUND TWIN SIDE KICK

General

Twin Kicks, in general, are somewhat anecdotic or overly spectacular for the power they really pack. As a rule of thumb, it is normally unnecessary to kick with both legs when you can kick with one and then follow-up. But no rule comes without exception, and they can have their uses, especially when considered as *Ground Moves* or as *surprise* maneuvers. We have presented a few Drop Twin Kicks in our book about *Essential Kicks*, and the Ground versions are very similar. The idea is pretty simple: you place both hands on the ground and lash out into two simultaneous Side Kicks through their classical chambering trajectories. The **Side Twin Kick** is relatively powerful because of the classic side chambering move, and because it is backed by a whole body thrust. It can be especially useful as a Ground Stop Kick and has the additional advantage to allow for connecting at two points simultaneously, both knee and groin for example. It is not too important a Kick though, and it will be presented here succinctly, mainly for the sake of completeness.

Lash out through airborne chambering position

Description

From a kneeling position, twist to present your side to the opponent while lowering the hands to the floor. Jump into a Twin Side Kick Chamber by pushing from your hands and throwing the body forcefully up. Kick from both legs simultaneously while thrusting the hips. Try to land on your feet. Follow up.

The classic Ground Twin Side Kick

Key Points

- This is a (Twin) Side Kick: Kick straight from a *fully-chambered position*, as you would regular Side Kicks.
- Thrust *your hips into the kick*, just like for any Side Kick.
- Slightly *chamber back* after impact and before landing; if not, it becomes a push.
- Kick a few inches *into the target* and try to time the impact with a full leg and body extension.
- Always *follow up*.

Targets

Knees, groin, lower ribs.

Typical Application

The next Figures show how to use the Kick after being pushed violently to the floor. Roll to smother the fall and then rebound back smoothly to the kneeling ready position, as fast as possible and using the same momentum energy. Kick out at the lower belly of the opponent as he closes in to follow up. Two feet around the lower belly will both stop him, -at the hip and at the upper leg-, and will propagate the impact in the general neighborhood of his groin. As a surprise stopper, this is a great unexpected move.

Thrown to the floor: Humpty-Dumpty move to roll back forward into the Ground Twin side Kick

Specific Training

- Practice the Kick, from the various starting positions, on the *heavy bag*. Drill for speed of set-up from the various starts. Separately, drill for power development of this special Kick, hitting the heavy bag as strongly as possible.
- For familiarity, drill the kick *as a follow-up of the various basic Ground Kicks*, like Front-, Side- and Roundhouse-kicks. Train to enhance the smoothness of the transition. Even if you will never use the Kick in itself, it is a great drill for familiarity of Ground Movement and for overall body conditioning.

Self defense

The next Illustrations show how to use the Kick (again as a Stop Kick) by luring your assailant forward with too much misguided confidence. Make sure the assailant has you categorized as a "fleer" by preceding fake moves. You will then evade his next attack with a full Roll-back (*Ushiro Ukemi*) ending smoothly in the required starting kneeling position. Kick out with no interruption as the assailant follows you cockily to conclude his attack. In this example you aim for both the forward knee and the groin area. Follow up, as always required.

Lure him to follow you, and ...twin-kick

Illustrative Photo

The Flying Twin Side Kick is closely related to the Ground version

11. THE GROUND DOUBLE SPLIT BACK KICK

General

This is a very special but not overly important *Double Ground Kick*. Its uniqueness comes from the fact that it is a <u>Split Kick</u> hitting two complementary targets: one foot hits the opponent's groin and the other foot hits the face. And it is the Groin Kick which causes the bend-down, thus drawing the face into the simultaneous Head Kick. When the set-up is right, it is a very effective maneuver which results are extremely surprising: on top of the direct damage from the Kicks, it causes the opponent to fall down backwards. Just like myself, after using it a few times, the reader will realize how easy the technique is and how surprisingly efficient it is in the right set-up. I shall have to agree, though, that the right set-up does not come along that often. But it will never come, if you do not drill for it.

The Ground Double Split Back Kick

Description

The Illustrations show the basic execution of the Kick from a full lying-down position, with the opponent *on your head side*. You roll back in chambered position, with your legs up. You then kick back over your head with a straight Penetrating "Front-type" Kick, always to the groin area. You nearly-simultaneously kick upwards with the other foot, in the direction of his face coming down. The head will be coming down from either the groin pain, or from the hip retraction at attempting to escape the Groin Kick. If possible grab your opponent's ankles or trousers, but it is not a requisite for a successful Kick.

Strike groin and face nearly simultaneously: the exotic Ground Double Split Back Kick

Key Points

- The Roll and Kicks are one *uninterrupted move*: Use the momentum of the Roll.
- Make sure you *kick*, not push. Some chambering back is a requisite.
- The power of the Kick will be enhanced if you can *grab* something with your hands, preferably your opponent's lower limbs.

Targets

Only as specified: Groin and face.

Specific Training

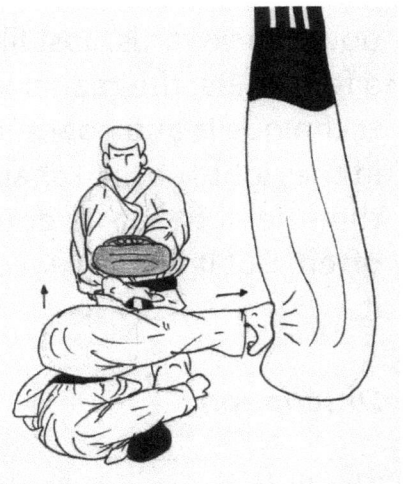

- Start drilling on a *heavy bag*, hanging or standing for coordination and precision; make sure you hit groin level smoothly from the rolling-back move.
- Then have a partner holding a *focus pad* for the nearly simultaneous head kick. Increase speed gradually only.
- The "feel" of the Kick can only be obtained by *cautious execution with a training partner.*

Roll back into double kick to hit both bag and focus pad

Self defense

The Typical Applications are limited to very specific self-defense situations. The Drawings at the top of next page illustrate how you deflect a head Stomp Kick from an assailant on your head side: with an Outside Block. You then hit his lower leg *hard* to both deflect and hurt. Immediately catch his trousers' legs. Roll back into the Double Kick while pulling yourself by his grabbed legs. Kick hard and watch him stumble back. Stand up or get into ready Ground Stance.

➙

1 2

Block head Stomp, grab and execute the Split Kick

3 4 5

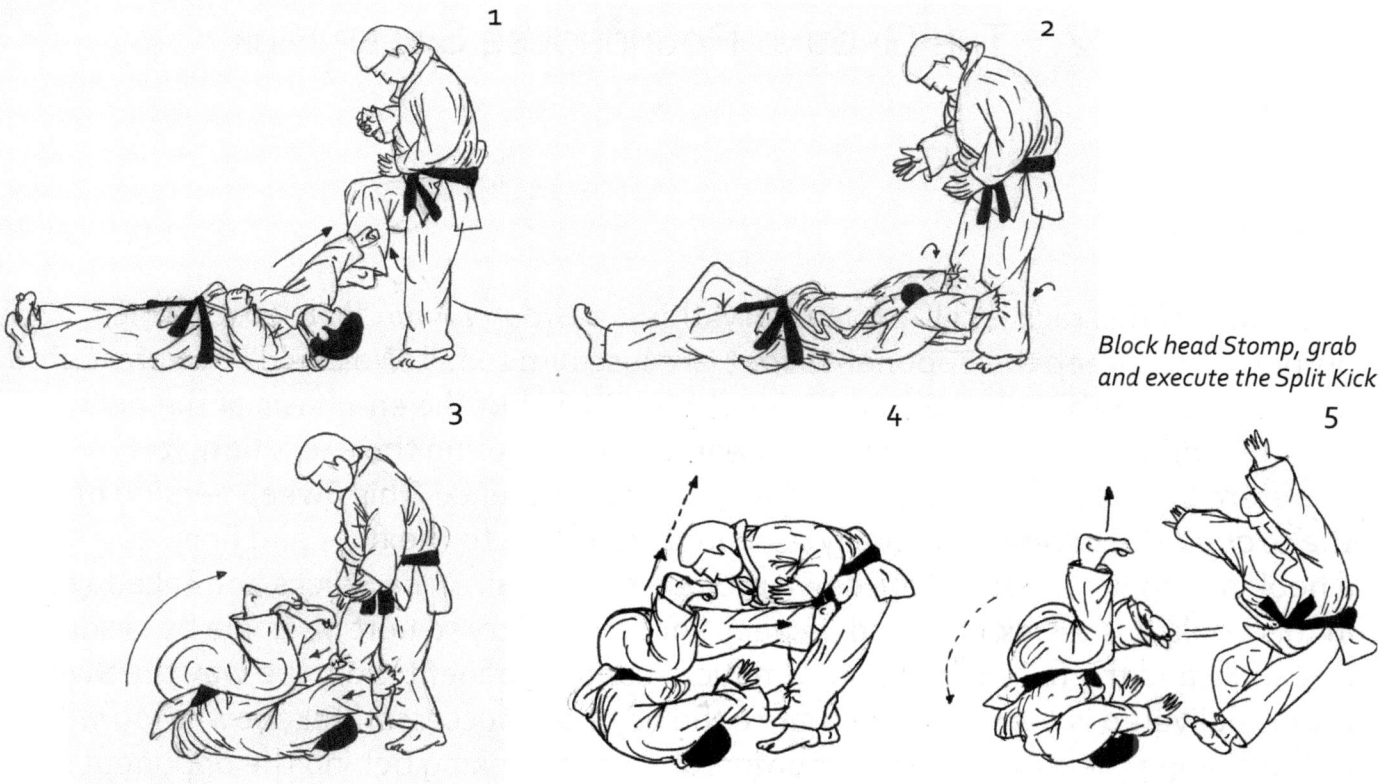

Illustrative Photos

Roll strongly into the kick

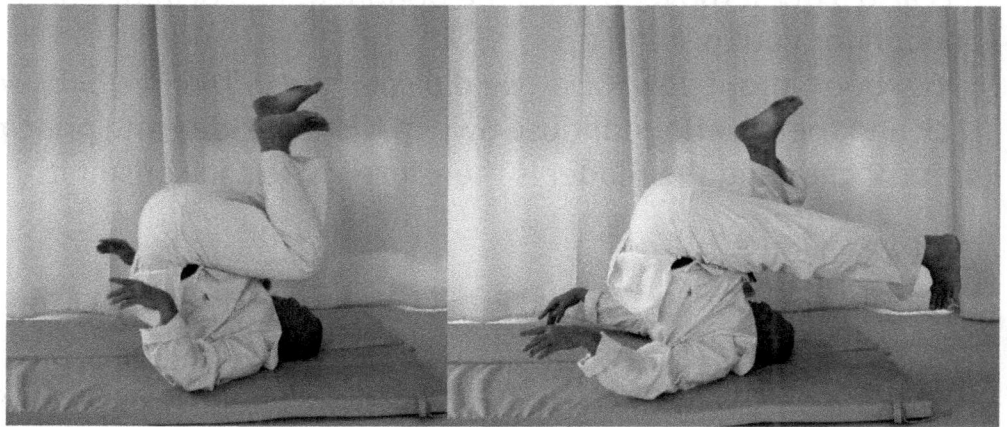

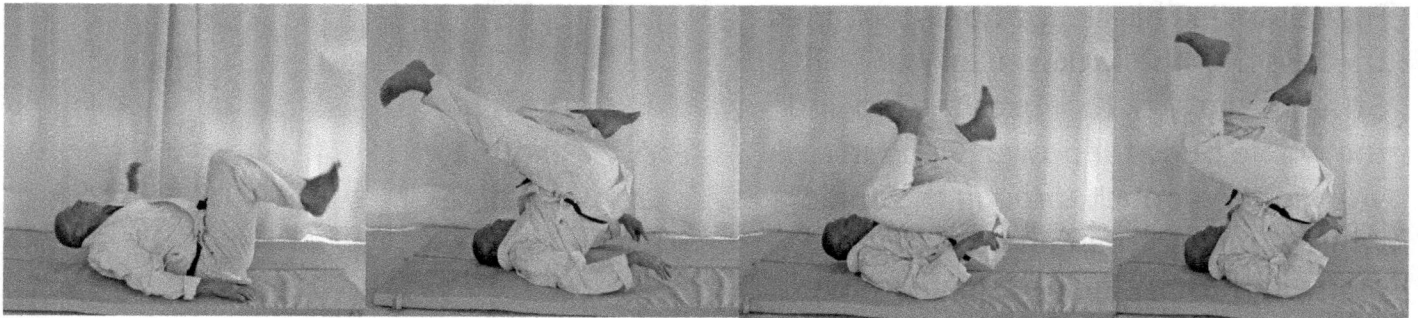

The one-leg version of this Double Kick: Kick groin then face with same foot in series

12. THE GROUND ROUNDHOUSE SWEEP KICK

General

The name of this Kick is self-explanatory: this is a *Ground Roundhouse Kick* which purpose is to sweep the opponent's foot to cause him to fall. We could have presented it in the section about the Ground Roundhouse Kick, but the emphasis of the delivery is slightly different and the leg is held nearly straight during the execution. It is therefore best presented separately for internal coherence. This **Sweep version of the Ground Roundhouse** is usually executed very close to the floor and finishes with a hooking move for better Takedown properties. Like all Sweep Kicks and Takedowns in this book, it is a **Kick** first, and a sweep second: You try to hurt his ankle by kicking it forcefully and the fall will be an automatic secondary benefit. Still, the way the Sweep Kick is delivered is designed to enhance the odds of a successful Takedown. You will be continuing the circular vector momentum while hooking behind the opponent's ankle: both these actions tend to pull the foot into natural off-balancing direction. This maneuver is very common in Capoeira (*Rasteira*) and in Chinese Kung Fu (*Iron Broom*). It is also a great move to keep the opponent at a distance or to make him retreat long enough for you to stand up.
In our book about *Low Kicks*, we did spell the difference between the Low Roundhouse Kick and the Low Roundhouse Sweep Kick; the idea and principles are similar in this present case and the reader is therefore invited to consult it.

Description

As a tribute to its *Kung Fu* roots, we shall present the basic Kick from which this Ground Kick is derived in its traditional style. The Drawings show the delivery of a *Roundhouse Sweep Kick* from a standing but low Bow Stance. This illustration underlines the fact that the Kick is nearly a Straight-leg Kick that uses the hip and the whole body for power. Of course, you kick very much *through* the ankle while "hooking" behind it to take it along in the continuing circular move.

Kung-Fu's Iron Broom: A Drop Roundhouse Sweep Kick

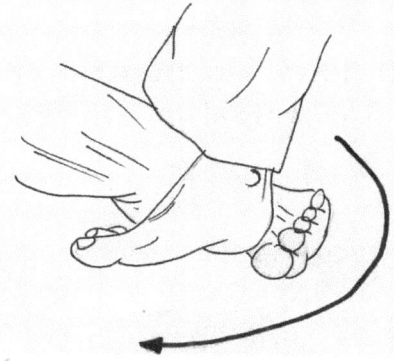
Hooking behind the opponent's ankle while kicking through

And the next Figures show, in turn, the delivery *Capoeira-style*. This example is a **Standing-up Kick** from a typical dynamic and nearly-sitting Capoeira position. And it really shows the meaning of 'Straight-leg Kick'. This is a fully kick-through Ankle Kick that completes a full circle rotation: half-a-circle until it connects, and then another half-turn afterwards.

It should now be clear to the reader that many variations are possible, with the following common traits:

- Straight-leg or near Straight-leg Roundhouse
- Fully kick-through
- Ankle Kick.

A Capoeira-like version of the Ground Roundhouse Sweep Kick using a medicine ball as a target

Key Points

- For this Kick, *timing* is of the essence: When the opponent kicks and stands on one leg, or when he just starts moving his target leg.
- This is a kick first; we shall not repeat it enough. *Kick* for maximum damage at impact and drill it as a power Kick.
- Kick *through* the target, and much more than a few inches. Kick through as a continuation of the wide arc trajectory of the Kick.
- This is a Takedown only: *always follow up* after your opponent's fall, or if the Kick is not a full success.

Targets

The lower leg, from the ankle to the knee. As a rule of thumb when talking 'Takedown', the lower is always the better for longest fulcrum.

Typical Application

The Figures show a more classical version of the Kick as a *Cutting Kick*. As you are in a kneeling position, a standing assailant gets menacingly close to stomp-kick you. Smother his stomp into your arms while committedly attacking his standing leg. Timing is of the essence here, and the Stop-Kick must be delivered while he chambers the Front Stomp Kick. Follow up.

The Ground Roundhouse Sweep Kick as a 'timing' Cutting Stop Kick

Specific Training

Drill the kicking of a basket-ball or a medicine-ball, from various ground positions. Kick the ball as hard as possible to send it as far as possible. Emphasize the kick-through.

Self defense

The timing of this Kick is key to its success, but is also quite difficult to achieve. You will not always be able to fell your opponent with one kick, or even with two. This is not important, as those are aggressive and painful kicks: so long as you keep kicking, you keep the initiative and you have the opponent on the defensive. The Figures at the top of next page show how you can attack an approaching assailant with the *Ground Roundhouse Sweep Kick*, trying to catch him just as he steps forward. Should he not be taken down, your opponent will still be off-balance, both mentally and physically. You can then follow up with a Spin-back Ground Hook (Sweep) Kick to the rear leg he is standing on. Kick *through* the ankle and that should bring him down. You could follow up with an Axe Kick (*Downward Heel Kick*) powered by a strong body twist. If you have not succeeded in taking him down, keep kicking from the ground without interruption.

1 2

The classic Kung-Fu Iron Broom series: Ground Roundhouse Sweep Kick followed by a Ground spin-back Hook Sweep Kick

3 4 5

As a last example, we shall again give a **Cutting Kick** application, but in a **standing-up version**, Capoeira-style. You are in Kneeling Guard when your assailant throws a Roundhouse Kick towards your head. Evade down while pivoting into the Kick. Kick *through*, as you should, and keep the momentum live in order to complete a full Spin-back Stand-up. The whole circular maneuver is smooth, with no interruptions.

1 2

Ground Roundhouse Sweep Kick into Spin-back Stand-up

3 4

13. THE GROUND INSIDE HOOK SWEEP KICK

General

This is a relatively weak kick that is not delivered in a very codified way. This interesting technique is kind of a Ground **hybrid** between an *Inside Crescent Kick* and a *Heel Hook Kick*; or it could be considered as a Roundhouse variation without turning the hip.
It is of the same family as the *Heel Outside Low Kick* presented in our previous book about 'Low Kicks'. All these small Hybrid Kicks are not very powerful, but annoyingly surprising and irritating to any opponent.
The **Ground Inside Hook Sweep Kick** is interesting as a Sweeping Takedown or as a part of a combination, but it will not do a lot of damage besides the takedown or the misdirecting combination start. But those results should certainly not be sneezed at. It is also a great transition maneuver and an important Ground Move by itself. Fittingly, a version of this Kick is used quite a lot in *Capoeira*, which practice is based on uninterrupted movement. It is a worthy move to practice if one remembers that it must be part of a dynamic set-up. The Kick can be "hooked" at the end, and it should certainly be if it is possible and relevant (For more theory about "hooking" with Hook Kicks, the reader is invited to refer to our work about *Essential Kicks*).

Description

The Drawings show the most relevant version of this Kick which is the one seen in *Capoeira* practice (**Corta Capim**). It is basically the full-momentum half-circle version of a straight-leg sweep travelling from the outside inwards. Starting from a side sitting dynamic position, your foot does a full half-circle close to the floor towards and *through* your opponent's ankle. The trajectory is akin to a Crescent Kick, not a Hook Kick, but it is very close to the floor and with at least a hint of "hooking" with the heel into the opponent's ankle (represented in the illustration by a medicine ball). Note the evolving position of the hands: this is a purely dynamic movement using the body shift as a leg-propeller.

Capoeira's Corta Capim

Key Points

- This is a momentum Kick needing *a full trajectory* to gather speed.
- Do not try to kick at the target, but *through* it for the full half-circle.
- Kick *as close to the ground as possible*, as this is a kicking Takedown.
- If possible, *"hook"* with the heel after impact: Bend slightly the leg after impact while keeping the overall movement.

Targets

Mostly the ankle as a takedown, though the full momentum version could hurt a knee or the head of a bent-over opponent.

Typical Application

This is a great opener for a ground combination that will keep your opponent off-balance. The Figures illustrate how you attack the front leg of your stepping-forward standing opponent, and then follow up with a Ground Roundhouse Kick with the other leg. It is your body going down that powers the Inside Hook Kick that will put him off-balance, and it is the body twist in the opposite direction that will power the Roundhouse Kick to the offered head.

The Ground Inside Hook Sweep Kick puts your opponent off-balance for a subsequent Roundhouse

Specific Training

- *Kick a basketball or a medicine-ball,* as far as possible. A powerful delivery will be achieved by serious drilling only. This kind of exercise can be done by students as a game, while allowing for the honing of a truly powerful hard Kick.
- Practice *combinations* for speed and smooth transitions.

Self defense

The next Illustrations show the more traditional hooking-version of the Kick against the standing leg of a kicking assailant. Again, it is the *body movement* that gives the power behind the Kick. This *Cutting Kick* will send him flying while you can keep rolling into position for a Ground Downward Roundhouse Kick to greet him at landing.

The Ground Inside Hook Sweep Kick from a regular floor sitting position, as a Cutting Stop Kick

Illustrative Photos

The closely related Heel Outside Low Kick

14. THE JUMPING ROUNDHOUSE KICK FROM THE GROUND

Chapeu de Couro/S-Dobrado (Capoeira)

General

This is a great Kick which looks rightfully acrobatic, but which is much easier to perform than it looks. It exists in a variety of forms, all legitimate. We have already presented the Kick briefly in a previous section (about the Ground Roundhouse Kick), as a variation of the basic Ground Roundhouse. We shall concentrate a bit more here on some variations, especially the ones in the *Capoeira* spirit. The **Jumping Ground Roundhouse** is a very effective Kick, and it is also helpful to keep an opponent away or to stand up safely. It is ubiquitous in Capoeira under several versions, but it can be adapted easily to most fighting styles. It has the advantages of being both surprising (as you jump off the floor) and powerful (as it has the whole body momentum behind the Kick). Use it to stand back up, or to confuse your opponent, or to stand up then back down for more Ground Kicks. This is certainly a must-drill technique, and one that you will certainly love to use once mastered.

One version of the Jumping Roundhouse from the ground

Description

The Figures at the top of next page show the most common *Capoeira*-style delivery of the Kick, from a side sitting position...

➡

...Leaning on your forward hand, you jump off your rear (bent) leg into the air, **up and sideways** like for a Side Cartwheel. You then scissor with your legs in the air to deliver a Roundhouse Kick with your former rear leg, while landing on the other foot after a nearly-full pivot. You can then stand up or keep hopping around close to the ground. Notice that this execution is in fact quite close to a simple Side Cartwheel.

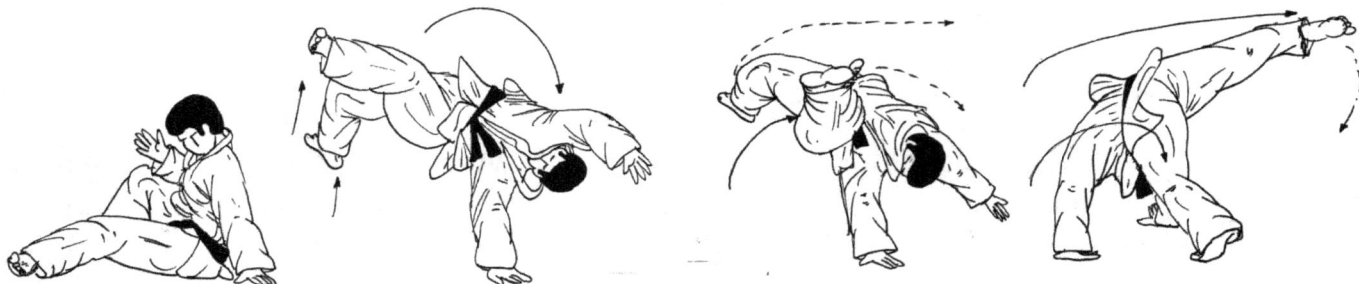

Capoeira's Flying Roundhouse Kick from the Ground

Key Points

- This is a *fully committed* Kick only. Fire-and-forget, until you land.
- The *jump-up and the body twist* do give the power to the Kick: start the Roundhouse Kick itself as late as possible.
- Land in guard and *always follow up*.

Targets

This is a *Go-through Kick*: The **head** is normally the only worthy target, though the **groin** is always a good choice too.

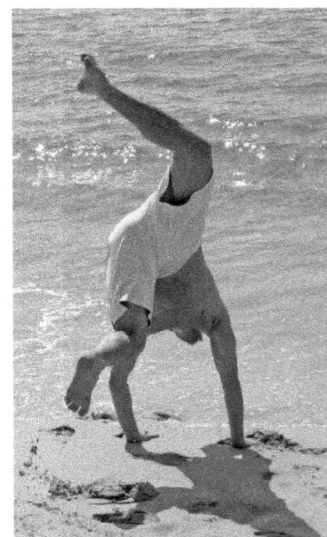

Capoeira-style Jumping Roundhouse Kick from the ground

Typical Application

The Illustrations at the top of next page show the Kick as a **natural follow-up** to a *Ground Outside Crescent Kick* that can be used as a punch block, as a guard disrupter or as keep-away move. The Outside Crescent Kick rebounds on the floor for a **'Stand Back Up' Jumping Roundhouse**. The extended range of the Jumping Kick should be very surprising indeed, especially if your opponent thinks you are vulnerable after the completion of the Crescent Kick. ➤

Outside Crescent Kick to Jumping Roundhouse, on the ground

Specific Training

- This Kick needs to be relatively accurate to be efficient: Drill with a partner holding a *focus pad* (See Figure), concentrating on accuracy and on the speed of the "kick-thru". This is also a very energetic kick and a great stamina-builder.

*Kick accurately **through** the focus pad*

- Great strength-builders, confidence-builders and agility-builders for this Kick are the *Cartwheel* and the *Forward Handstand Flip*. Proceed carefully, but those exercises will help your progress towards proficiency for this Jumping Kick (and many others).

The Cartwheel drill

The Front Handstand Flip: another great exercise to improve kicking proficiency

Self defense

The Drawing is here to remind the reader that the unexpected jump will provide the (unexpected) range needed to surprise and stop-kick an incoming assailant. To keep the maneuver surprising, make sure you do not overuse it.

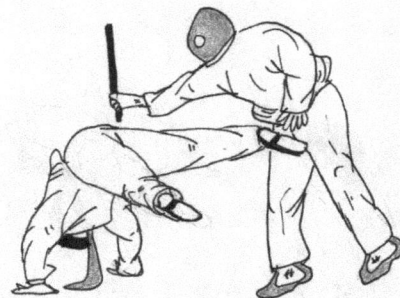

The Jumping Roundhouse Kick from the ground in self-defense

And the next Illustrations show the Kick used for you to stand up from the ground while overwhelming your would-be assailant with Circular Kicks to keep him away. Keep going after him as he retreats, hopefully surprised by the range of your **Preemptive Jumping Roundhouse Kick from the ground**.

Standing up from the ground with a series of circular kicks: Jumping Roundhouse, Spin-back Hook and standing Roundhouse Kick

Illustrative Photo

The Jumping Roundhouse Kick from the ground

15. THE GROUND DOWNWARD INSIDE SHORT HOOK KICK

General

This is a small, very natural and easy Kick; but it is also one which is <u>very important to practice</u> in order to become able to use it *instinctively* and to do so while delivering Power. The **Ground Downward Inside Short Hook Kick** is only applicable in very specific situations, for example against an opponent bending over you. Being very fast, it can be used as soon as your opponent bends towards you. And it should be on your mind immediately if you get pushed or swept to the floor in such adequate relative positions. It is also the Kick of choice if you lie on your back and have grappling control of the opponent between your legs (Ground Grappling Guard).
This is not intrinsically a very powerful Kick, but it can be drilled to become very painful. It would be a mistake to neglect thorough training because of the easy execution: surprisingly great power can be achieved by stubborn training!
The Kick should be directed to sensitive points like the neck, the head or the kidneys, and it can be extremely effective, especially with the added effect of unexpectedness. Remember that the Kick comes to the opponent from behind; if you can make the first impact count on account of high developed power, you have an important new weapon in your arsenal.

Description

The Kick in itself is simple and will remind the reader of the *Heel Outside Low Kick* described in our previous book about 'Low Kicks'. Lying on your back, you lift a straight leg diagonally to the outside and then proceed to kick by lowering the leg while bending it towards you. Anything in this trajectory should be struck by your heel, with some added 'hooking' effect. The Photos at the top of next page are more explanatory than many words could be. As it is a relatively weak *Attrition Kick*, it is best delivered in series in a quick succession; <u>but you should make the first Kick of the series a surprise that counts on account of its maximum power delivery</u>. The subsequent Attrition Kicks will be expected and therefore less effective.

➤

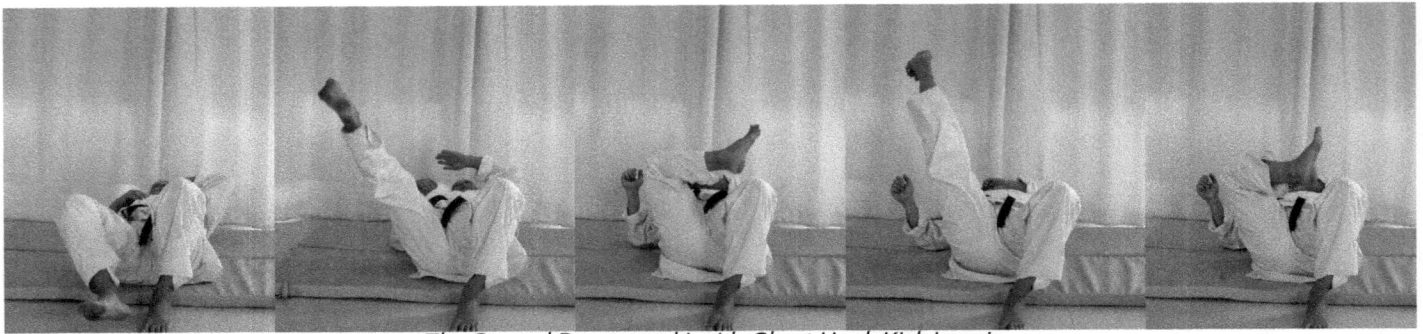

The Ground Downward Inside Short Hook Kick in pair

This is an exclusively Situational Kick, and mostly in a dynamic situation. The Illustrations below describe the classic use: as your opponent bends towards you, between your legs, when you are lying on the floor. You lift the leg, straight and then kick the back of his neck with your heel, by bending the leg at the knee. Repeat and keep hitting. The experienced reader will notice how suitable to a Juji-Gatame arm-bar the situation is: nothing easier than to grab his extended arm and to roll the kicking leg over his head (*Not illustrated*).

Target the back of the neck of an opponent bending over you to punch you

Key Points

- Make sure you kick with the *heel* and strive to "hook" into the target with said heel.
- Chamber by *lifting the leg fully*: you need momentum for the Kick to be effective.
- Kick *through* the target and chamber back; do not "push-kick".
- Always *follow up*, by repeating the kick or by switching attacks.

Targets

The back of the head, the back of the neck, between the shoulder blades, and the kidneys. And the groin if you are on your back and have your opponent's back in a grappling situation.

Typical Applications

The most frequent use of this Kick is kidney attrition in grappling ground guard. Photos below are self-explanatory.

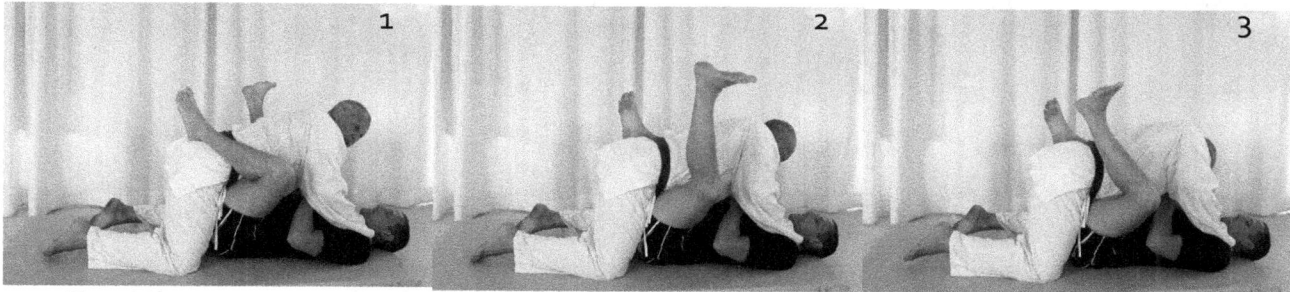

Target the kidneys for attrition of a grappling opponent; connect with the heel

***

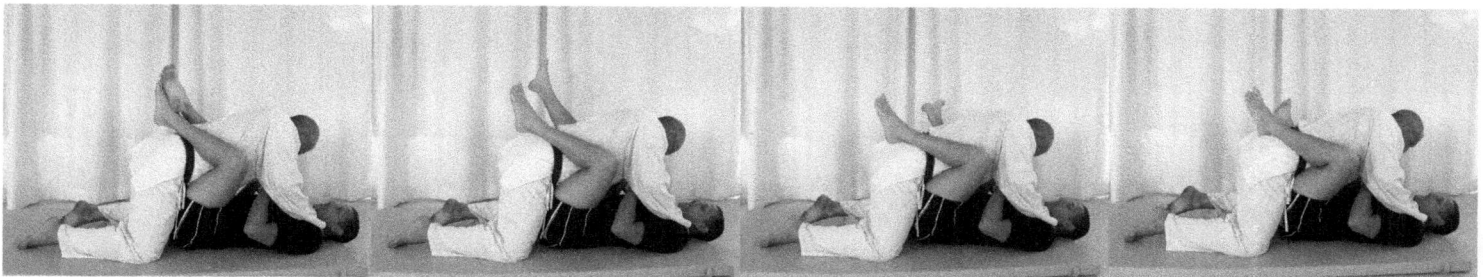

Kicking with the other foot; you can and should alternate

The Figures at the top of next page illustrate the use of the Kick as a natural follow-up to a Ground Groin Kick. In this example, you deliver an Upward Ground Front Kick to your opponent's groin as he comes close. As he bends over from pain, you can use the other leg to kick the back of his head, hooking at impact for further damage. The best execution of this combination (*but that requires training*) is when the chambering of the Downward Small Hook Kick is executed **simultaneously** with the Groin Front Kick as illustrated; the two complementary Kicks therefore hit in close succession for synergistic results. A great follow-up would be a lifting knee strike, using the leg from the groin kick, all the while chambering another Ground Downward Inside Short Hook Kick.

➡

Already chamber the Downward Kick while you deliver the Groin front Kick with the other leg

Specific Training

- The Kick is easy to deliver but you need to *practice it in relevant situations*. Drill being swept to the floor by your partner. Kick him as he tries to follow up by punching you as you fall, or pull him down with you while setting up the Kick. See Figure below.
- You <u>need</u> to drill the Kick *on a heavy bag* you hold, in order to learn to develop power. This is very important, because the impact energy can be greatly increased by practice; it then becomes a surprisingly painful kick, worth the work you have invested in it. Kick the bag as hard and as fast as possible. See other Figure.

Drill executing the kick immediately as you are taken down

Drill for power on the heavy bag

Self defense

The Figures at the top of next page illustrate the use of the Kick as you are taken down with an Inner Reap Throw (*O Uchi Gari – Judo*). Pull the opponent down with you while chambering the Kick. Follow up. It should be noted that the principle stays valid for a whole array of Takedowns and the reader is invited to experiment. Another example will follow.

➡

The Ground Downward Inside Short Hook Kick as a counterattack to a successful O Uchi Gari

And the next Drawings show how suitable this Kick is against a 'one-leg lock shoot takedown'. As your assailant throws you down by pulling your ankle and pushing your knee rearwards, you exaggerate the fall in order to gather momentum for your raising (other) leg. This a very natural move, and the exaggeration is in the Judo spirit of yielding for a better counter. Kick the back of his neck, a few times if necessary. Follow up with a same-leg Ground Side Kick to his throat or face in order to push him away while you pull your leg free.

1   2

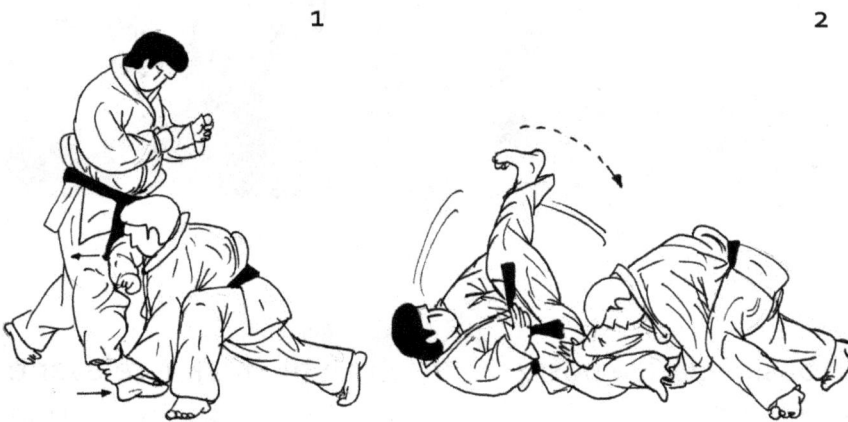

The Kick as a counter for a one-leg tackle; the Ground Side Kick follow-up will push him away

3   4

16. THE GROUND DOWNWARD OUTSIDE SHORT HOOK KICK

General

This is, again, a *Situational Kick*, and even more so than the previous (*Inside*) one. It is very fast and relatively easy to deliver, but it is suitable only for very specific situations. Again, should you find yourself into one of those relative positions to your opponent, it should flow immediately and naturally. This is a very surprising technique, and painful if well targeted. The Kick's first phase is similar in principle to the previous one, but instead of kicking to the inside, you are delivering the same kick *to the outside*, as that is where your opponent is. You simply twist the knee on the other side while bending it. It is easier to understand from the photographs below.

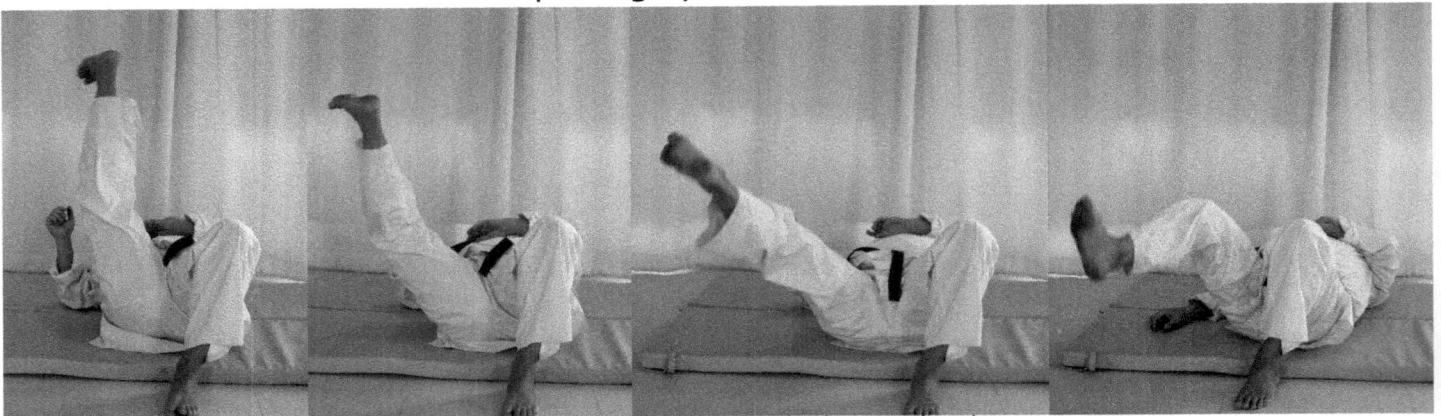

The Ground Downward Outside Short Hook Kick

Description

The Drawings below show the two basic relative positions in which the Kick is relevant: an opponent bending towards you from the side, and an opponent lying on the ground with you side-to-side. Both these situations are, of course, extremely dynamic and you will have to kick as soon as *passing through them*. You lift the leg high and bend it forcefully into the target: the back of the head or the groin, as illustrated. If possible, 'hook' into the target. This is, in these special situations, a very surprising Kick. It will need following up in any case, but you can so stun your unexpecting opponent.

The two possible situations for the use of the surprising Ground Downward Outside Short Hook Kick

Key Points

- Lift *the leg high*: you will need momentum to gather power.
- Use the *heel* to connect and "hook" into the target.
- Kick *through* the target, at least a few inches.
- Always *follow up*; this is not a powerful kick but a sneaky surprising one.

Targets

The back of the head, the back of the neck and the groin.

Self defense

As this is an easy-to-understand Situational Kick, we shall present only one classic self-defense application: the next Illustrations show the use of the Kick at the end of a release from a straddled Naked Choke, once you have successfully caused your assailant to lie to your side.

As your assailant reaches to choke you in a natural hands choke from his superior straddling position, you cross-catch a wrist while immediately finger-spearing his throat violently (*Nukite – Karatedo*). This is a life-and-death situation: time and efficacy are of the essence. You then hit the inside of the elbow of his controlled hand to bend it and initiate a classic *Gooseneck Wrist-lock*. Unless you are an adept *Ju-Jitsu* or *Aikido* Artist, it is recommended to switch at this stage to a cruder control method: catch a few of his fingers with your other hand (but keep him in 'gooseneck' position). You can now easily force him to roll sideways off you, especially with the help with a hip lift. You now are lying side-to-side with your assailant while still controlling him with an extremely painful Finger Lock; this is the perfect position for our little Kick. You lift the leg sideways and Hook-kick downwards into his groin. Keep control of his wrist and fingers, and repeat the kick.

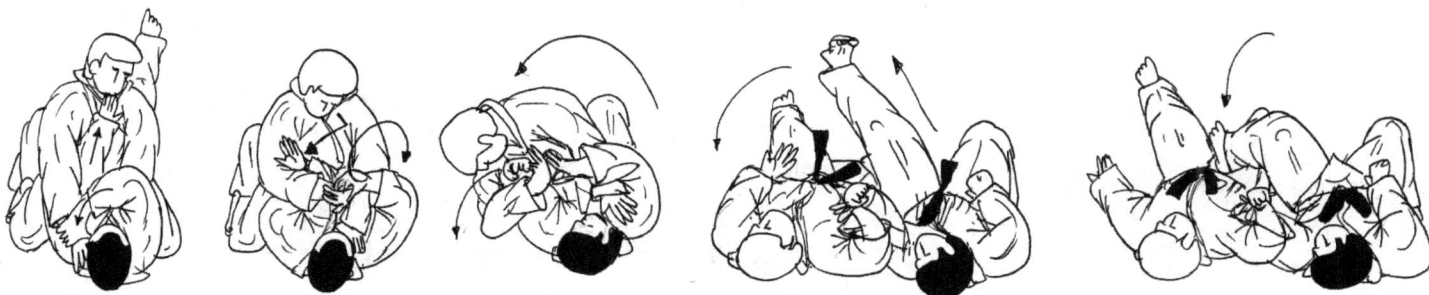

Cap a ground choke-release with the Downward Outside Short Hook Kick

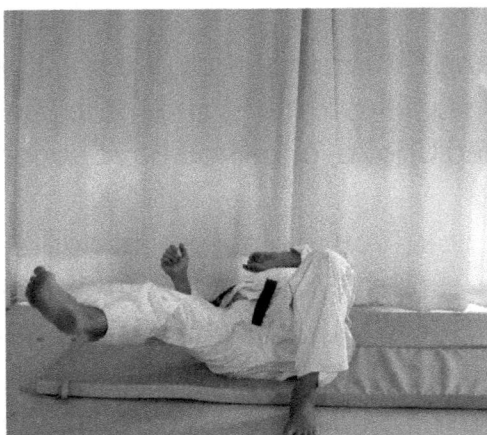

*Comparative trajectories of the Ground Downward **Inside** Short Hook Kick, the Ground Downward **Outside** Short Hook Kick and the **Straight** vertical Ground Axe Kick*

Don't wish it were easier, wish you were better.
~Jim Rohn

17. THE GROUND CRESCENT KICK

General

The Ground Crescent Kick (or more completely named: **Ground Inside Crescent Kick**) is a very simple Kick to understand, very easy to deliver, often surprising because coming from a blind side, always very fast but... it is never very powerful. Unlike its standing parent, well anchored in the ground and where the hips allow for a lot of energy, the Ground version cannot muster a lot of raw power. Serious training will certainly help to learn to optimize energy delivery and make it an important instrument of your ground fighting. But, in order to achieve reasonable impact power, it will require using the whole body, and therefore extra momentum after impact that will keep you going and sometimes rolling sideways; this will have to be taken into account and it is important to learn to put it to your advantage. The Ground Crescent Kick is an important Kick though, especially useful as a block, as a distance keeper or as part of redoubtable combinations; and examples will be given below.

Basic Crescent Kick from Ground Guard Position; the body is rolling with the kick

Description

The Ground Crescent Kick is usually delivered from a dynamic position, not a static guard, as explained above. The wider the arc of the Kick, the more powerful will it be at impact, just like for the *Essential* standing version. For this reason, the more open the starting position is, the more energy can be gathered during execution, but at the cost of earlier detection, and of 'opening' yourself. This trade-off and the specific situation will decide on how much "chambering" to invest into and on from which starting position to initiate the Crescent Kick itself. But you usually will arrive to your starting position by previous kicking or by purposeful Ground Movement.

The coming Photos illustrate a **wide** Ground Crescent Kick, from lying on your back, into an opponent's guard. Of course it will necessitate following up.

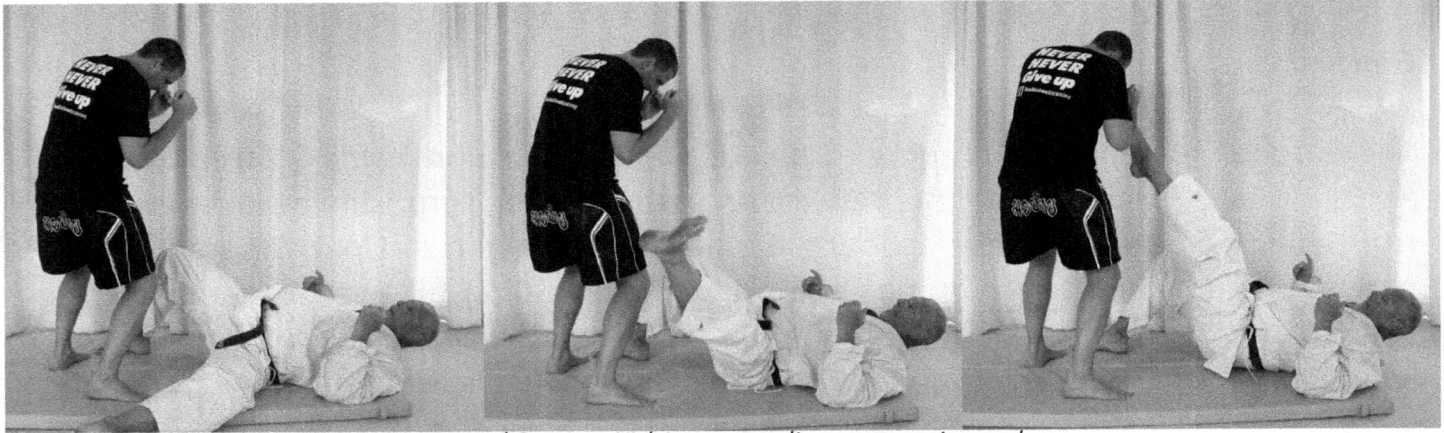

Ground Crescent Kick into a standing opponent's guard

The coming Drawings illustrate the delivery of the Kick from a *natural ground-sitting position*, and they try to underline that the Kick must be followed up by:

- **Either** kicking back in the direction the kick was coming from. In this first example, with a Hook Kick.
- **Or** standing up by making use of the extra momentum of the pivot. Illustrated by the subsequent Figures at the top of next page.
- **Or** keeping the spin in the same direction and executing a Spin-back Kick (like a Spin-back Hook Kick or a Spin-back Outside Crescent Kick). See the set of Photos that follows on the next page.

1   2   3

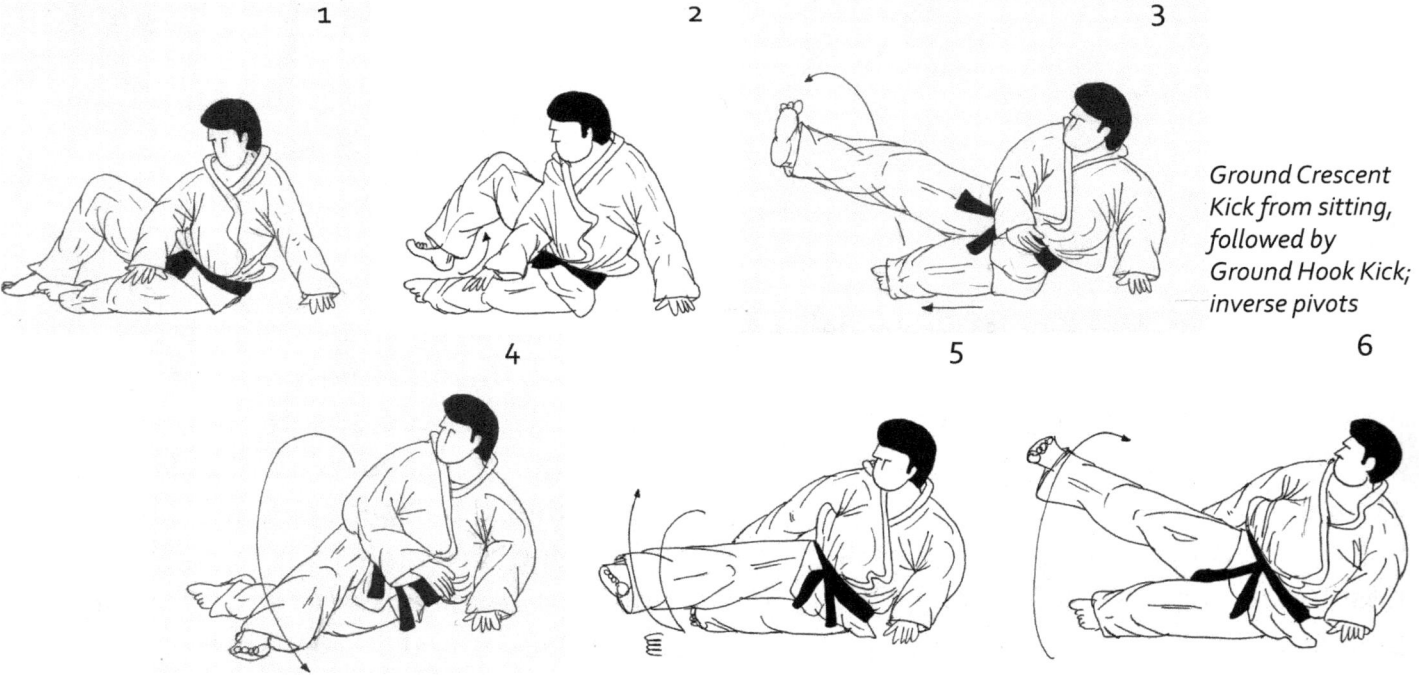

Ground Crescent Kick from sitting, followed by Ground Hook Kick; inverse pivots

4   5   6

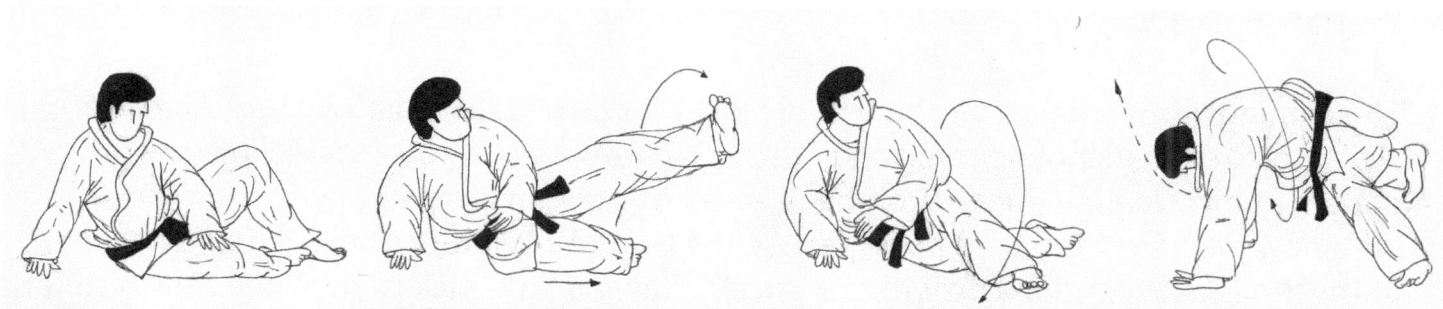

Sitting Ground Crescent Kick all the way to stand-up; use momentum

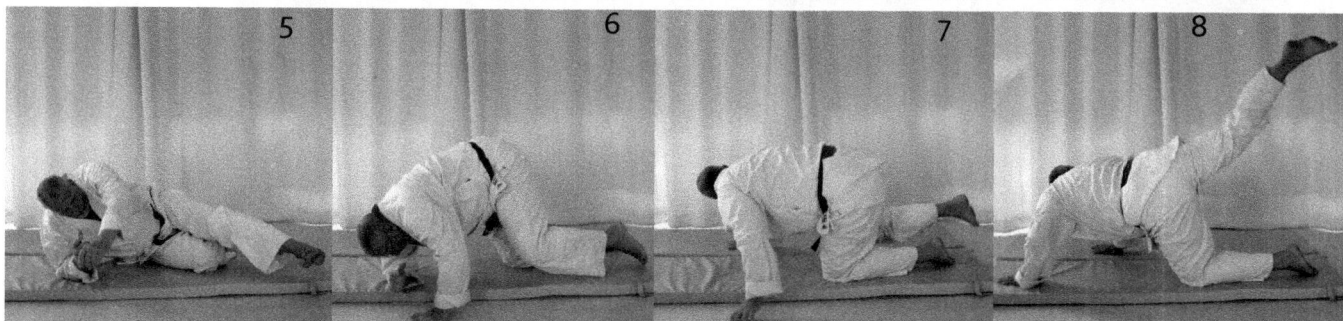

Ground Crescent Kick from lie-down, followed by Spin-back Hook Kick; use momentum

Key Points

- Kick with *straight leg* for maximum acceleration-building trajectory.
- Kick with the *whole body*.
- Always *follow* up.

Targets

The head, the groin, the knee or the elbow joint.

Typical Application

The coming Illustrations show how to use the Kick **as a block**, painfully targeting the elbow joint of an incoming punching arm. Start from a sitting position to lure the opponent into an easy punch. Roll-back, away from his attack, and twist while kicking his elbow joint as strongly as possible; use the Humpty Dumpty principle to add energy to the 'Roll & Kick'. Follow up with a naturally-flowing Side Kick to the knee (The natural flow from kick-through Crescent Kick to Side Kick Chamber is similar to that of the standing version of the Kick).

Ground Crescent Kick Block followed by Ground Side Kick

Specific Training

- Practice the Kick in *combinations*, starting with those presented here.
- Learn to kick hard *through* a partner-held focus pad (See Figure).

Self defense

The Figures at the top of next page show a very typical use of the Kick *as part of a ground kicking combination*. The Crescent Kick is ideally delivered after a kick with the same momentum direction, in this case a Ground Outside Crescent Kick. The combination presented below is similar to the previous one, *but for the initial Block Kick*. As your assailant tries to punch you, you *block his punch by attacking his elbow joint with an Outside Crescent Kick this time. You use full body momentum into the Kick, which will lead you naturally into the (Inside) Crescent Kick with the other leg,* aiming for his head. You keep rolling and flow naturally into a Ground Side Kick with the same leg to his lower belly. You keep rolling in the same direction and find yourself into an ideal position for a Ground Back Kick, preferably to the throat.

Outside Crescent Block, Inside Crescent Kick, Side Kick and Spin-back Back Kick, in series on the Ground

And remember that Crescent Kicks used as **Block Kicks** can also be very effective against Stomp Kicks from your standing assailant.

The Ground Inside Crescent Block Kick against a Stomp Kick attack

Illustrative Photos

The Essential standing high Inside Crescent Kick from close-up

Classic standing Crescent Kick into the opponent's guard

18. THE GROUND OVERHEAD TWIN FRONT KICK

General

This is a simple Kick, easy to grasp and easy to deliver, but again conditional to a very specific position in relation to your opponent: you are lying on the floor and your opponent is standing at your head side (one could say behind you in some way). This is, of course, a very dangerous position to be in, and this Kick, or one of its relatives, should then be automatic.

*The ground Overhead **Single** Front Kick*

You can also maneuver yourself dynamically into this position to surprise him, although it is a dangerous and tricky move. Should you like the Kick and drill it a lot for proficiency, it can be a sneaky technique with very high chances of scoring. We shall present such an offensive application below.

In essence, the Kick is simply a Ground Front Kick delivered overhead with both feet simultaneously. Before learning the technique, the reader is invited to check the closely related: Overhead version of the Ground Front Kick (Chapter 1), Ground Twin Front Kick (Chapter 2) and Double Ground Split Back Kick (Chapter 11).

Description

The Figures at the top of next page show the classic execution in which you catch hold of the opponent's ankles while kicking back over your head. This has the quadruple benefit of:

- Giving you more power by anchoring you to the ground,
- Neutralizing his feet as potential stomping instruments,
- Preventing him from evading back and/or from smothering the power of the Double Kick, and
- Generally causing his fall after the Kicks' impact.

Of course, the Kick can be delivered without catching his ankles, or even by catching only one ankle, and still be effective.

➡

The classic ankles-hold Ground Overhead Twin Front Kick

Key Points

- Push *the hips into the Kick* by strongly rolling back while kicking.
- Make sure to *chamber* the kick, just like for a regular Front Kick.
- Always be ready to *follow up*, or to take an appropriate ready-position.

Targets

The groin, the lower belly, the face and the solar plexus. Requiring more precision: the throat, if possible.

Typical Application

The coming Illustrations (top of next page) show an interesting variation as a *surprise Drop Kick* from a standing position. This is the promised example of an <u>offensive</u> sneaky version, to be executed out of the blues. It can also be used as a *Stop Kick* against high punching attacks, but such a use would require even more training, timing and commitment. Turn your back to your opponent while falling backwards, -towards him-, into a Back Roll. At the end of this Downward Spin-back to Back Roll, catch his ankles or trousers. Kick him in the solar plexus or groin, while pulling strongly on the ankles. Immediately after impact, release his ankles to let him fall rearwards, while you roll away forwards (Humpty Dumpty-style) into a standing position. Be ready to follow up or to deal with any further attack.

➡

1 2

The offensive Drop Overhead Twin Front Kick

3 4 5

Specific Training

- Drill the *abdominal Plyometric exercise* in which your partner throws back your straight legs towards the floor while you resist the fall. Repeat for at least ten reps. See Figure extracted from our 'Plyo-Flex' book.

- Drill with *a protected partner*. Do ten repetitions holding his ankles, then ten more without a hold. See Figures.

- Drill for power *on the heavy bag*, with and without a hold. As a hold, you can either hold the bag itself, or a rope, or elastic band tied to the wall. See Illustration.

Plyo-Flex drill for specific muscle development

Drill with a body-protected partner

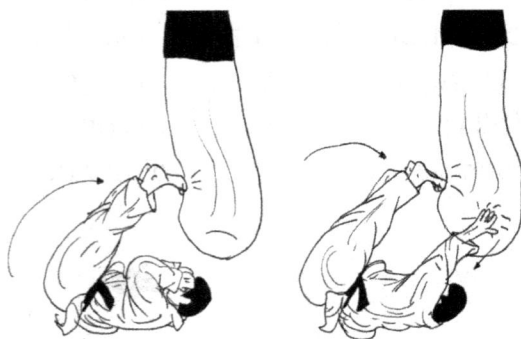

Drill for power by hitting the hanging heavy bag, with or without a holding prop

Self defense

The next Illustrations show the use of an old Jiu Jitsu throw named *Gyacku Tomoe Nage*. This dangerous Takedown had already been watered down in the original Judo, and it was finally discarded and removed from Modern Judo's curriculum. Like with all old Jiu Jitsu versions of Judo throws, the leg movement in the Takedown was originally a **Kick**. This fantastic maneuver is adequate when you have control of the opponent's wrists in the same position as before, instead of his ankles. You could be in this position after having been thrown to the ground, or after having caught his wrists as he reaches for you, or even purposely from a previous standing position. It could even be that it is the opponent himself who has grabbed your wrists to try to drag you on the floor!

In any case, in this version, you will not use his ankles as an anchor point <u>but his wrists</u>. If it is he who holds you, encircle and catch his wrists to execute the Twin Kick to his lower abdomen. In this technique, it is important to kick low, close to the groin, as you do not want to send him flying back; you want him to bend over forwards. You can then pull on his arms while lifting him forward in this scary **Inverse Wheel Throw** (Gyacku Tomoe Nage – Jiu Jitsu). Follow-up with a Downward Heel Kick (*Axe Kick*) to his head as he lands. Ouch!

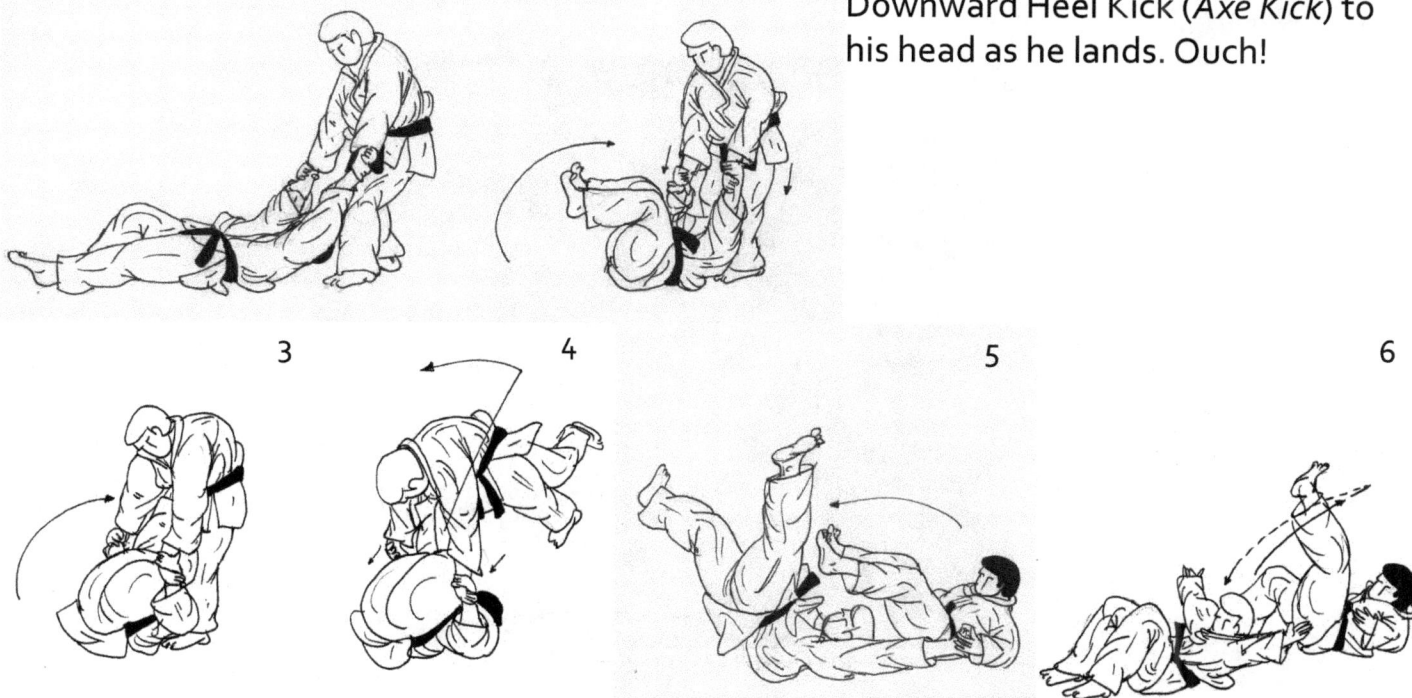

3   4   5   6

Hold assailant's wrists and kick into **Gyacku Tomoe Nage**

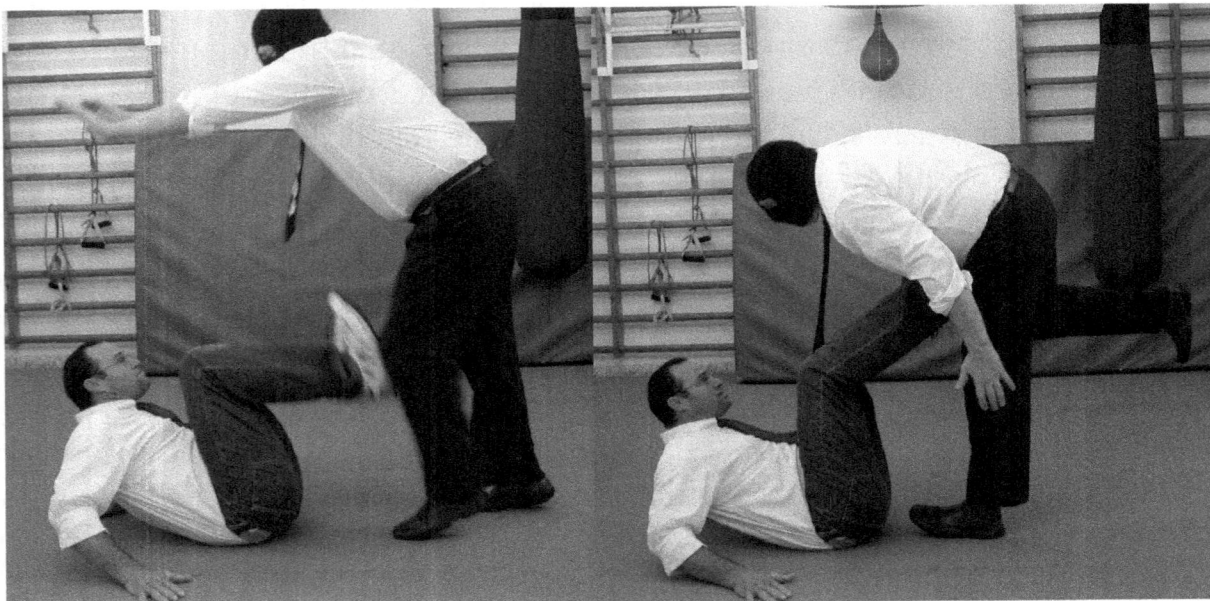

The regular forward Ground Twin Front Kick

The no-grip Overhead Ground Twin Front Kick

The successful warrior is the average man with laser-like focus.
~Bruce Lee

19. THE GROUND HOOKED DOWNWARD HEEL KICK

General

This is a very simple, versatile, and easy to master Kick, with the added benefit of being very painful when well delivered. It is a short and **hooking** version of the classic Ground Axe Kick, - better named Ground Downward Heel Kick- , and that we shall present later on. This is an *Attrition Kick* and a great combination opener. It is a typical Kick to execute in series, with the same foot or alternating feet, in order to repel an opponent and keep him away. It will usually not be powerful enough in itself: it is very simply *a bent-leg "hooking" Downward Heel Kick to sensitive areas* of a close opponent. As illustrated, the most common targets are a standing opponent's upper thighs.

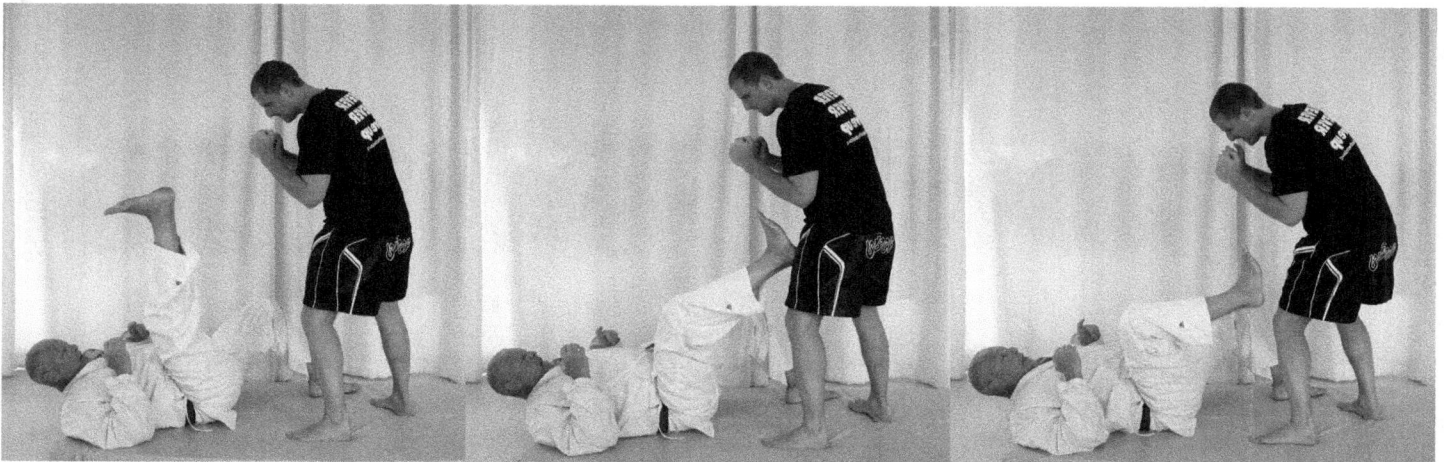

The Ground Hooked Downward Heel Kick to the thigh

Description

The Illustrations show the classic delivery of the Kick to the front of an approaching opponent's thigh. Chamber by lifting the straight leg as high as the situation allows for and drive your heel downwards into the nerves of the thigh; "hook" at contact and strive to penetrate a few inches. Preferably repeat in series: this is an annoying *Attrition Kick* that screams convincingly: "Keep away!".

The Ground Hooked Downward Heel Kick to an approaching assailant's thigh

Key Points

- Kick *into* the target, but then chamber back to be able to repeat the Kick.
- Lift the straightened leg to chamber as *high* as the specific circumstances allow for; this is the only way to maximize power, although at the expense of early detection.
- Always "*hook*" into the target at impact (=bend the leg slightly just after impact).
- Aim for *sensitive points*; this is not a powerful kick.
- Always *repeat*, -with same or with other leg-, or *follow up*.

Targets

The front thighs mainly. But also the top of the feet, the groin, the head, the back of the neck and more. Basically, anything that is in range in the relative position to your opponent. See Figures below.

Target the feet, the groin, the back of the neck, the head and more

Typical Applications

The first set of Figures show how to open an aggressive combination with this Kick as soon as the opponent gets in range; you then follow up immediately with a Ground Front Kick. Note that the Ground Front Kick can become an *Assisted Kick* as a direct follow-up of a **Hooked Downward Kick**, if the connecting heel stays on the opponent's thigh (as illustrated). Of course you could also use a regular Front Kick from the other leg after the foot from the first Kick is lowered closer to the opponent and with the hips raising for more range and more power (Illustrated in the second set of Drawings at the top of next page).

Offensive Ground Hooked Downward Heel Kick immediately followed by Assisted Ground Front Kick

Offensive Ground Hooked Downward Heel Kick followed by 'bridging' Ground Front Kick

With all this said, the best use for this Kick in the author's opinion, <u>is attrition when you do control your opponent with a lock</u>: you can thus both cause him pain and hinder his efforts to release himself from the hold. The coming Illustrations present an MMA-type application, very effective if you can pull it through. It is, in any case, very important to drill. As your opponent who is caught in your guard (=*between your legs*) attempts to "pound" you, you get hold of the hand on your chest that controls you while blocking his incoming punch by kicking his biceps. Immediately kick his head with an Inside Hook Kick (or a Front Kick) while twisting his wrist to bring his elbow to face upwards. In an uninterrupted transition, do lower your kicking leg on to the elbow as you push away his hips with your other leg. Twist your body and pull his arm; you have him in a painful Arm-lock. Now you can start hammering his back with painful "small" Downward Heel Kicks! It should keep him busy.

Hold your opponent in an arm-lock and keep kicking him continuously with Hooked Downward Heel Kicks to the kidneys

The Kick is also an interesting Reflex Kick to use as you reach the ground together with your opponent, or as you get into position as you grapple. It is fast, and it can get more powerful if it makes use of a falling or rolling body movement. In the example illustrated at the top of next page, it is a natural follow-up to a *Twin Inside Crescent Kick Takedown* (which is an important technique presented later in the book). This example presents the Kick, with an added Head Butt before the takedown, and the seamless follow-up with a body-powered ***Hooked Downward Heel Kick***. The illustrations tell it all, and the reader is invited to consult the section about the Twin Kick itself.

THE GROUND HOOKED DOWNWARD HEEL KICK

1 2

*The Hooked Downward Heel
Kick after a suitable Takedown*

3 4 5

Specific Training

- "Run" after a protected partner in *Crab Walk* and attack his thighs as soon as in range. See Illustration.
- Hit a *target*, like a bag, a soft step, a tire. Drill for precision, <u>power</u> and speed of repetition.

Deliver fast from Crab Walk

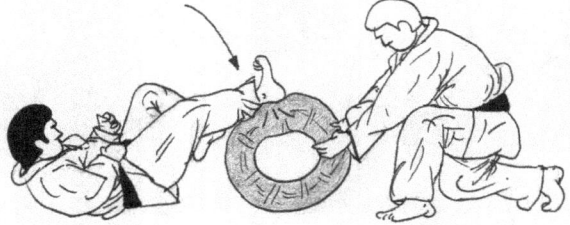

Hit an old tire for precision and power

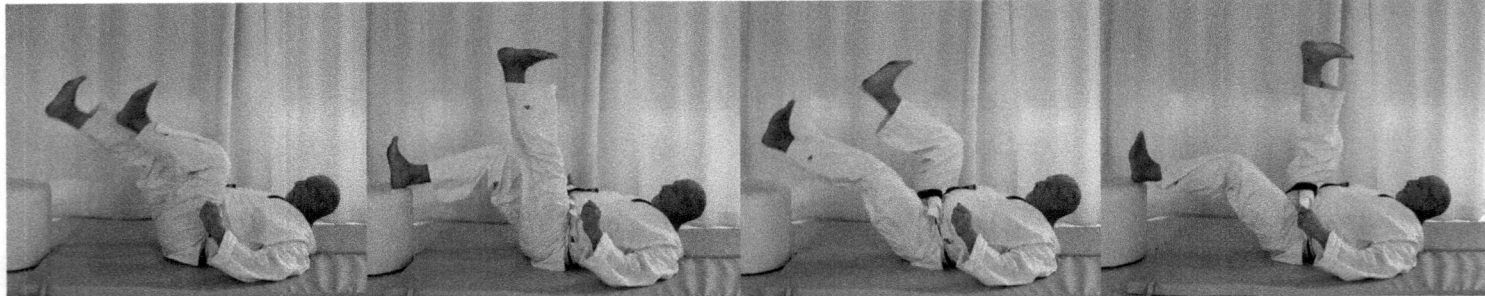

Hit a soft step repetitively for speed and power

Self defense

The coming Drawings illustrate another example of the Kick as an annoying attrition while you hold the opponent in a Lock. In this case, you take an assailant down with a one-legged shoot or after having caught his own kick. You get hold of his leg in a preparatory move for the following Ankle Lock, and you then let yourself fall back into old Jiu-Jitsu's classic *Kata Ashi Hishigi* Leg Lock (technically, an Ankle Lock pressuring Achilles' tendon). Make sure you press his knee between yours for full control. Kick him while holding the lock and maintain the knee pressure.

The Ground Hooking Downward Heel Kick in Ankle-lock position

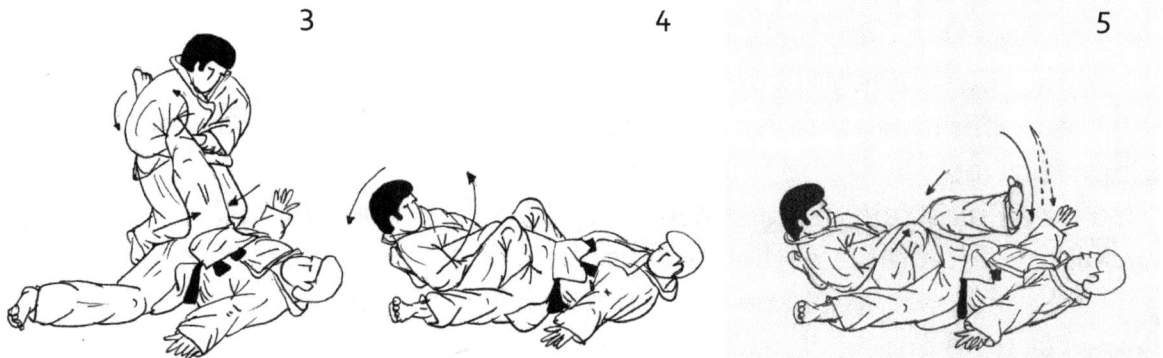

3

4

5

The Figures at the top of next page illustrate the **Pressing/Assisted version** of the Kick, delivered from a "Shell" lying-down position, with no hand support. The Assisted version will allow for much more chambering and, therefore, for a much more powerful Kick (it is, as always, at the cost of detection). But in this case, the high chamber is in some way a feint for a much higher kick towards his face and it should be executed with that in mind. And while your opponent will lift his hands against what seems a High Kick, you still will exert some control on his front leg with your foot check. As illustrated, you place your foot on the thigh of the front leg of your assailant, and use it immediately as support to lift your hips and chamber your other leg. You chamber fast and as high as possible, *before kicking down on the controlled thigh*. Hook at impact and follow up. Your checking foot stays on his thigh until the last moment, or, if it is not in the way, even stays there. This Kick is surprisingly easy to deliver successfully. In any case, it is also an important drill for instinctive positional kicking. If successful and delivered with precision, this is a crippling strike.

➤

The Assisted Ground Hooking Downward Heel Kick

And the next Figures illustrate the use of the Kick as a **Stripping Kick**, to release the assailant's hold on one of your feet (We have already met the *Stripping Ground Roundhouse Kick*). When you are lying on the ground and your assailant has control of one of your feet, you have to react fast, before he takes the advantage, for example by twisting your ankle to cause you to pivot. Bend the caught leg while lifting the other one, and *kick down into his hold, aiming for his wrist with your heel*. Hook into the hold. Repeat if necessary and follow up to keep him on the defensive. The Stripping Kick could also be a Full straight-leg Downward Heel Kick (that we shall meet later on), but it then would be detectable earlier and would lack the important "hooking" into the hold (on the other hand it would be more powerful and more damaging if the opponent tries to keep his hold on). Such a Kick to an immobilized wrist can be seriously joint-damaging.

The Stripping Ground Hooking Downward Heel Kick

An interesting version of this Kick, that is illustrated at the top of next page, sees you **compound it with a straight Heel Kick**. In the relative positions of the Illustration, you can nearly-simultaneously execute a Hooking Downward Heel Kick to the head of the opponent, all the while delivering a straight Front Heel Kick to same head with the other leg. You can reach this position after rolling towards your opponent, or during a grappling episode on the ground. *This is a very dangerous technique to be practiced carefully*.

➤

A dangerous combination kick

To close off this section, the Figure below reminds the reader of the versatility of the Kick as an attrition or a mollifying technique. In this example, you hammer your opponent as you hold him in a classic *Juji Gatame* Arm Bar (*Ju Jitsu*).

Softening an opponent held in classic arm bar

If you always put limit on everything you do, physical or anything else. It will spread into your work and into your life. There are no limits. There are only plateaus, and you must not stay there, you must go beyond them.
~Bruce Lee

20. THE GROUND TWIN INSIDE CRESCENT KICK

General

This is, again, a very specific *Situational Kick*. It is also showy and exotic, and it could have been classified in our future book about *Joint Kicks* because its most common version targets the elbow joints of an assailant choking you on the ground. But, the Kick being also applicable with the head and ribs as targets (and having witnessed its successful use to the head in hard free fighting), the author has decided to classify it here as a Ground Kick. It is an interesting technique, quite easy to execute, and that certainly needs to be described for completeness. After some training, a skilled Artist could find the opportunity to use it, though probably more in an asymmetric fight that he dominates.

Description

The coming Figures describe the classic execution of the Kick as an attack to the elbow joints of a choker sitting between your legs. As he sets the choke, you immediately straighten his arms with your hands to prepare them for impact and then twin-crescent-kick them, making contact with the inner thighs. Ideally catch his wrists as you kick to keep his arms in place and extended, and with the elbows pointing out. If possible pull his wrists outwards as your legs kick his elbows inwards. The natural follow-ups are all kinds of arm-lock maneuvers, compliments of *Judo* and *Jiu-Jitsu*.

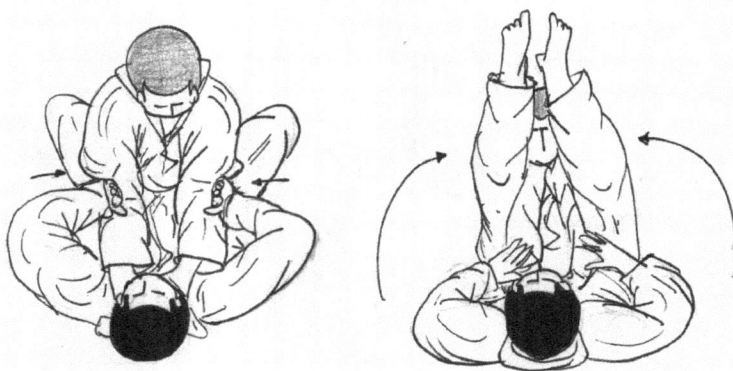

The Twin Inside Crescent Kick to the elbows against a Ground front Choke

Key Points

- Kick *into* the targets, the elbows in this instance.
- *Straighten the legs* at impact.

Targets

The elbow joints of course, but also the *ribs* and the sides of the *head* (See Illustration). You connect with any part of the inside leg from thighs to feet, according to the target and the specific situation.

Ground Twin Inside Crescent Kick to the assailant's head as he bends towards you to punch

Typical Application

The next Drawings illustrate an application with the *Drop version of the Kick* that targets the *ribs*. Against a standing common Front Choke attempt, you immediately hit the assailant's elbows downwards and get hold of his upper arms or shoulders, in a typical release. Using him as an anchor, you jump up into a ***Twin Inside Crescent Kick***

to the ribs and let yourself fall (you can then knot your ankles up in his back). You have to aim to hit his offered lower ribs powerfully with the lower leg (the lower the more powerful the kick). Treat this maneuver as a **Kick,** and *not* as a scissor Hold. A great follow-up would be spear-fingering his throat or eyes when landing, and then, for good measure, Twin Crescent-kick his head (with as much or as little re-chambering as the situation warrants).

3   4   5

Drop Twin Crescent Kick to the ribs, followed by Ground Twin Crescent Kick to the head

Specific Training

This is a Situational Kick; it needs to be *drilled with a partner*. You can also drill it on a heavy bag which you hold 'as if' a grappling partner.

Self defense

And the last Illustrations show a follow-up combination to the classic elbow delivery against the Ground Choke (described earlier). Once you have delivered the Twin Crescent to the opponent's elbow joints, you immediately repeat the Kick to the sides of the head, connecting with the heels if possible. The legs will be slightly bent at impact, but the spirit behind the Twin Kick stays the same. Catch one of his wrists while pushing away his opposite hip. Twist and use your other leg to place him into classic straight arm-lock position. Once controlled, you can bend his arm, twist his wrist and switch to a twisting elbow arm-lock position, from which you can repeatedly Downward Heel-kick him in the kidneys.

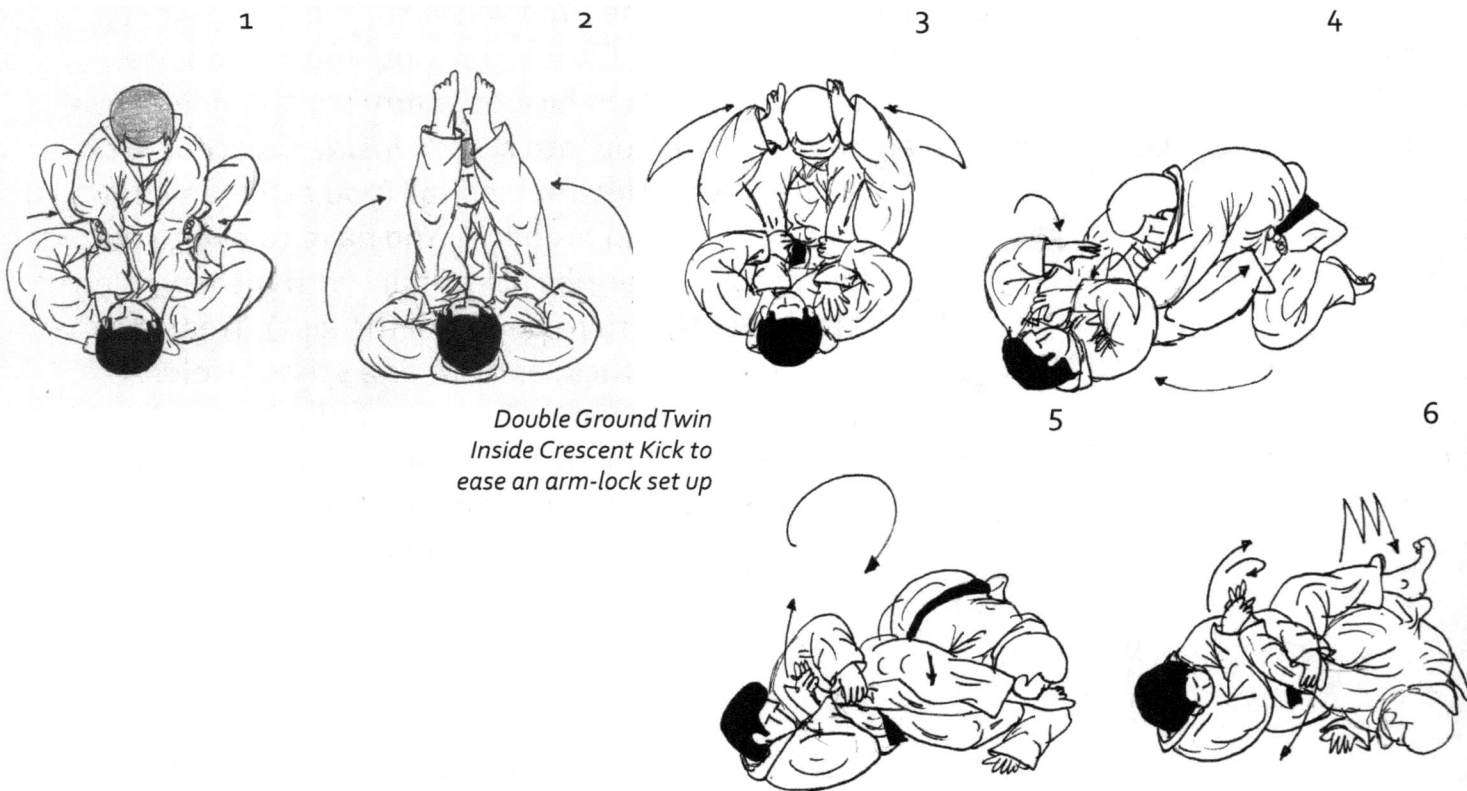

1   2   3   4

Double Ground Twin Inside Crescent Kick to ease an arm-lock set up

5   6

Don't judge each day by the harvest you reap but by the seeds that you plant.
~Robert Louis Stevenson

21. THE PULL-IN ASSISTED KICK

General

This is a very exotic Kick, typical of Indonesian *Silat* styles, but surprisingly efficient. We will describe it briefly. These special kicks need thorough training to become natural, but they then become very unexpected maneuvers at the disposal of a skilled fighter. The Kicks described will also provide the basis for variations and personal research by the interested Artists. *Pull-in Kicks* are great because they help the smooth delivery of the kick, they pull the opponent into the kick and they prevent him from executing evading moves. In the specific case presented here, the wrist hold even allows for a Double Kick: placing the foot on the opponent's leg for "Assistance" can become a full-fledged staying kick. Remember that your hold will prevent him from pulling away. Several following kicks are possible in this set-up: Front, Side, Roundhouse and even more. Keep reading and all will become clear.

Description

The Drawings illustrate the basic *Assisted Roundhouse version*: you catch your opponent's forward hand and then kick his front knee with a Ground Outside-tilted Front Kick, while leaning onto your free hand. Of course, you do not chamber back, but you leave your foot on his knee/upper thigh as an Assist for the coming main event. You do use (1) your free hand on the floor, (2) his checked knee and (3) his caught hand to pull yourself up into an airborne pivot and a Roundhouse Kick to the head. The first Kick could also be delivered to the hip joint and the second kick could also be a Side Kick; all up to you. Feel free to explore all possibilities.

The Pull-in Assisted Ground Roundhouse Kick

Typical Application

And the next Figures show the *Side Kick variation* of the same basic move.

The Pull-in Assisted Ground Side Kick

Self defense

The last Illustrations will show the Kick delivered as a **Drop Kick** after having caught the opponent's front hand. The principles are identical, and it is a powerful and sneaky move, if mastered. You deliver the first Kick to the knee while letting yourself go to the ground; the second Kick starts as soon as your free hand has reached the floor. Even if you will never use it, drill this interesting maneuver for general proficiency and for ... fun

The Pull-in Assisted Drop Roundhouse Kick

Quickness is the essence of the war.
~Sun Tzu

22. THE GROUND BACK KICK

General

The **Ground Back Kick** is probably the most powerful of the Ground Kicks because of the muscles involved, much like its classic standing counterpart. But, just like for the standing version, it sports the disadvantage of limited vision of the opponent who is ... behind you.

The Ground Back Kick is extremely useful in dynamic situations and in kicking combinations that bring you to the right chambering position. A few examples will be given.

The Ground Back Kick is also, in the author's opinion, one of the best Ground Kicks to be used for subsequently standing up.

The Ground Back Kick

Description

Just like for the corresponding standing Essential Kicks, the two basic **Ground Back Kicks** are the *Spin-forward* version and the *Spin-back* version. The reader is invited to consult our previous book about 'Essential Kicks' for the basics of the standing Back Kicks. The difference between the versions is clear from the comparison of the Figures below. In the Spin-forward, it is the leg that moves that also kicks. In the Spin-back, the legs that moves first gets on the floor while the other leg delivers the Kick. Whether you spin one way or another, it is imperative that the Kick is delivered <u>straight</u>, regardless of the twisting momentum. Just like for the Standing Kicks, the key to success is switching from circular momentum to straight momentum; any overlapping of the two will cause a diagonal kick that misses its target.

The Spin-forward Ground Back Kick compared to the Spin-back Ground Back Kick

Key Points

- Kick *straight*, with no influence from the spinning momentum.
- *Push the hips* (backwards) into the kick by using your three anchor points to the ground (two hands and one knee/foot).
- *Chamber back.*
- Strive to *minimize the blind period* in which you do not see the opponent

Targets

This is a very powerful Kick, *all targets are relevant* from the shin up to the face.

Typical Applications

The most appropriate use of the *Ground Back Kick* is after a Circular Kick which momentum provides the spin into the chamber. We shall not repeat enough though, that the circular motion must be fully stopped before the Kick can start developing *straight* from the chamber.

The next Drawings show the *Spin-forward* version of the Kick as a natural follow-up of a Ground Crescent Block Kick. The very natural movement from Crescent to Back Kick is identical to that of the standing versions. In this particular example, the Ground Back Kick aims at the front knee of the opponent.

Ground Crescent Kick to knee Back Kick

The dynamic *Spin-back version* will be illustrated as a follow-up of a Ground Roundhouse; the spinning principle is the same and both Kicks blend in smoothly in the same circular pivot. In this example, a 'Timing' Ground Roundhouse Stop Kick to the groin will stun the menacingly approaching opponent. It will then evolve into a powerful Spin-back Back Kick straight into the same area. See Illustrations at the top of next page. ➡

Groin Ground Roundhouse to Spin-back Back Kick

As mentioned, the Back Kick is probably one of the best **'Standing-back-up' Kicks**, because it can be delivered while straightening up, and because the chamber-back puts you in an easy position from which to stand fully up. Last but not least, it is a powerful <u>Push-back Kick</u> that should send your opponent flying and give plenty of room and time to get back into a standing guard.

One example of standing-up with the Ground Back Kick

All Back Kick variations lend themselves to Ground versions. Our previous book about *Essential Kicks* includes a full Chapter about normal standing Back Kicks. We shall give a few examples in the Self-Defense section, but the reader should experiment and extrapolate from the Essential Kicks what work for him on the ground. One example, -of which I am particularly fond- , is presented at the top of next page: it is the **ground version of the Drop Overhead Back Kick**, an extremely surprising and efficient Kick. ▶

The sneaky Ground Overhead Back Kick

Specific Training

- The Ground Back Kick, in all its forms, needs to be drilled for power *on the heavy bag*, whether the bag is standing, is hanging or is thrown at you. It is a powerful Kick and needs to be drilled as such. The best exercises are stop-kicking the heavy bag powerfully *thrown at you by a partner*; it could be a long hanging bag or a free bag.

Drill the Ground Back Kick on a heavy bag thrown at you by a partner

- It is important to drill *the standing version of the Kicks* in order to fully master the basic principles involved in back-kicking, especially the transition from spinning to straight vectors.

Self Defense

The Figures at the top of next page illustrate the important *Groin "hooking" version* of the Back Kick: you kick the groin from under and then hook back forwards with the heel to make sure to hit and pull the testicles. In the example presented, you execute the Kick as your assailant is pinning you down with a classic behind-the-back arm-lock. In this instance, you have only two anchor points to the ground (One hand, one knee), but less power is needed to hook into the groin than for a regular full Back Kick. Let yourself go down more to the ground as you kick and make sure to hit the groin. To follow up, you simply extend your legs and roll to take him down. If you do this violently, you will also cause him joint damage.

➤

The Ground groin Hooking Back Kick against an arm-lock attempt

And the last Frawings illustrate the use of the Kick in a classic escape from a 'Low Kick' in standing position. You evade and smother the Low Kick to your front knee by twisting back while bending the knee to the ground (= you "go with the kick"). Your opponent has certainly not taken these moves and ranges into account and will feel as if pushing through an open door. Your twisting pivot turns seamlessly into a Ground Spin-back Back Kick to his hip, sending him flying away. Chamber back the leg while completing the pivot into ready position. The end posture could, for example, be crab-like to allow for keeping going after him.

Evading knee into Drop Spin-back Back Kick

Illustrative Photos

The classic Essential standing Back Kick

Illustrative Photos (Continued)

The Essential standing **Spin-forward** *Back Kick*

The Spin-back Short Back Kick

The close-combat Short Back Kick

A few Hooking Back Kicks

The evading Drop Back Kick

The Uppercut Back Kick

The Essential Downward Back Kick

The classic Ground Back Kick

The Overhead Back Kick

23. THE GROUND TWIN BACK KICK

General

The name says it all: This is the Ground version of the Essential Drop Twin Back Kick, a very powerful but blind maneuver sometimes called the *Mule Kick* for obvious reasons. This Kick is especially useful as a *Stop Kick*, as it is powerful enough to neutralize even the strongest of opponent's forward momentum. Of course, it has the disadvantages of being without eye contact, of being fully committed and of necessitating a lot of energy to execute. It is an important Kick to know though; drill it and you could one day be in the perfect position to use it.

Description

Just like a mule (or maybe you prefer a horse comparison), you lean on your hands or fists (as per your preference) to jump up and launch both legs simultaneously into two airborne Back Kicks. The Photos illustrate this clearly.

The Ground Twin Back Kick leaning on fists

Key Points

- Execute only if *fully committed.*
- These are Back Kicks delivered from *full chambers* and exploding into legs-straightening.
- Push *your hips and whole body* into the Kick at impact by pushing from your hands as well
- *Chamber back*, at least slightly, before landing.

Targets

This is a Blind Kick, destined to stop a forward momentum: *it needs to aim for the general center of the assailant.* Aim for the groin, the lower belly, the ribs and the solar plexus.

Typical Application

The next Figures illustrate the use of the Kick as a *Stop Kick*; probably the most common and adequate use. As the opponent closes in, roll into starting position and kick out.

The Ground Twin Back Stop Kick

Specific Training

This is a Kick to drill for *the speed of setting up into starting position* first and foremost; and then only, also for power of delivery: the best training is execution against a swinging heavy bag.

Self defense

The series illustrated in the Figures below shows how to lure your opponent in with a missed (purposely or not) Roundhouse Kick, just to have him impale himself onto a Twin Back Kick when he tries to counter. As your assailant comes menacingly towards you, edge forwards towards him and punch in the direction of his groin. Follow up by rolling down while delivering a Ground Roundhouse in the general direction of his head. The Roundhouse will probably not connect, though if it does, it is even better! You use the momentum of the Roundhouse to roll into starting position for the Back Kick. The assailant, seeing you having missed or nearly-missed, and seeing you presenting your back, will have the utmost difficulty to refrain from initiating a counterattack. *Twin Back Stop Kick!*

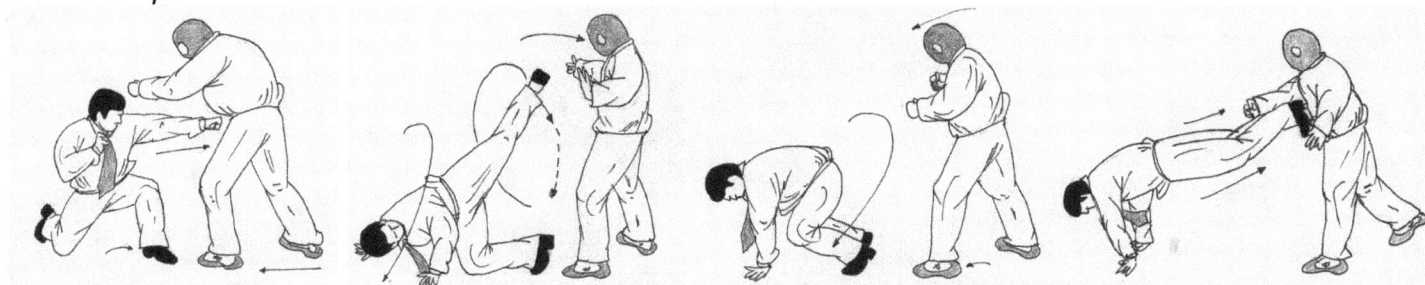

Lure your opponent in for a Ground Twin Back Stop Kick

Ground Twin Back Kicks

If you want to learn to swim jump into the water. On dry land no frame of mind is ever going to help you.
~Bruce Lee

24. THE GROUND TWIN ROUNDHOUSE KICK

General

We introduce this Twin Kick for the sake of completeness, in the spirit of the previously encountered Side- and Back-Twin Kicks. The *Ground Twin Roundhouse* is simply, again, the Ground version of the basic Drop Twin Roundhouse Kick, illustrated here and also described in our previous book about *Essential Kicks*. This is a surprising and very powerful Kick, especially useful when directed towards the groin area. The shock wave in the general groin area on impact makes it unnecessary to be accurate, and it will rattle any opponent into carefulness. The Kick needs to be started in a dynamic movement though, and it requires total commitment: once started, there is no way back.

The Drop Twin Roundhouse Kick against a high-kicking opponent

Description

From a kneeling position, pivot to place both hands sideways on the floor. From this ready starting position, jump up off your hands into double chamber and extend both legs in a classic circular Roundhouse trajectory. Strive to hit target just at legs extension, and with both feet simultaneously. Kick through.

The Ground Twin Roundhouse Kick

Key Points

-       The Kicks are *real Roundhouses*, needing classic Roundhouse chambering, "whipping" extension and some chambering back after penetrating a few inches into the target.
-       *Commit fully* to the Kick, there is no way back
-       Use the *hips and the full body* move to drive the Kicks

Targets

This is a "Concussion" Kick which must send a rippling vibration; the whole body is a good target, from knee to head, but the most appropriate will be the *groin* area.

Typical Applications

As mentioned, the Kick should start in a dynamic context, just like the corresponding Drop Kick. You need to kick or to move on the ground to get into the adequate starting position. And remember that there is no stopping before kicking, but just a continuous smooth movement that will negate any inertia problem. In the example below, you surprise an opponent by going aggressively after him, starting with a Forward Roll that blends into the starting Kick position.

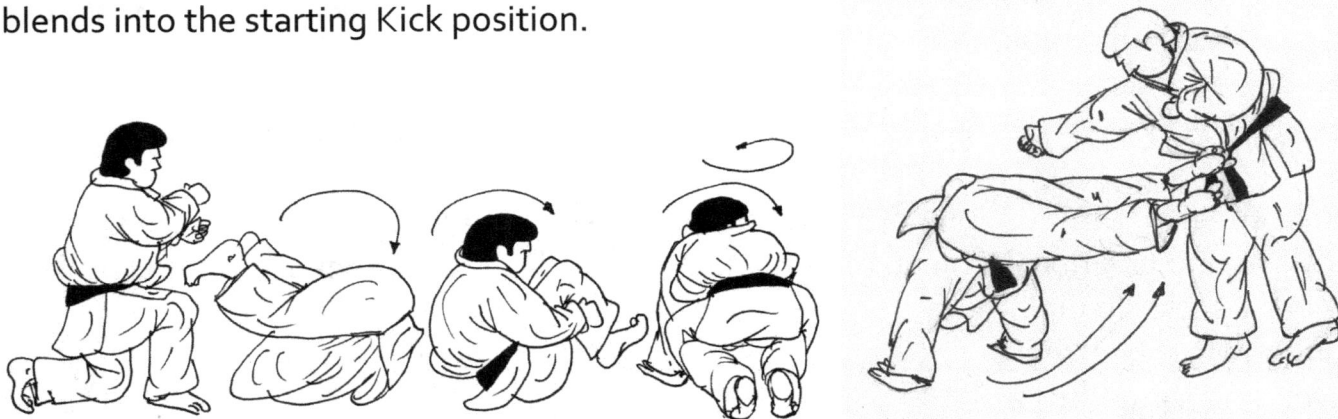

Forward Roll into Ground Twin Roundhouse Kick

Many variations are possible. The illustrations at the top of next page show a complex but interesting **Assisted Downward version**. The reader can clearly see how the Knee Check to stop the assailant's advance turns into an Assist Point to jump up into the Twin Kick. Please note that the Downward variation adds the weight of your legs to the energy of the Kick itself.

➡

The Ground Assisted Twin Downward Roundhouse Kick

Specific Training

- Drill for power on the *heavy bag.*
- Drill for speed and precision on a *medicine ball* held by partner: aim to kick the ball as far as possible.

Self defense

As mentioned, the *Ground Twin Roundhouse* is a great Kick for self-defense if targeting the groin, because of its concussive effect. Remember to always follow up though.

The Ground Twin Roundhouse Kick to the assailant's groin

Good, better, best. Never let it rest. 'Til your good is better and your better is best.
~St. Jerome

25. The Ground Outside Crescent Kick

General

The Ground version of the *Outside Crescent Kick* is quite powerful because of the body movement involved, just like for the Inside Crescent Kick. But it is, again, a dynamic maneuver that needs to start after a Spin-back or to al least start from a cross-legged position. It is a natural Kick to follow (and/or precede) an Inside Crescent Kick or a Roundhouse Kick. In one word a great technique, but not a stand-alone one.

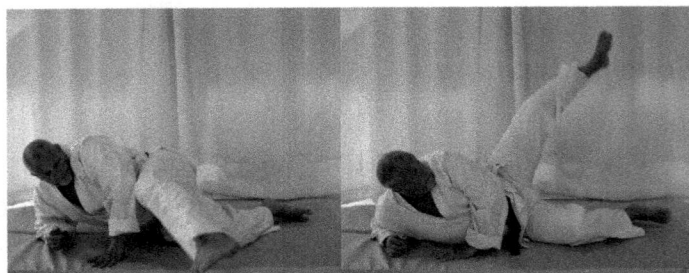

Ground Outside Crescent Kick starting from crossed-leg position

Description

The coming Figures illustrate the delivery of the Kick with emphasis on the starting position and on the end position. This Kick being just the mirror image of the Inside Crescent Kick, this is pretty straightforward to the trained reader.

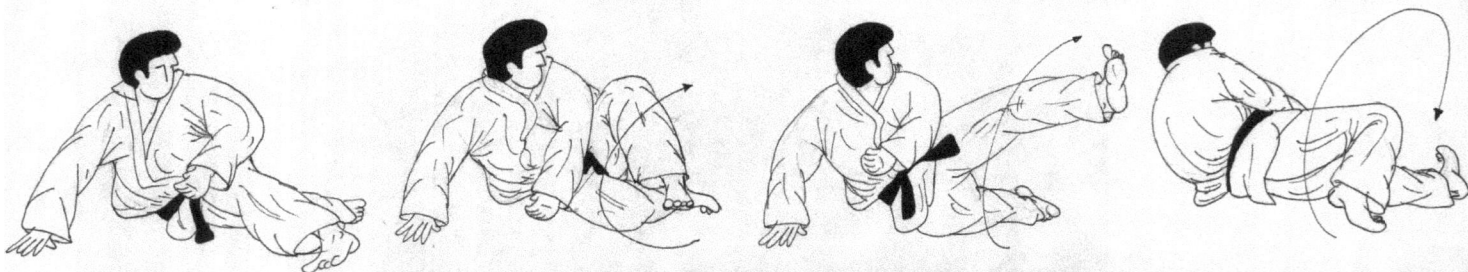

Basic Ground Outside Crescent Kick

An often-encountered variation of the Kick is its delivery when impact to target is made **with the ball of the foot**. In order to do that, the foot must pivot early in a Kick that is delivered in a more "whippy" way. In fact, this is simply a Ground version of the **Inverse Roundhouse Kick** (*Gyacku Mawashi Geri – Karatedo*) . [The Inverse Roundhouse Kick, which is presented in our book about Essential Kicks under the name Outward-tilted Front Kick will be shown in the **Illustrative Photos** section below.] The principle is the same, and easy to understand. ➤

The Ground Inverse Roundhouse Kick, a very close relative of the Outside Crescent Kick

The other preferred preceding move to the Outside Crescent Kick is the Spin-back. The next Drawings are self-explanatory. One could refer to the Essential standing version of the Spin-back Outside Crescent Kick, or to the very close Ground Spin-back Hook Kick already encountered. It is obvious that the Spin-back takes you naturally into a powerful Outside Crescent.

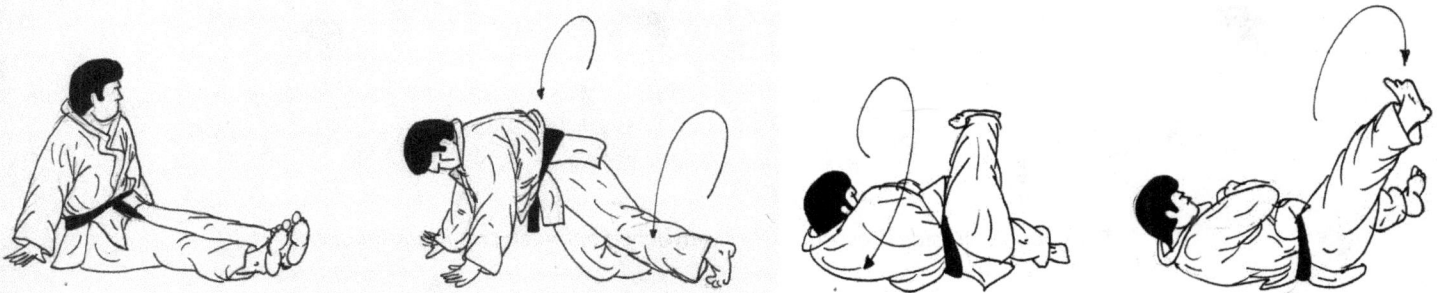
The Ground Spin-back Outside Crescent Kick

Key Points

- The Kick is delivered with the *twisting of the whole body*, not with the leg only
- Pull *the hips first,* then the kicking leg
- Always start from a *dynamic* inertia-free position

Targets

Aim for the head, the groin or a limb extending in your direction. Other targets are not really vulnerable to that Kick.

Typical Applications

The coming Figures illustrate the most classic use of the Kick: in between two Ground Roundhouses! The first Ground Roundhouse kicks 'through' the opponent and the foot "rebounds" on the floor to help switching the direction of the pivot into the fully-hipped same-leg Outside Crescent Kick. This Outside Crescent will pull the hips into a naturally-flowing Roundhouse Kick from the other leg. The whole move must be smooth and uninterrupted.

The Ground Outside Crescent Kick, sandwiched between two Roundhouses

The other most complementary kick to the Ground Outside Crescent is the (Inside) Crescent Kick, as it is also fully circular. Just like with the Roundhouse Kick, the Outside Crescent is a naturally following or a naturally preceding Kick to the Ground Inside Crescent Kick. In the Illustrations, the Ground Outside Crescent is used to block the incoming punch of a looming opponent. The momentum of the first Block Kick is naturally used for a smoothly following powerful Crescent Kick to the head.

Ground Outside Crescent Block Kick naturally followed by Ground Inside Crescent Kick

Specific Training

- This is a *kick-through* Kick; it needs to be drilled for speed and power on a focus pad held at the right height by a partner.
- Kicking a *medicine ball* held by a partner is also a good exercise.

Self defense

The Crescent Kicks are obviously great *Block Kicks*. They can also be very useful to block Stomp Kicks or crushing Downward Heel Kicks from standing assailants. Following up would obviously be Crescent Kicks or Roundhouse Kicks, as discussed above.

Ground Outside Crescent Block Kick against Stomp

And the last Illustrations show the fast roll from a full powered Ground Roundhouse Kick into a **Spin-back Outside Crescent Kick**; this is clearly a very natural movement that also takes you away from the centerline. In this example, you get ready as your assailant approaches menacingly and you aggressively kick him in the groin area as soon as he gets in range. The momentum of this first groin Ground Roundhouse Kick takes you into a spin that you boost on purpose to get into position for an Outside Crescent Kick after a full turn. The Spin-back Roll gives your Outside Crescent Kick a lot of energy and you kick *through* his head. Keep the momentum going for yet another Spin-back Kick. In this example a Ground Spin-back Hook Kick, though it could also be another Spin-back Outside Crescent as well.

Two full turns in this ground combination: Groin Roundhouse Stop Kick, Spin-back Outside Crescent Kick and Spin-back Hook Kick

Illustrative Photos

Three executions of the standing Essential Outside Crescent Kick

A close combat execution of the standing Outside Crescent Kick

The Essential Spin-back Outside Crescent Kick

The Essential Outward-tilted Front Kick, also known as Inverse Roundhouse Kick

Another Essential Outward-tilted Front Kick, also known as Inverse Roundhouse Kick

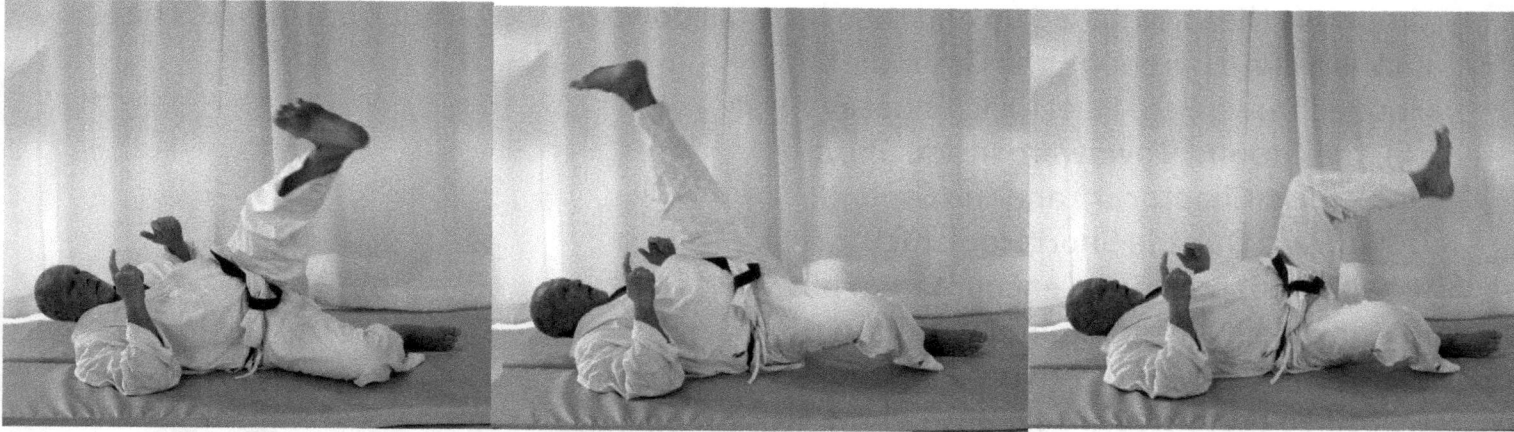

The high version of the Ground Outside Crescent Kick, generally a Kick Block against an opponent fully above you

The measure of who we are is what we do with what we have.
~Vince Lombardi

26. THE GROUND AXE KICK

General

The 'Axe' Kick is the common name of the **Downward Heel Kick**, a basic Essential Kick described in detail in our previous books. The Ground version is very important because extremely powerful when well executed, as the weight of the leg adds itself to the power of the kicking. Gravity helps you; therefore, accept its help gracefully. Of course, the Kick is not always suitable to every situation; but when it is, use it! You simply lift the straight leg up and then let it fall down on the target from above. The Kick is a close parent of: the Ground Hooked Downward Heel Kick (Chapter 19), the Ground Downward Inside Short Hook Kick (Chapter 15) and the Ground Downward Outside Short Hook Kick (Chapter 16) previously encountered; but it is now delivered straight down, with the leg straightened and with no "hooking". Of course there would be many hybrid possibilities between all these similar Kicks; choose according to your physique and your temperament.

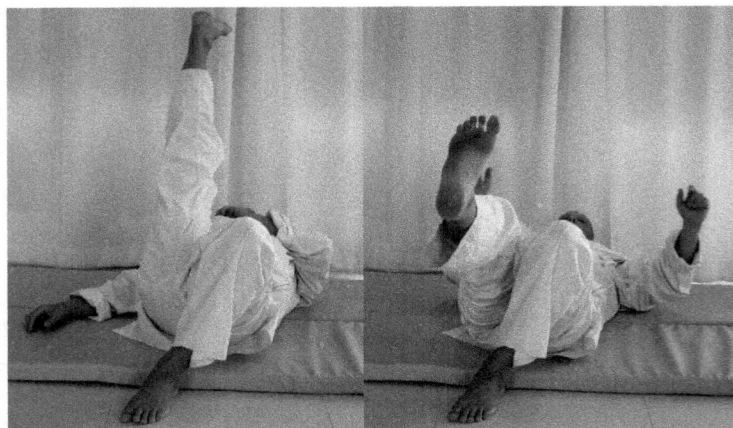

Lift the straightened leg up, and kick down

Description

As mentioned, and as easily understood from comparison to the standing basic Kick, you just crash your straightened leg down onto the target. If the way up (=the chambering) is encumbered by the target itself or by something else, you lift the leg in an Inside Crescent or in an Outside Crescent trajectory and you lower it powerfully straight down from the apex.

The basic Ground Axe Kick

Of course, the Kick is usually used in a *dynamic* context and not from a set immobile position. One of the most interesting and powerful versions is the Kick executed at the end of a Forward Roll. The Roll gives a safer and surprising approach, while adding energy to the Kick; it is also Ground Movement difficult to deal with by any opponent. This rolling version of the Kick, when delivered from a standing position, is often referred to as the **Rolling Hill Kick**, a very effective maneuver common in Korean and East Asian Arts. The Downward Heel Kick at the end of the Roll can in fact be delivered with either leg as illustrated below. Kicking with the second leg to "arrive" (meaning the opposite side of the shoulder you roll onto) is more powerful but slightly delayed; it could be relevant for a *coup de grace* for instance.

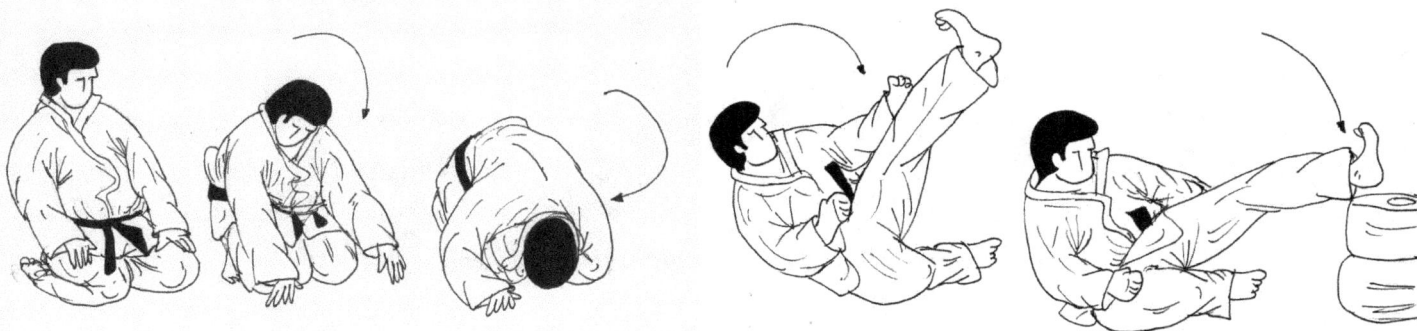

The regular Front Roll to Ground Axe Kick

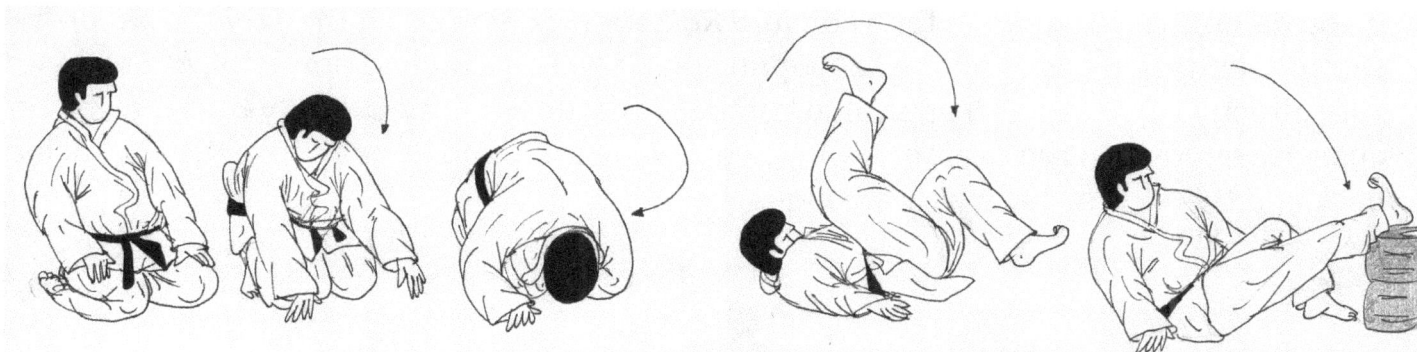

The Front Roll to 'second-leg' Axe kick

Key Points

- The Kick is delivered with the *power of the abdominal belt*, of which the straight leg is only an extension.
- Kick *through* the target; there is no chamber back and no hooking.
- Use *the whole body*, its momentum and the acceleration of gravity; this is a full commitment-kick.

Targets

This Kick is very powerful and is suitable to target anything that can be attacked from above downwards, according to the relative positions of the protagonists. Most commonly *the top of the foot, the upper thigh, the groin and the head*, but everything else too. For example should you get in a situation in which your opponent lies on the floor, the whole of the side facing the sky is open to you: if he is lying on his belly: the back of the neck, the back of the head, the spine between the scapulae, the kidneys, the sacrum, the Achilles' tendon,...Should he have landed on the back: the face, the throat, the solar plexus, the groin, the knee, the shin...

The most common targets of the Ground Axe Kick: toes, thigh, groin, head

Typical Applications

If you do not have the range for a *Forward Roll Axe Kick*, you could then try the **Humpty-Dumpty variation** based on the same principle. It will be a bit less powerful, but still very effective. You can also apply it in combat with the Humpty-Dumpty Back Roll being an evasive move. In the example below, you evade a Ground Roundhouse Kick by rolling back and then, come back with a vengeance.

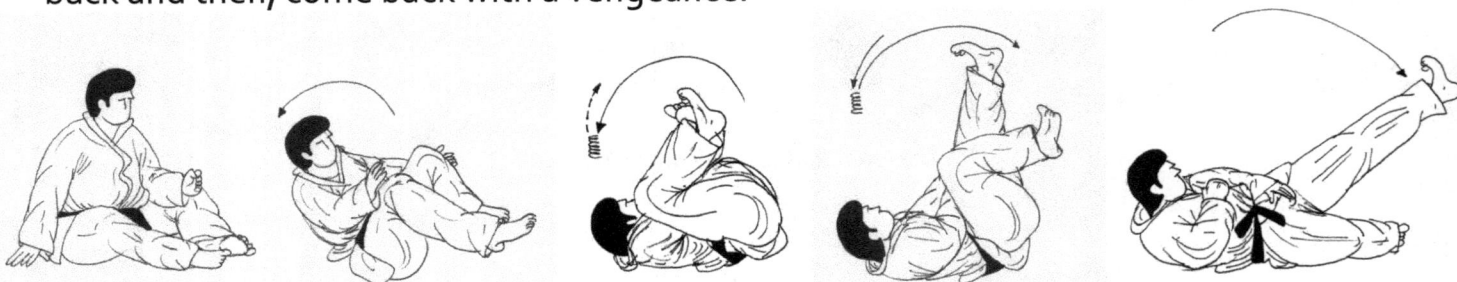

The Humpty-Dumpty version of the Ground Rolling Axe Kick

Roll back to evade a head Roundhouse and Humpty-Dumpty back into Ground Downward Axe Heel Kick to the offered hip joint

Specific Training

This is a no-pull back Kick that needs to be drilled for even more power. The best target for drilling is the old tire, or a stack of them as illustrated earlier. A lying heavy bag is also a worthy training prop. The Kick is simple to execute and understand, but it does not mean it should not be trained for!

Self Defense

We have mentioned previously **Stripping Kicks** to release holds to one of your ankles. If you use the *Axe Kick* with no 'hooking' the kick will be much more powerful and will likely hurt the wrist joint of your assailant. It is only applicable in some situations though. If the assailant is already close and your caught leg is bent, then a Hooking Kick is a better option. In any case, Stripping Kicks are meant to be used immediately as your leg is caught, with no delay.

The Ground Axe Stripping Kick

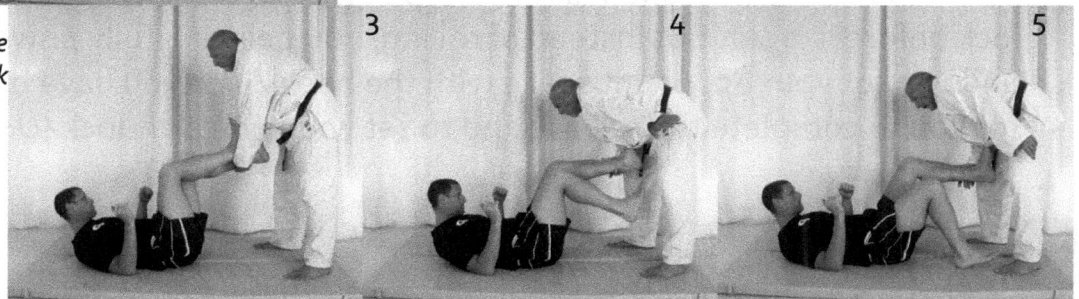

A fully powered Downward Heel Kick **to the groin** will certainly end up a fight. In the example illustrated by the Figures below, you stop an approaching assailant with a forward-surging preemptive Front Kick to the groin. You then follow up immediately by a leg-opening Takedown. As soon as your opponent starts falling back, you chamber the Axe Kick. Kick down into his open groin as he lands. Ouch!

The Ground Axe Kick to the groin should always follow a Ground Takedown

A sophisticated but interesting Takedown technique based on the **Humpty-Dumpty Ground Axe Kick** is now presented. You evade an incoming assailant from your rear side by rolling back and sideways out of the centerline. Your Back Roll turns into a Humpty-Dumpty Axe Kick to the back knees of your assailant who has kept to his forward momentum. The impact of the Kick can be light for a Takedown, or hard for a *Joint Kick*. This is not an extremely practical maneuver, but a great drill for Ground Movement.

Humpty-Dumpty Ground Axe Kick around an assailant

Many of the grappling moves executed on the ground are learned and taught as pushing and wriggling techniques, but they could be and *should be turned into powerful Kicks in self-defense situations*. The example below will make this clear and can be expanded to nearly all grappling moves of Judo, Jiu Jitsu and Wrestling. Just get used to kick any time you are using your legs.

As you have been caught in a *Nikyo*-type ground Arm-lock (*Aikido*), you pivot into the lock before it is set. But instead of rolling, you deliver a fully powered Hook/Axe Kick and aim for your opponent's face with the heel. Once you have hit him, it will be easier for you to complete the release and to set your own arm-lock (*Ude Hishigi Juji Gatame – Judo*).

In grappling situations, kick whenever you can; the Axe Kick can be used in many wrestling set-ups

Illustrative Photos

Examples of basic Essential standing Axe Kicks

The Rolling Ground Downward Heel Axe Kick

27. THE GROUND SCISSOR KICK

General

We shall complete this overview of the main Ground Kicks with the **Scissor Kick** which is technically a simple Double Kick on the ground: Roundhouse Kick with one leg and simultaneous Hook Kick with the other. This Kick is essentially a Joint Kick and we will classify it as such in our coming book about *Joint Kick*s; but as it is executed on the ground, it deserves a mention here. The Kick mainly targets the knee, but is sometimes used viciously to attack the elbow, and even the neck in some styles. The basic idea, - well translated by the name 'scissor' -, is to attack the joint from above and below in opposite directions. If the attack is <u>against</u> the normal range of allowed movement, it is a dangerous *Joint Kick*; if the attack is <u>into</u> the normal range of allowed movement, it is more of a *Takedown*, although quite painful and not much conducive to joint health.
The **Scissor Kick** comes from old Jiu Jitsu, and was also a very effective takedown when applied <u>at hip level</u>; this basic technique called *Kani Basami* has now been banned from the Judo curriculum because judged too dangerous. Delivered as a Kick, it is indeed an aggressive technique.

The Scissor Kick above is mainly a Takedown, the Scissor Kick below is a dangerous Joint Kick that will also take him down

*Classic **Kani Basami**, naturally followed by an Axe Kick*

Description

The coming Figures illustrate the execution of the milder 'takedown' version of the Kick, an image is worth a thousand words.

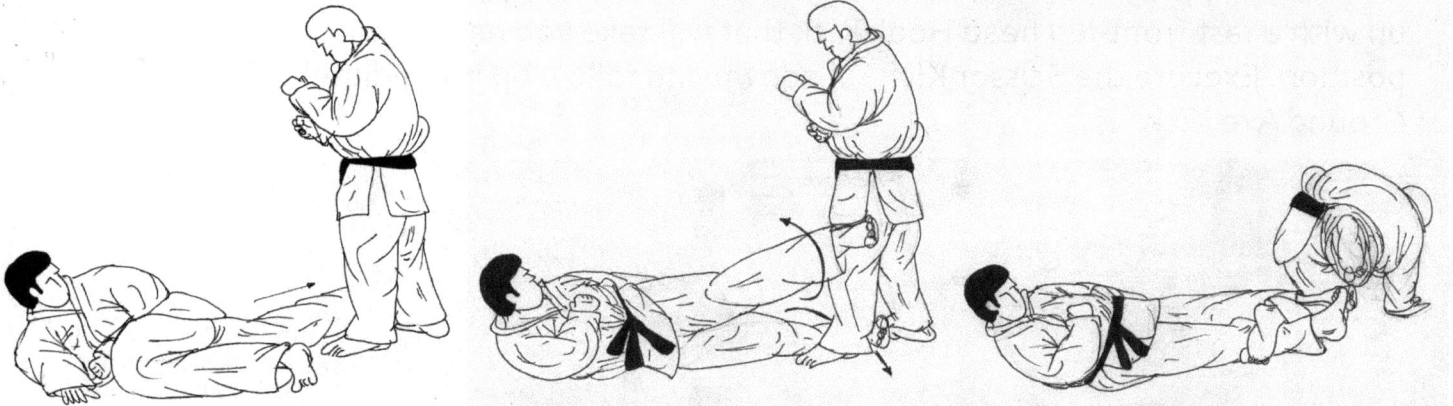

The Ground Scissor Takedown Kick

Key Points

- Execute those as Double Kicks: fast, hard and *simultaneous.*
- Kick *through*!

Targets

The knee, the arm, the neck. That's it! But most commonly, the *knee joint* from all sides.

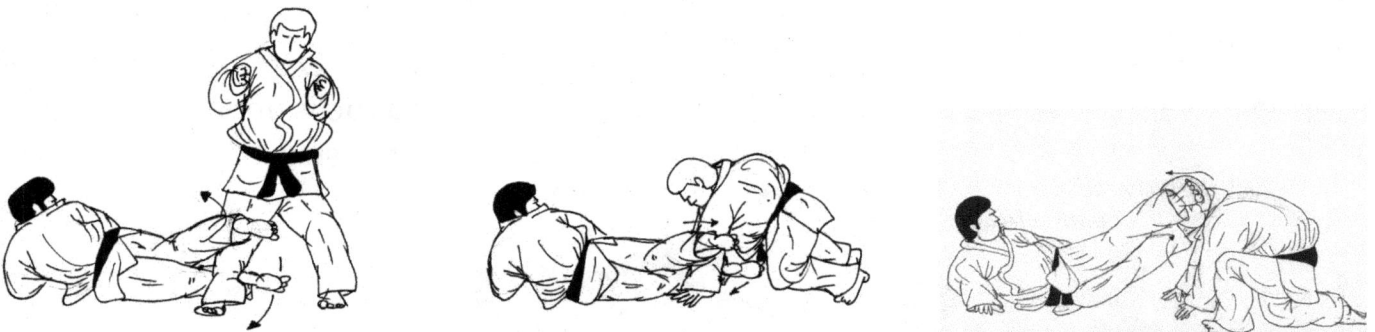

Ground Scissor Kick joint targets: knee, elbow, neck

Typical Application

The basic Kick is quite straightforward. We present here a dynamic application of Jiu-Jitsu's great *Kani Basami* Takedown <u>at the end of a standing combination</u>. Open with a front-leg Hopping Roundhouse to the kidneys followed by a high Back-fist Strike. Follow up with a fast front-leg head Hook Kick that will take you naturally to hands-on-floor position. Execute the Scissor Kick Takedown and follow up immediately with a head Ground Axe Kick.

Drop Scissor Kick Takedown in the middle of an offensive combination

Specific Training

This Double Kick is coming from opposite sides and it needs to be drilled as a **<u>double 'kick-through';</u>** the best prop to use for training is a big focus pad/body shield. One could use two focus pads hold by a partner, but it tends to force the trainee to focus unnecessarily on precision.

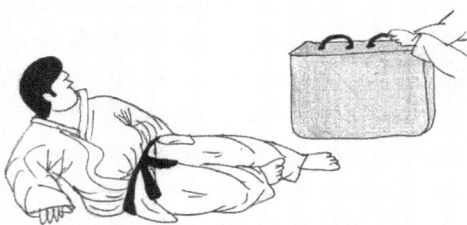

Kick the body shield from both sides

3

4

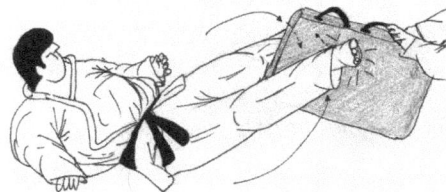

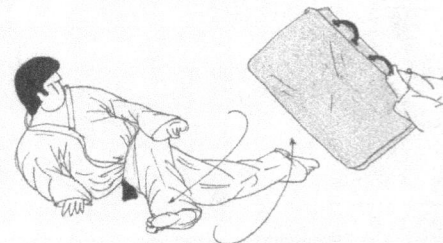

Self defense

This is a great maneuver for any situation in which you can get one of your assailant's leg between yours, or in which you can achieve the set up. The effectiveness of this Double Kick should not be underscored: it is easy and it hurts bad.

Another example of the Ground Scissor Kick in action

The *Flying Scissor Kick to the neck* is emblematic of the Vietnamese Arts of *Viet Vo Dao* and *Vovinam*, though it is also present in other East Asian Arts. It is more of a violent twisting maneuver once you have jumped to catch your opponent's neck between your legs, than a clean Double Kick. But it is still a close parent of the Ground version of the **Neck Scissor Kick** that we shall present here for completeness. In this example, you throw a Pressing/Assisted Side Kick across your opponent head, in order to be able to come back with a Hook Kick that will stop and rest on your opponent's shoulder. This 'Assistance' is the parallel to the jump in the Flying version, and it has the additional advantage to limit possible movement of the opponent. You then start twisting and deliver a clean Assisted Spin-back Hook Kick to the other side of his neck (Your points of support are the hands and the foot that is on his shoulder). Press his neck from both sides and keep twisting to hurt his neck while taking him down. Be careful in training; this is a very dangerous technique!

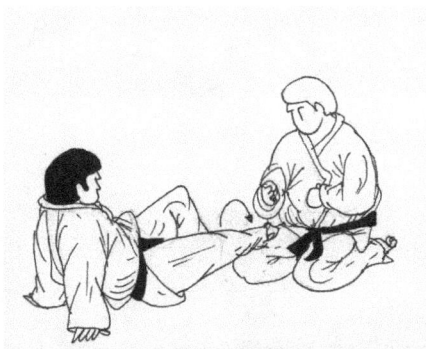

4

5

The dangerous Assisted Ground Neck Scissor Kick

3

And we shall finish with a reminder of the fact that you should scissor-kick automatically in any case you get your legs on both sides of the leg of a standing assailant. This is even especially true if he is starting a kick of his own. In this example, the standing assailant approaches and steps near your leg to chamber his stomp. Big mistake!

A Ground Cutting Scissor Kick against a Stomp attempt

Illustrative Photos

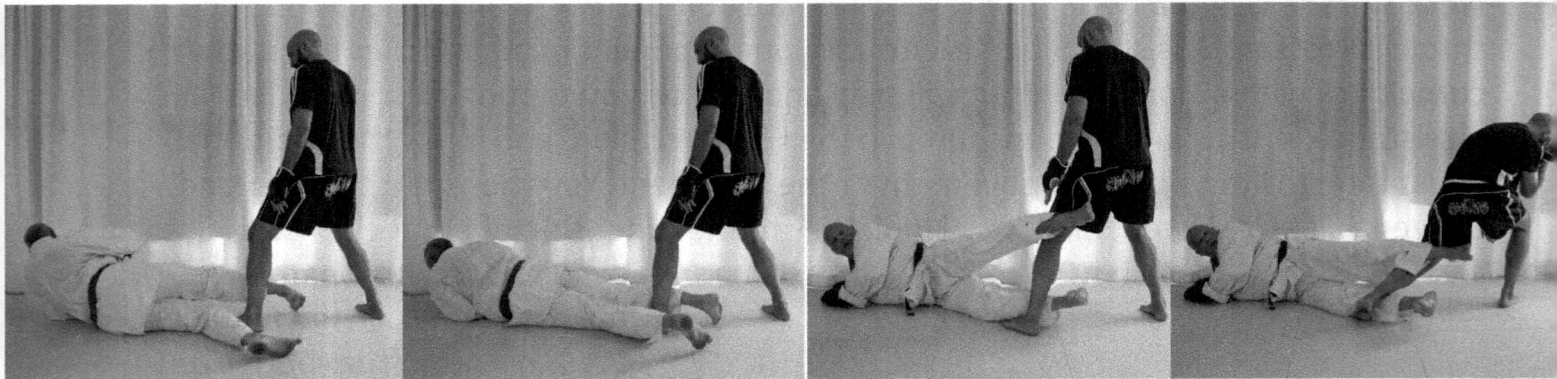

The Outwards Ground Scissor Kick Takedown

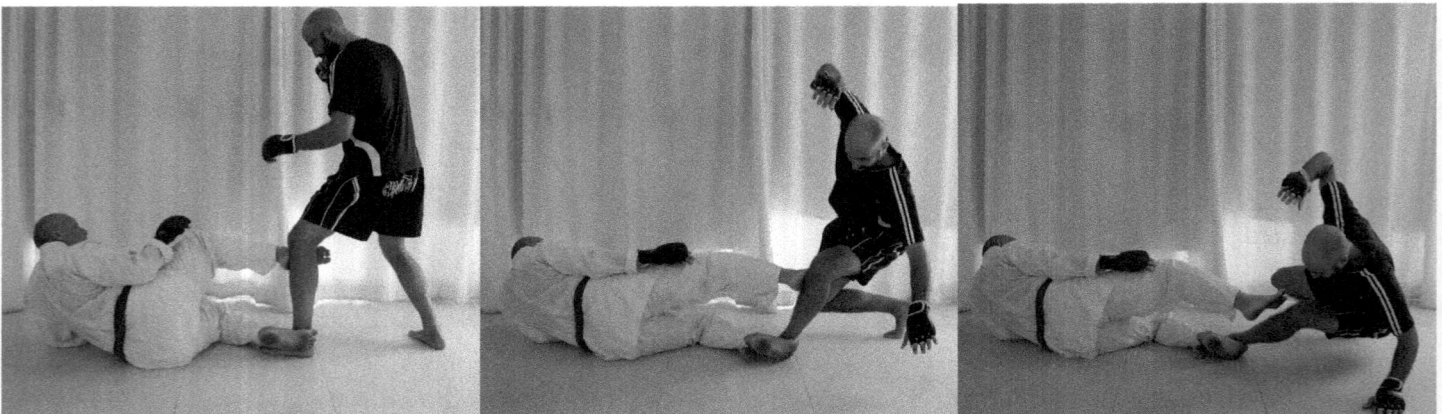

The Inwards Ground Scissor Kick Takedown

AFTERWORD

I've missed more than 9000 shots in my career. I've lost almost 300 games. 26 times, I've been trusted to take the game winning shot and missed. I've failed over and over and over again in my life. And that is why I succeed.
~Michael Jordan

We have come to the end of our overview of the main *Ground Kicks*. Our presentation has strived to be exhaustive, but probably is not. There will be many variations that we have not covered. Many Arts have are more complex, complete and sophisticated in their handling of Ground fighting. A *Capoeirista* will be much more comfortable on the Ground, and will be able to link Grounds Kicks more dynamically than Artists from other Arts. But the author hopes that the current work will be a good basis for personal exploration and adaptation to one's own chosen Art or School.
After drilling the Kicks presented, only free-fighting will allow the trainee to develop his own Ground Kicking style and link it to Ground movement and to more traditional Ground Fighting, like grappling, locking and choking.

So, try the Kicks presented here. Try your own variations. Once you have got the principle right, try your own preferred Kicks in loads of set-ups and sandwiched into various Ground Moves. Then try them in free-fighting, there is no shame in failing at the first attempts. If you persevere, you will certainly get there.

Ground Kicking is definitely underused. Today's fighters do not drill Ground Kicks enough. Try to hold your ground standing in front of a Ground Kicker, and you'll be convinced of the validity importance of Ground Kicks. Having such an uncommon proficiency in your arsenal will only make you a better Artist. And, it is good to remember that even only *training* for Ground Kicks will make you a much better *standing* Kicker.

As a last word, I would like to encourage the aspiring Ground Kicker to also develop his Ground Grappling skills. He could obviously need them once he is on the ground...

He who conquers others is strong, he who conquers himself is mighty.
~Lao Tsu

If you have enjoyed the book and appreciate the effort behind this series, you are invited to write a short and honest review on Amazon.com…

It has become extremely difficult to promote one's work in this day and age, and your support would be much appreciated. Thanks!

Remember:

I fear not the man who has practiced 10,000 kicks once, but I fear the man who has practiced one kick 10,000 times.
~ Bruce Lee

And now, dear reader, what is left is for you to start sweating.

Pain is the best instructor, but no one wants to go to his class.
~Choi, Hong Hi, Founder of Taekwon-Do

All questions, comments, additional techniques, special or vintage Photos about Kicks and Krav Maga are welcomed by the author and would be introduced with credit in future editions. Just email:**martialartkicks@gmail.com**

Strength does not come from physical capacity. It comes from an indomitable will.
~Mahatma Ghandi

The author is trying to build a complete series of work that, once finished, could become an encyclopedic base of the whole of the Martial Arts-Kicking realm, a base on which others could build and add their own experiences. In his endeavors the author has already penned:

- **The Essential Book of Martial Arts Kicks** – *Tuttle Publishing* (2010)
- **Plyo-Flex** - Training for Explosive Martial Arts Kicks (2013)
- **Low Kicks** - Advanced Martial Arts Kicks for Attacking the Lower Gates (2013)
- **Stop Kicks** – Jamming, Obstructing, Stopping, Impaling, Cutting and Preemptive Kicks (2014)
- **Ground Kicks** – Advanced Martial Arts Kicks for groundfighting (2015)
- **Stealth Kicks** - The Forgotten Art of Ghost Kicking (2015)
- **Sacrifice Kicks** - Advanced Martial Arts Kicks for Realistic Airborne Attacks (2016)
- **Krav Maga Kicks** - Tested in Battle: Kicking for No-nonsens Self-preservation (2017)

In the same frame of mind, the following works are in preparation:*Combo Kicks, Advanced Krav Maga and Joint Kicks*

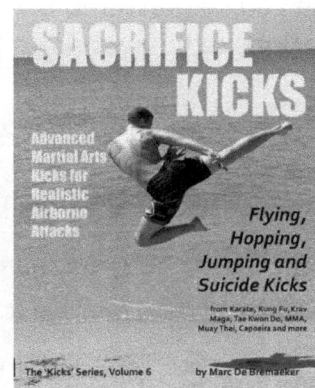

Only one who devotes himself to a cause with his whole strength and soul can be a true master. For this reason mastery demands all of a person.
~Albert Einstein

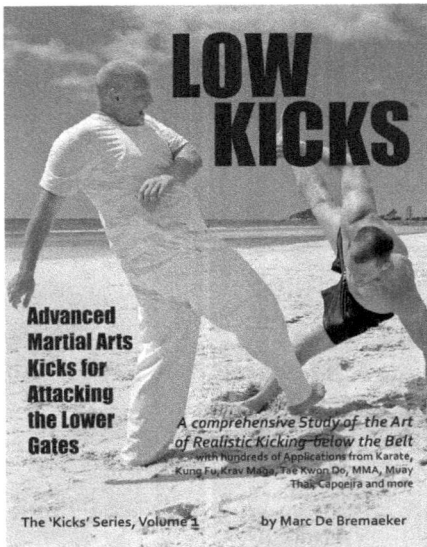

Low Kicks are powerful, fast, and effective exactly what you need to defend yourself in a real life confrontation. And because they are seldom used in sport fighting, they can be a surprising and valuable addition to your free fighting arsenal. While they may seem easy to execute, not all low kicks are simply low versions of the basic kicks. There are specific attributes and principles that make low kicks work. Marc de Bremaeker has collected the most effective low kicking techniques from Martial Arts like *Krav Maga, Karatedo, Capoeira, Wing-Chun Kung-Fu, MMA*, and *Muay Thai*. In this book, he analyzes each kick in depth, explaining the proper execution and outlining applications and variations from self-defense, sport fighting and traditional practice: Hundreds of examples in over one thousand photographs and drawings.

Plyometrics and Flexibility Training for Explosive Martial Arts Kicks and Performance Sports Plyo-Flex is a system of plyometric exercises and intensive flexibility training designed to increase your kicking power, speed, flexibility and skill level. Based on scientific principles, Plyo-Flex exercises will boost your muscles, joints and nervous system interfaces to the next performance level. After only a few weeks of training, you should see a marked improvement in the speed of your kicks and footwork, the power of your kicks, the height of your jumps, your stamina and your overall flexibility. Hundreds of illustrations and photographs will guide you through the basic plyometric and stretching exercises. Once you've mastered the basics, add the kicking-oriented variations to your workout for an extra challenge.

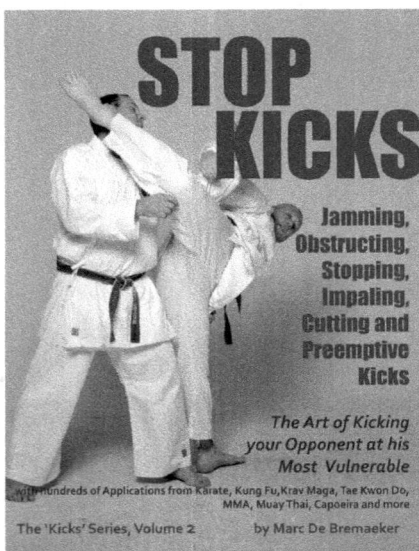

Stop Kicks are among the most effective, sophisticated kicks a fighter can use. And because they hit your opponent at his most vulnerable, they are also the safest way to pre-empt or counter an attack. Stop Kicks are delivered just as your opponent is fully committed to an attack, physically or mentally, meaning it is too late for him to change his mind. Hitting an opponent in mid-attack gives you the added advantage of using his attacking momentum against him. Stop Kicks: Jamming, Obstructing, Stopping, Impaling, Cutting and Preemptive Kicks presents a well organized array of stop-kicking techniques from a wide range of martial arts. Learn Pushing Kicks, Timing Kicks, Cutting Kicks, Obstruction Kicks, and Block Kicks from the hard-hitting styles of Muay Thai, Karatedo, Krav Maga, Tae Kwon Do, MMA and more.

Krav Maga is recognized as one of the most efficient fighting systems around today. Based on common sense, it has evolved by necessity in a region ravaged by fighting for over a century. The first part of this book details and illustrates the preferred Kicks used in Krav Maga, and the second part presents the vital points to be targeted when kicking or striking. The Last part of this work is basically a full Krav Maga Self-defense course that also includes offensive techniques. The defenses against strikes, kicks, grabs, holds and chokes do often include kicking, but only when it is the most adequate reaction. This book is the first to underline in print the important principle of _Retzev_, with dozens of examples of continuous motion until the opponent is fully vanquished. Suitable for beginners and trained Martial artists from other Schools. Over 1500 Photos and Illustrations!

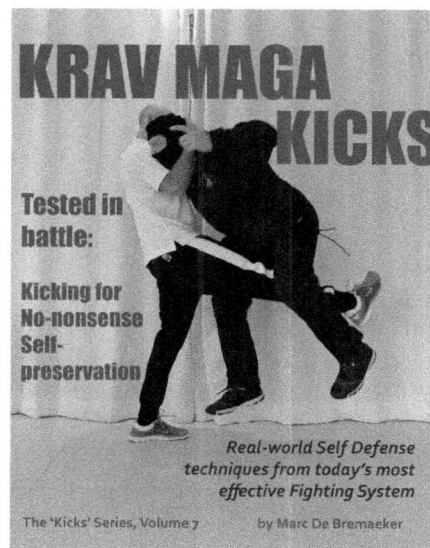

KRAV MAGA KICKS

Tested in battle:

Kicking for No-nonsense Self-preservation

Real-world Self Defense techniques from today's most effective Fighting System

The 'Kicks' Series, Volume 7   by Marc De Bremaeker

STEALTH KICKS

The Forgotten Art of Ghost Kicking

He will not know what hit him: Feint Kicks based on _Misdirection_ and _Dissimulation_

from Karate, Kung Fu, Krav Maga, Tae Kwon Do, MMA, Muay Thai, Capoeira and more

The 'Kicks' Series, Volume 5   by Marc De Bremaeker

Stealth Kicks will introduce you to the Art of executing Kicks that your opponent will not see coming. This subject has never been treated comprehensively before. Whether you are a beginner or an experienced Artist, you will find suitable Kicks or tips to modify your current techniques to give them stealth. It will help you to score in Sport confrontations or make sure to come on top in real life Self-Defense situations. The _Feint Kicks_ presented are based on misdirection: they will aim at provoking a misguided reaction that will open your adversary to the real kick intended. The _Ghost Kicks_ presented are based on dissimulation and will travel out of your opponent's range of vision to catch him unawares.
Together with general feinting techniques and specific training tips, hundreds of applications will introduce you to the sneaky Art of stealth kicking and will make you a better and unpredictable fighter. Crammed with over 2300 photos and drawings for an easy understanding of the concept of Stealth.

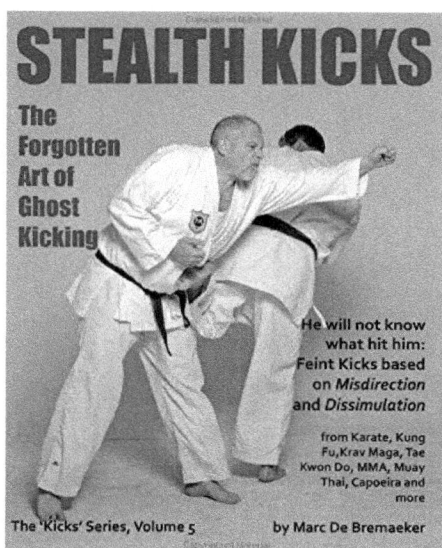

'Sacrifice Kicks' will comprehensively present the most important Martial Arts Airborne Kicks: Flying Kicks, Hopping Kicks, Jumping Kicks and Suicide Kicks. They have been dubbed 'Sacrifice' in the spirit of Judo's redoubtable Sutemi Takedowns in which one sacrifices his balance in order to throw his opponent down. _Flying Kicks_ are not about showmanship, they are very effective techniques when used judiciously. They need not be necessarily high and spectacular; they can be surprising _Jumping Kicks_ and _Hopping Kicks_ executed long and low. And _Suicide Kicks_ take the Sacrifice principles a little further: they are extremely unexpected techniques delivered airborne, but with little hope of landing on one's feet, unlike classic Flying Kicks. All these realistic maneuvers, coming from Karate, Krav Maga, Kung Fu, TaeKwonDo, MMA, Capoeira, Muay Thai and more, are described with applications and training tips. Over 1000 Photos and Illustrations.

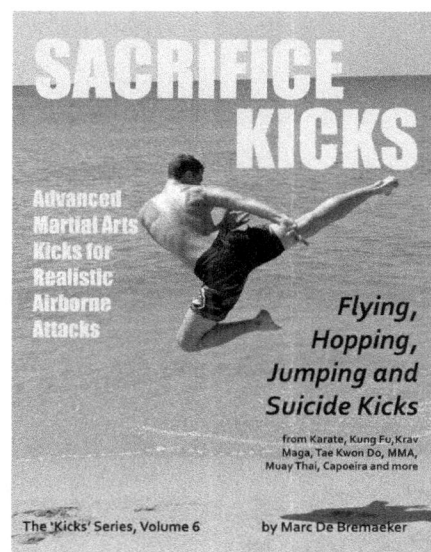

SACRIFICE KICKS

Advanced Martial Arts Kicks for Realistic Airborne Attacks

Flying, Hopping, Jumping and Suicide Kicks

from Karate, Kung Fu, Krav Maga, Tae Kwon Do, MMA, Muay Thai, Capoeira and more

The 'Kicks' Series, Volume 6   by Marc De Bremaeker

OTHER GENRES FROM FONS SAPIENTIAE

AVAILABLE IN PAPERBACK AND KINDLE FORMATS ON AMAZON

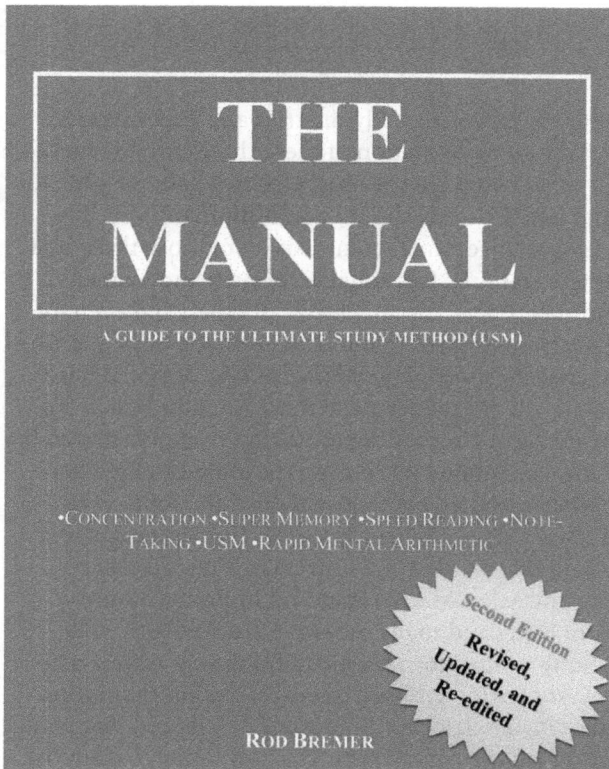

THE MANUAL

A GUIDE TO THE ULTIMATE STUDY METHOD (USM)

•CONCENTRATION •SUPER MEMORY •SPEED READING •NOTE-TAKING •USM •RAPID MENTAL ARITHMETIC

Second Edition
Revised, Updated, and Re-edited

ROD BREMER

The Manual is the definitive guide to Enhanced Concentration, Super Memory, Speed Reading, Note-Taking, Rapid Mental Arithmetic, and the *Ultimate Study Method* (USM).

The techniques presented are the culmination of decades of practical experience combined with the latest scientific research and time-tested practices. The system described herewith will allow the practitioner to:

• Read faster with higher comprehension.
• Remember any type of information instantly.
• Store information in long-term memory.
• Enhance concentration and focus.
• Access deeper levels of the mind.
• Induce relaxation.
• Rapidly perform complex mental arithmetic.
• Master the Ultimate Study Method (USM).

USM is a synergistic combination of established techniques for Concentration, Long-Term Memory, Speed Reading, and Note-Taking. It involves a systematic procedure that allows the practitioner to study any topic fast, efficiently and effectively. USM can be applied to all areas of educational study, academic research, business endeavours, as well as professional life in general.

Rain Fund: A riveting thriller

"...For the safety of the readers, this book ought to come with the disclaimer: leave this book read half-way at your own risk. Unless you are Superman, you won't be able to concentrate on much else until you have read the last page of "Rain Fund". The time has come for Patterson, Ludlum, Dan Brown et al to slide over and make space at the top for Marc Brem." - Shweta Shankar for Readers' Favorite

"...In the good tradition of Ludlum and Grisham. Five Stars" Aldo Levy

"Autistic geniuses charting financial markets; Mobster-fuelled Ponzi schemes; sophisticated hardware viruses; spies; and a rising superpower that strives for dominance – so realistic it is frightening."

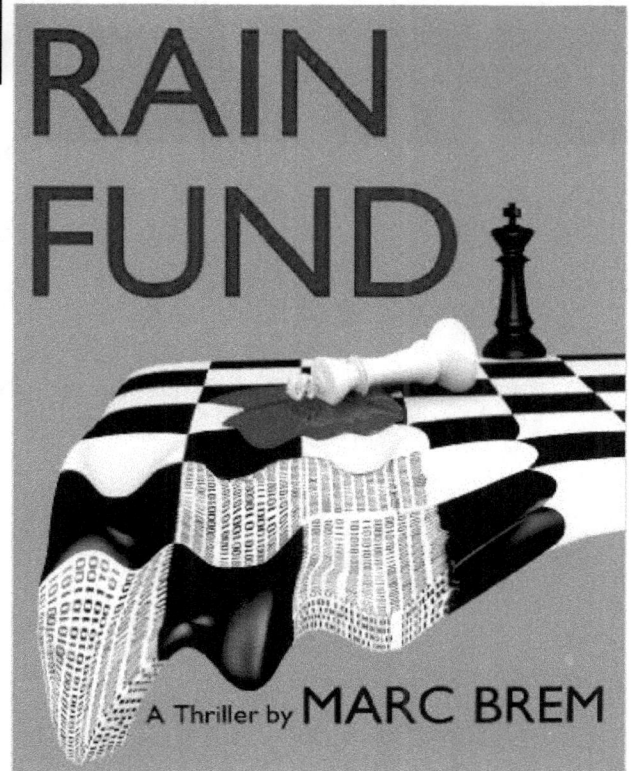

RAIN FUND

A Thriller by MARC BREM

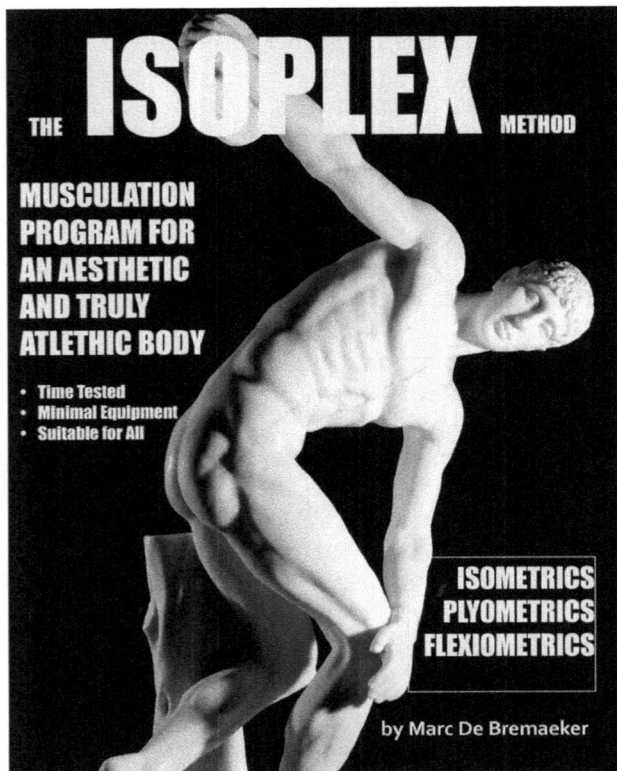

THE ISOPLEX METHOD

MUSCULATION PROGRAM FOR AN AESTHETIC AND TRULY ATLETHIC BODY

- Time Tested
- Minimal Equipment
- Suitable for All

ISOMETRICS PLYOMETRICS FLEXIOMETRICS

by Marc De Bremaeker

Isoplex stands for Isometrics, Plyometrics and Flexiometrics. The well-organized combination of these three training methods will give the serious trainee the most effective path possible to powerful and aesthetic muscles, in a minimum of time. The method is simply the optimal combination of those three basic tenets of fitness training. It is suitable for men and women. It is suitable for beginners, for athletes of all types, and even for bodybuilders. It is designed to build an aesthetic physique which is also conducive to sport performance and to personal health. ISOPLEX is in fact the modern and more scientific version of the training ideals of Greco-Roman Antiquity. As illustrated by many well-known antique sculptures, the athletes of old had aesthetic bodies based on core musculature and long, well-defined and necessarily efficient muscles. These synergistic training principles are and were universal. They were to be found in ancient Asian Martial Arts and in Body Cultures like Yoga, Chi Kung and many others. A truly athletic and functional body needed for realistic fighting was achieved by a mixture of Isometric exercises, intensive flexibility training and dynamic (Plyometric) drills. Martial Artists and Yogis will immediately grasp the connection. This is the way to train the body for effective and natural aesthetics, and that is what Isoplex concentrates on through an optimal and synergistic time-saving program.

With hundreds of Photos and Drawings and detailing Five complete weekly Programs for all levels.

www.ingramcontent.com/pod-product-compliance
Lightning Source LLC
Chambersburg PA
CBHW062040090426
42740CB00016B/2967